P9-BII-541

God & the History of Art I

by
Barry Stebbing

Art History & Art Lessons

How Great Thou Art Publications

God
& The History of Art I

by
Barry Stebbing

"The Last Supper" by Leonardo da Vinci
Copy by Matt Watson   Age 16

This book is dedicated to God, who is my main purpose in life.
It is also dedicated to my wife, Saundra, my rock and comforter.
Thank God for Christian women.

How Great Thou ART Publications
Box 48 McFarlan, N.C. 28102
2nd Edition
Copyright 2001

(Lessons within texts are reproducible for "in home use" only)

Professor Solomon

Dear Students,

Welcome to *God & the History of Art.* For many years my wife and I traveled across the United States and Canada specifically to teach art to homeschoolers. What we found was a wealth of disciplined students with a great attitude and a willingness to learn. As you page through *God and the History of Art I & II,* you will find artwork done by many of these students. Our prayer is that God will use you and many others to lay hold of the art world and claim it for His kingdom, touching the heart of man.

God & the History of Art is recommended for students ages 10 and up. It is comparable with *Feed My Sheep* in level of ability, but was especially created for those families who have both a desire to learn art and art history.

We recommend that the student go *in and out* of the text. You may want to do unit studies like *Impressionism* or the *Reformation* instead of starting with the first chapter *Egypt.* The painting program does not formally begin until the end of *God & the History of Art I* (with the advent of 17th and 18th century art). However, the introduction to painting begins on page 55 with our studies of the Christian artist Albrecht Dürer. We believe that students like variety, and painting is a wonderful addition to the learning experience. Notice that each *paint card* has the page number on the top where the lesson may be found. *God & the History of Art* has been created at about a 4th grade reading level. Much of the terminology has been simplified to give everyone a clearer understanding of the various periods and styles of art. If a lesson is too difficult for the student, have them return to it later. Remember, our artistic skills develop as our motor skills develop.

Finally, a word about the set of full color postcards of works by the masters which are included with your curriculum. These have been carefully chosen to give you a well rounded collection of great works through different periods and styles of art. We believe the reproductions are not only of exceptional quality but also very practical. You will be thumbing through them for *comparative studies* time and time again. May we all grow in our appreciation of art in the way which God has intended us to.

In Christ,

Barry Stebbing
How Great Thou ART Publications
Box 48
McFarlan, NC
28102

Christ is Risen!

"Why do you keep filling gallery after gallery with endless pictures of the one ever-reiterated theme of Christ in weakness, of Christ upon the cross, Christ dying, Christ hanging dead? Why do you stop there as if the curtain closed upon that horror? Keep the curtain open, and with the cross in the foreground, let us see beyond it to the Easter dawn with its beams streaming upon the risen Christ, Christ alive, Christ ruling, Christ triumphant.

For we should be ringing out over the world that Christ has won, that evil is toppling, that the end is sure, and that death is followed by victory. That is the tonic we need to keep us healthy, the trumpet blast to fire our blood and send us crowding in behind our Master, swinging happily upon our way, laughing and singing and recklessly unafraid, because the feel of victory is in the air, and our hearts thrill to it."

Michelangelo (1564)

Stephanie Hobeck   Age 10   Ruckersivlle, Virginia

God & the History of Art I
Table of Contents:

(The High Renaissance through the 20th Century continues in *God & the History of Art II*.)

Planning Your Curriculum

God & the History of Art I & II includes the *picture postcard gallery,* a set of 34 full color postcards of works by the great masters. You may want to review your collection of these masterpieces. Make sure to keep them in a safe place for future references. Listed below, and in the forward to *God & the History of Art II* are the titles of each masterpiece as well as where the assignments may be found pertaining to the artwork.

Title of Artwork	Name or Style of Art	Pages
1. *"Stag Beetle"*	Albrecht Dürer	54
2. *"Portrait of the Artist's Son / Titus"*	Rembrandt	72
3. *"Man with a Hoe"*	Jean-Francois Millet	85
4. *"Black-Figured Neck-Amphora"*	Greek pottery (540 B.C.)	161
5. *"Portrait of Caligula"*	Roman (40 A.D.)	171
6. *"Saint Dominic"*	Gerard Horenbout	183
7. *"Saint Luke"*	Constantinople (1133)	211

Art Materials Needed for Text

Colored Pencils (set of 12 or 24)

Pure Pigment Acrylic Paints
(yellow, red, blue & white)

Set of 3 or 4 Brushes (#1, #3, #5, #7, or #9)

Set of Drawing Pencils & Kneaded Eraser

1 Extra-Fine Black Marker Pen

Set of Washable Markers

Student Art Gallery

"Daniel in the Lions' Den"
Jared Kellog Age 10 Ada, Mi.

"Jonah & the Big Fish"
Tate Swanson Age 10 Herdon, Va

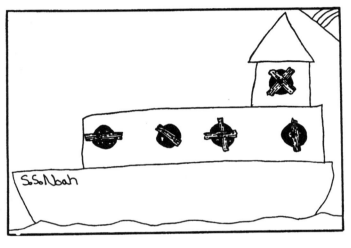

"Noah's Ark"
Casi Woods Age 11 Ft. Myers, Fl.

"God Made the World"
Natalie Salim Age 7 Midlothian, Va.

"Hosanna to the King" Laura Owens Age 8
Cucamoga, Ca.

"The Preacher sought to find acceptable words; and what was written was upright - words of truth."

Ecclesiastes 12:10

Introduction

"The Ten Commandments" Rachel Dow Age 16 Rochester, New York

"Jesus" by Melissa Gilreath Age 4
Gastonia, North Carolina

"Jesus, Mary, and Joseph"
by Angela Matthews Age 9

"Jesus Feeding the Thousands"
Abigail Lisner Age 11
Manomet, Illinois

"Adam and Eve"
Angela Hamby Age 15
Danielsville, Georgia

"Finally, brethren, whatever things are true, whatever things are noble, whatever things are just, whatever things are pure, whatever things are lovely, whatever things are of good report, if there is any virtue and if there is anything praiseworthy - meditate on these things."

Philippians 4:8

Man & Art

Have you ever read the children's fable, *The Emperor's New Clothes?* I believe that is how most of us perceive art. The fable was written by Hans Christian Andersen, and is about two swindlers who convinced the king that they could prepare a royal robe for him made of the most exquisite material, wonderful pattern and delightful color. The material had the peculiar quality of being invisible to every person who was not fit for his office or who was impossibly dull. Well, no one wanted to think this of themselves, so when they saw the invisible robe everyone commented about its beauty. At last there was a grand ceremony, and the king paraded through the town wearing his new robe. Everyone marvelled. Finally, a little boy looked up at the king and exclaimed, "But he has no clothes on!"

So it seems with art that we have been dictated to and influenced by what others believe to be good and acceptable. This is especially true of what has been produced during the 20th century with its new approach called *modern art.* Sadly, much of modern art has been created to shock its audience and many times to offend.

Art was intended to be *sublime*, to make us feel better about ourselves and to be uplifting, elevating man to a higher level. Art was intended to touch our hearts; to inspire us to think on those things which are good and pure. It seems as if with today's art, our hearts are set aside. Instead, the mind, or the intellect is what art strives to captivate.

There is much to be said about the older, more traditional values in art. For example, Buchanan stated, *"All that is beautiful shall abide..."* Michelangelo said, *"Art is the shadow of Divine Perfection."* Sister Beckett observed, *"Looking at art is one way of listening to God."* Chuck Colson commented, *"Art is any expression of form and beauty that elevates and inspires."* Ruskin wrote, *"Fine art is that in which the hand, the head, and the heart of man go together."* St. Francis of Assisi echoed, *"He who works with his hands, his head, and his heart is an artist."* A Latin proverb states, *"A picture is a poem without words."* Even George Bernard Shaw remarked, *"I believe in Michelangelo, Valasquez and Rembrandt...the redemption of all things beautiful."*

"An Angel Descending from Heaven"
Elaine Nichelson Age 13
Zeelard, Michigan

"Man is a maker. This is part of what it means to be in the image of our Creator God. As we learn to collaborate with Him, He confirms and mightily blesses the work of our hands....When we allow God to bestow His favor and beauty and delightfulness on the work of our hands, He makes artists of even the humblest among us." Leanne Payne

Lesson #1: A Lesson on Frustration

Before we begin, let's say a word about *frustration*. Many students become frustrated when it comes to learning the fine art of drawing and painting - they believe that art is something you have a talent for. But the truth is that art is a *learned discipline;* the more you practice, the better you will become. We become frustrated with our lack of ability to draw or paint because we cannot do it the way we want. Yet we need to understand that frustration is a part of the process of becoming an artist.

Throughout all of history, artists have become frustrated with their artwork. The great Renaissance artist, Michelangelo, destroyed many pieces of his artwork out of frustration. So did William Mallard Turner, the English landscape painter of the 19th century. It is said that Frederic Remington, the great artist of the American West, destroyed 50 of his paintings in 1908, one year before he died. And Claude Monet, the French Impressionist, at the height of his success as a painter said, *"Every time I start a canvas I think I'm going to create a masterpiece, and it never, ever happens. It's appalling, never being satisfied. I suffer terribly."* So you see, frustration is part of being an artist. If you understand this, you will be able to relax and enjoy the learning process involved in drawing, coloring and painting.

 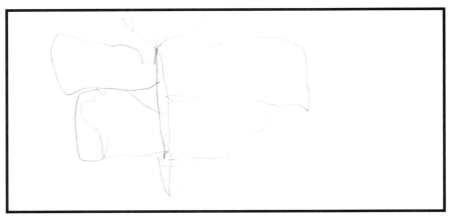

The story of Joni Eareckson Tada is a very good one for every student who becomes frustrated in art. Joni was a young girl of 17 living on the Eastern Shore of Maryland. One day she went swimming. Unfortunately, when she dove into the water she did not realize it was shallow and broke her neck. She was placed in traction for many months, paralyzed (to this day), crying her heart out as her life was seemingly over. Then, as time passed, she committed her life to God. From that day forward Joni began doing artwork by drawing and painting with a brush held between her teeth.

For your first assignment in *God & The History of Art,* draw the picture of the butterfly above (A) in the figure box to the right (B). However, do it the way Joni does by using only your mouth. Before beginning, set your pencils close to you in a jar (points down) and situate this text in front of you in a comfortable position. Then, start drawing and coloring your picture with colored pencils. I'm sure when you are finished you will have more respect for Joni's artwork and a deeper appreciation for the hands which God has given you to work with. The quote above by Leanne Payne seems to sum it up, *"When we allow God to bestow His favor and beauty and delightfulness on the work of our hands, He makes artists of even the humblest among us."*

God & the History of Art

My name is Professor Solomon and I will be your guide throughout the text. Studying the great masters is a wonderful endeavor for the student of the arts. Researching the lives of great Renaissance masters like Michelangelo, Raphael and da Vinci can inspire you to great heights in your own artwork. Studying American Western artists like Charles Russell and Frederick Remington can also be very exciting and interesting. Likewise, the works of English landscape artists, John Constable and William Mallard Turner are remarkable. And we can't forget masters like Norman Rockwell, Claude Monet and Vincent van Gogh, each of whom changed the way we think about art. However, what this text will focus most on is the lives of great Christian artists like Fra Angelico, Rembrandt van Rijn, Jean Francois Millet and the modern artist Georges Rouault. Studying the great masters along with godly periods of art is not only a wonderful source of inspiration, but can also influence what we appreciate in art and what we choose to draw and paint.

Professor Solomon

....

The History of Art in a Nutshell

Throughout history, man has labored to recreate the images of the world around him. Likewise, people at various points in history have had different reasons for creating. For example, the Egyptians believed art was a form of storytelling that when placed in tombs, would accompany those who passed into the hereafter. Egyptian art also portrayed their many gods and goddesses. These ancient artists would use art to tell simple stories of the lives of their great leaders and also of their gods. Their style of painting and sculpture changed very little throughout the centuries as it was handed down from generation to generation. The Egyptians believed that the ability to copy the exact style of those before them was more important than making artwork unique or creative.

Then came the ancient Greeks. At first they were influenced by the Egyptian tradition with their rigid style of painting and sculpture. Eventually the Greeks became more imaginative and created some of the most beautiful and perfect artwork in the history of mankind. They also began to have an exalted opinion of man. Thus, the first seeds were planted for the *Age of Enlightenment,* meaning that man, through his own reasoning, could control the world around him and create a better life. Like the ancient Egyptians, Greece was a culture of many gods and goddesses. However, their artwork exalted human beings by glorifying man and placing him at the center of the universe. Hence, *humanism* was born, a term created by a Greek philosopher the fifth century B.C. who said: *"Man is the measure of all things."*

"Christ is Risen" Seth Holmen Age 12 Lakeville, Mn.

The next to come along were the Romans who conquered the once powerful Greek empire. However, the Romans never really conquered the Greek culture, but more or less took it and many of the Greek artists with them. They made Greek art a part of their own.

Then came the birth of Christ. With Christianity a new era in art was also birthed. Like the Egyptians who lived centuries before them, early Christian artists were more concerned with spiritual matters and telling a story than they were with beauty or man's perfection. Unlike the Egyptians, Greeks and Romans, the Christian artists only had one God to portray. It was the Christ of the gospel that became the focus of attention in art during this time, which lasted from the second century through the Middle Ages. Most other forms of art were considered forms of idol worship.

However, a conflict arose within the Church. First there was contention between the world *glorifying man* and the Church *glorifying God.* Then there was the question within the body of Christ whether art should be beautiful, glorious and uplifting, as the Greeks had achieved, or whether it should simply tell the Gospel in pictures for the common man who could not read, as the Egyptians had done. Some Christians strongly believed that when artwork became too beautiful, it would also become a source of *idol worship,* idolizing the art more than the Creator. As the Bible reminds us, idol worshipping has been a major concern with God ever since Aaron and the Israelites built the golden calf.

During the early years of Christian art which is best known as the *Byzantine Period,* the artwork remained simple, pure and holy, with Christ as the focal point. There were other godly periods of art during and after this time, such as Romanesque, Gothic and Reformation. The Church modestly wanted artwork to lead the people on the right path. During the sixth century, many ancient Greek and Roman pieces of art were destroyed by the Church because of what they stood for. Throughout the history of mankind, the Byzantine Period probably stands out as the period that best glorified God in its simplicity and purpose.

"Goliath" Tyler Horton
Age 9   Scottsdale, Az.

Then came the *Renaissance*, which means *rebirth*. Italy was the art center of this rebirth in the 1400s, the period following the *Middle Ages*. Another title many gave to the Middle Ages was the *Dark Ages*, because hoards of barbaric Huns and Goths overran most of civilized Europe.

The Italians believed that great art came out of ancient Greece and Rome and that these barbarians were responsible for destroying the wonderful influences these ancient cultures made on the civilized world. However, this is not true. Rather, a simple, Christ-centered art prevailed throughout the Middle Ages. Nevertheless, the artists of the Renaissance labored to reclaim the art lost during these ancient times and began to create classical art once again. Most of the artwork during the Renaissance was dedicated to the Church, however, there began to be a subtle shift in purpose from *glorifying God* to once again, *glorifying man* or *humanism*.

In the beginning of the 1500s, along with this great *awakening* of the Renaissance, arose another approach to art called the *Reformation*. The followers of this movement rebelled against the authority of the Roman Catholic church which was all-powerful at the time. These northern protesters would eventually be called *Protestants,* ones who desired purer relationship with God. The artists from this period turned away from the classical style of Renaissance art and returned to a more simple approach.

Purposes for art continued to ebb and flow with new periods and philosophies like *Mannerism* and *Baroque*. France gradually became the center for the arts in the 18th century. Humanism became popular again, this time packaged under the title of *the Age of Reason*. Man once again placed himself in an exalted position, returning to the belief that he was the center of the universe. Another style of art surfaced called *Romanticism*. The artists of this movement embraced passion, mythology and glorifying nature as their themes.

The latter part of the 19th century brought forth *Impressionism* with its great splashes of color and brush strokes. This was followed by the *Modern Art* of the 20th century, identified by its seemingly abstract defiance against the things of God.

Well, that's art history in a nutshell. To sum it all up, man has continually used art to glorify himself, while the Church has strived to use art to glorify God and spread the gospel.

"I am the Lord your God, Who brought you out of the land of Egypt, out of the house of bondage. You shall have no other gods before Me. You shall not make for yourself any carved image, or any likeness of anything that is in heaven above, or that is in the earth beneath, or that is in the water under the earth, you shall not bow down to them nor serve them."

Exodus 20:2-5

Before we study the history of art, we should take a moment to ponder, *What exactly should the purpose of art be?* In Exodus 20:4 the Lord says, *"You shall not make for yourself any carved image, or any likeness of anything that is in heaven above, or that is in the earth beneath, or that is in the water under the earth; you shall not bow down to them nor serve them."* Throughout the centuries, Christians have been very concerned with idol worship and its relationship to art. During earlier years of Christianity, much of the artwork from ancient Greece was destroyed by Christians because of the 2nd commandment. The Greeks had erected statues to their gods and goddesses and had also glorified man. However, that is not what the Lord is saying. God is telling us not to make art an idol. It is similar to having a Christmas tree. God created the tree, but not to make it an idol of worship. Instead, Christmas is when our hearts need to be nestled in the birth of Christ.

Today, many hold artwork in such high esteem that it has, once again, become a god to them. The Lord wants us to have focus, balance and understanding in our appreciation of art. As it states in Matthew 6:33, *"Seek ye first the kingdom of God and His righteousness, and all these things shall be added unto you."*

Think with me for a moment about the nature of God. The first five words of the Bible declare, *"In the beginning, God created..."* God is a creator, and we are made in His image and likeness to create. He has factored creativity into our DNA.

I believe that God, the supreme Creator/Artist, would like to see His Body, the Church, lead the way in creative excellence. Let us then, be compelled to look for a modern-day renaissance led by artists who love God.

"Coat of Many Colors" Mandi Simpkins Age 12 Statesville, North Carolina

"Years of patience, discipline and effort are the price of access to a strict and personal vision. An artist is not born but made."

Jean-Max Taxier

Fundamentals of Drawing

Tom Pellegrini Age 13
Hales Corners, Wisconsin

"To learn, you must want to be taught." Proverbs 12:1

Drawing: A Sure Foundation

It's always good to start with a drawing program. Learning to draw will add joy and variety to the art history studies. It is also good to start with drawing because drawing is the essential ingredient needed in learning art. This curriculum includes many drawing lessons on the pages that follow. I believe that God gives each and every child a joy for art. Since God is an artist, He has given this joy and a certain amount of *ability* to everyone as a free gift so that we all may participate in creating! However, this ability in art has to be developed. Remember, ability means you are *capable* of doing something. Joni Eareckson Tada had a measure of ability to draw and paint, and even though she became paralyzed from the neck down, she developed this ability into a *talent* through discipline and practice. Talent simply means practicing until you have developed your abilities to the point where you have become good at it, or *talented*. Your abilities will become better and better the more you practice. Observe a dancer, baseball player or pianist. They all become better with practice. The same is true with art! Everything takes practice, practice and more practice.

The question is raised, *"What should I practice?"* Well, you can always start by practicing the *fundamentals*. Fundamentals are the building blocks of art. The two most important fundamentals in drawing are learning to draw with *line* and how to draw an *ellipse*. Practicing these and other building blocks in drawing will improve your abilities.

Fundamentals: *Building Blocks of Drawing*

line	ellipse	form
light source	line variation	texture
axis line	overlapping	plumb line
proportions	foreshortening	crosshatching

Lesson #2: *"Draw lines, young man, plenty of lines."*

When, the French Impressionist artist, Edgar Degas was a young student he went to visit the great French master, Ingres (pronounced Angs). The one question that young Edgar asked the venerable teacher was, *"What do you consider the most important thing to learn in art?"* The wise, aged master replied, *"Draw lines, young man, plenty of lines."* Line is the main element in art. It teaches the student *control*. It also offers the student a wealth of beauty in drawing through a wonderful assortment of lines, called *line variation*. Drawings by the great masters are so divine because each and every line was done with exquisite control. Therefore, the practice of drawing lines is a fundamental that should be exercised continually. For this lesson practice drawing long, straight, horizontal lines below. Keep them close together and draw them as straight as if they had been drawn with a ruler. Then, take another sheet of plain white paper and fill it with more long, horizontal lines. Practice the fundamentals!

Long, Horizontal Lines

Note: The glossary, with terms and definitions, is found in the back of *God & the History of Art II* (pp. 441-451).

6

"You must accept drawing as a thing to challenge your best effort. It cannot be taught or learned in 10 easy lessons."
Arthur Guptill

Lesson #3: *Long Lines & Short Lines*

Let's practice drawing more long lines. This time you are going to complete the pencil and the paintbrush below by drawing long, straight lines. Notice that the handle of the paintbrush becomes wider the closer it is to the hairs of the brush. When you are finished, draw the entire pencil and brush in the figure box below (A).

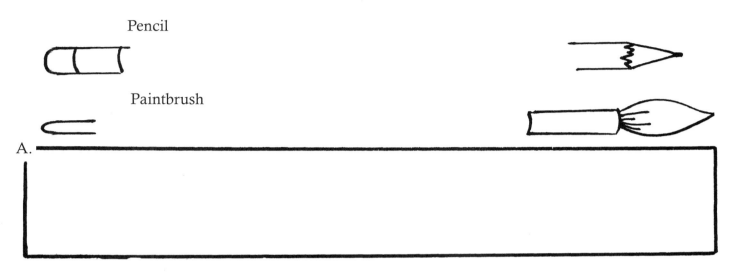

Pencil

Paintbrush

A.

Vertical
Lines

Horizontal
Lines

Diagonal
Lines

Now let's practice drawing short lines. Fill each box to the left using the correct type of lines: vertical lines, horizontal lines, and diagonal lines. Finally, shade each object below (B) with lines as shown. Use your black pen or dark pencil for this assignment.

B.

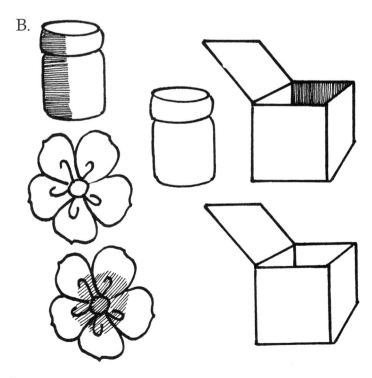

"Jacob Wrestling with the Angel"
Yuba Grant   Age 13 Ontario, Canada

Lesson #4: *Ellipses - Going Around & Around*

Leonardo da Vinci, the great artist from the Italian Renaissance, was one of the most talented people who ever lived. He was great at many things. However, notice what Leonardo said, *"Thou, O Lord, dost sell us all good things at the price of labor."* King Solomon, one of my great, great ancestors, stated in Ecclesiastes 3:22, *"So I perceived that there is nothing better than that a man should rejoice in his own works, for that is his heritage."* Thus, we are called to be an industrious people and in art, that means practice, practice, practice.

Let's learn another fundamental - *ellipses*. An ellipse is a circle seen on an angle, looking much like a perfect pancake shape. Literally hundreds of objects are drawn with ellipses: the tops and bottoms of jars, bottles, pots, bowls, cups, glasses, a basketball rim, a tire seen on an angle, a watch going around a wrist, and so on. To draw an ellipse, hold your pencil 1 or 2 inches from the point and lightly go around 4 or 5 times to make its shape (A). For this assignment, take out your colored pencils and fill the box below with colorful ellipses, using a different color for each.

* Ellipses * Ellipses * Ellipses * Ellipses * Ellipses * Ellipses * Ellipses *

A.

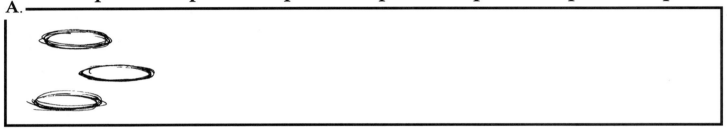

Now let's see if you can draw objects that are formed with ellipses. Copy the objects below (B), drawing an ellipse for the top and bottom of each. Notice that ellipses are even used to draw a label on a round jar. Start with a light colored pencil.

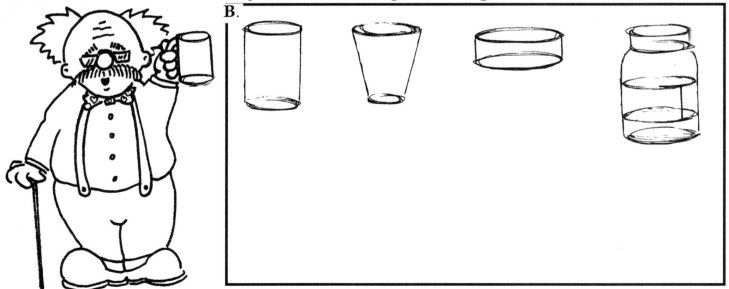

B.

Lesson #5: *Independent Studies:*

Take your sketchbook or some drawing paper and see how many things you can draw around the house that are formed with ellipses. Remember, jars, pots, cups, glasses, bottles, rolls of tape, lamps, and basketball rims are all drawn with ellipses. Make sure to go around lightly 4 or 5 times for each ellipse.

Lesson #6: *Around & Around*

The great French Impressionist Paul Cezanne said, *"Pleasure must be found in study."* Mr. Cezanne is stating that students need to practice the fundamentals of art in order to nurture their God given abilities. Most students do not like to practice the fundamentals but would rather draw and color the things they like. Paul, the apostle of Christ, seems to sum up this attitude in Romans 7:15, *"For what I am doing I do not understand. For what I will to do, that I do not practice..."* Many students want to draw and color pretty pictures, but it takes an effort to learn the basic fundamentals. When we practice fundamentals such as *line* and *ellipse* over and over again, our artwork will be of a much higher quality.

Let's draw *Wally the Worm*. First, fill another figure box (A) with ellipses using a different colored pencil for each. Then, draw *Wally the Worm* starting with two long, controlled lines for his body (B). Notice that the lines go to a point at his tail just like the handle of a paintbrush. Then put stripes on his body, but remember, his body is round so the stripes have to be curved or go around. Next, see if you can draw *Wally the Worm* wrapping around a pole. Draw lightly with your yellow pencil and then darken *Wally* with your orange pencil when you have drawn him just the way you like. Finally, draw the objects below (D) using ellipses to show they are round.

C.

A. *"Pleasure must be found in study."*

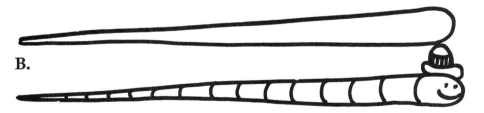

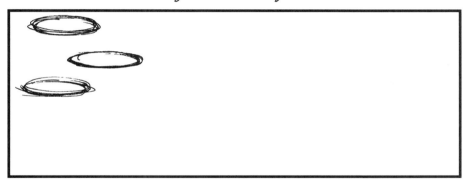

B.

D.

"Tower of Babel"
Marie Eichman Age 13
Ft. Wayne, Indiana

Lesson #7: *Let's Go Around & Around Again*

Michelangelo was one of the greatest artists of the Renaissance, being both a painter and a sculptor. Yet, when asked by a student, *"Master, how did you become a great artist?"* his reply was brief and to the point, *"I drew, and I drew, and I drew some more."* Sorolla, the great Spanish painter said, *"Don't paint as I do, draw, draw, that is everything."* Tintoretto, the great 16th century Venetian master (from Venice) stated, *"One can never do too much drawing."* He also added, *"Without faith and draftsmanship (the ability to draw) your paintings will crumble. Faith is needed to keep the subject matter holy, while drawing is a cable that bind's one's convictions together."* Remember, drawing is the key cornerstone in art! Upon this rock you shall build your house.

    Let's practice drawing circles. A circle is not drawn by going around once with a heavy line (A). It is much like drawing ellipses, going around and around 4 or 5 times. However, a circle is not thin like an ellipse (B) but perfectly round (C). Practice drawing 3 circles in the figure box below (D) using a different colored pencil for each. Then draw a hot air balloon, a Christmas ball, and a balloon in the clown's hand. Make sure to draw a round circle by going around and around. Color everything with your pencils when finished.

A. No!   B. No!   C. Yes!   D.

"Talent is like the grease on a wagon wheel. The grease makes it easier to get to town, but you can still get there without it....you just squeak more along the way." Paul Strisik

Lesson #8: Thick & Thin Lines & Wavy Lines

There are many types of lines you can use in drawing. One type is thick and thin lines. Thick and thin lines are great for outlining something delicate like a glass pitcher or a flower petal. They are also good to use to show texture on a piece of wood. Drawing thick and thin lines is done by putting more or less pressure on your pencil. The more pressure you apply, the darker the line; the less pressure, the lighter the line. First, fill the figure box below (A) with long, thick and thin lines. Then, take your orange and brown pencils and color the tree trunk and piece of wood (B & C) with long, thick and thin lines.

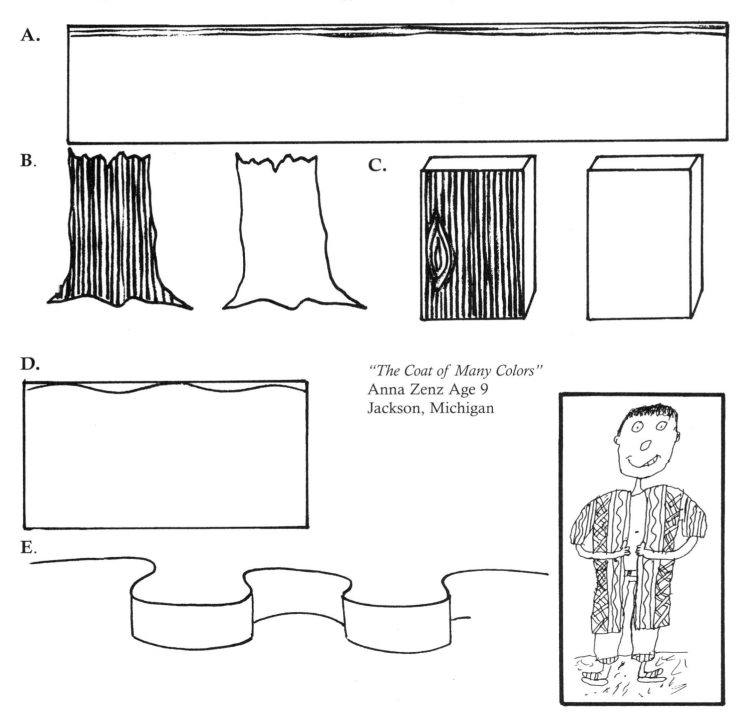

A.

B.

C.

D.

"The Coat of Many Colors"
Anna Zenz Age 9
Jackson, Michigan

E.

11

"I don't know a better definition of an artist than one who is eternally curious."

Charles Hawthorne

Lesson #9: Overlapping

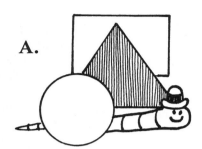

A.

Overlapping simply means placing one object slightly in front of another (A). When we overlap things in our picture, it helps to show depth. For this lesson, copy the geometric shapes below and place Wally the Worm behind each. Geometric shapes are circles, squares, rectangles, and triangles. When you are finished, use a different colored pencil for each geometric shape and color them in with lines, using a different series of lines for each: horizontal lines in one, vertical lines in another, diagonal lines in the next, and then any type of line you like in the last shape.

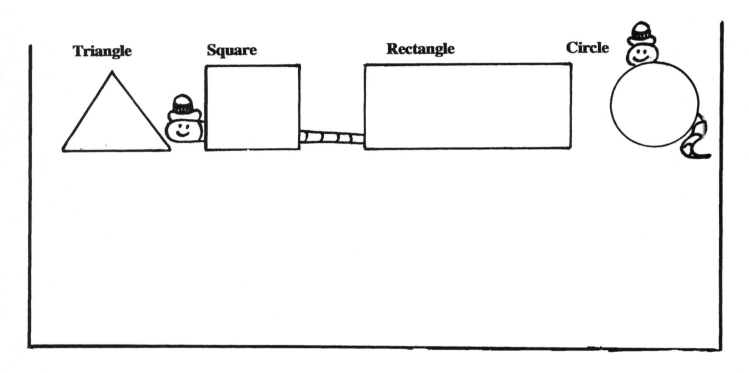

Triangle   Square   Rectangle   Circle

"God Made the Animals" Morgan Decker Age 11 Moseley, Virginia

12

Lesson #10: *Pen & Ink*

Pen and ink, or working with a black pen, will help teach you many of the basic fundamentals of drawing. For this exercise, draw the objects below with your drawing pencil and then go over each with your black pen. As with pencil, it is good to draw and shade with line. The closer you place the lines together, the darker the area will be (A). For real dark areas try cross-hatching (B). To cross-hatch, simply lay down a series of vertical lines and then place a series of horizontal lines over them to create a darker, criss-cross value. One of the keys to doing nice drawings is not to outline everything (C). Leave some areas open, allowing the light to shine in. You can also outline your objects by shading the background behind them (D). Draw the objects below and then go over each with your black pen practicing the different techniques.

A. **B.** **D.**

C. Do Not Outline

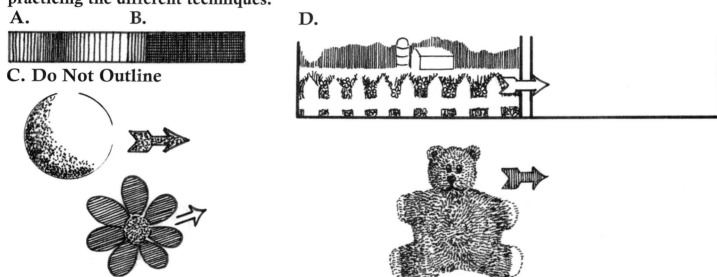

Lesson #11: *Shading with Line*

Many students shade by blocking in large dark areas with their pencil or pen (A). It is much better to shade with lines (B). Shading with lines makes your shaded areas lighter. In the beginning, many students draw their lines carelessly (C). For this assignment, use your black pen and shade the objects below with diagonal lines (D), placing in the shaded areas of the tree, can, box and pyramid with nice diagonal lines. It is always good to know where your light is coming from and to draw a small sun with an arrow to remind you what the light side and shaded sides will be.

A. **B.** **C.** **D.**

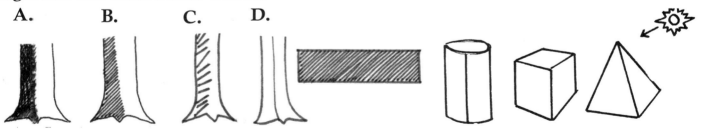

Lesson #12: *Cross-hatching* Finally, shade the objects below with cross-hatching using your black pen.

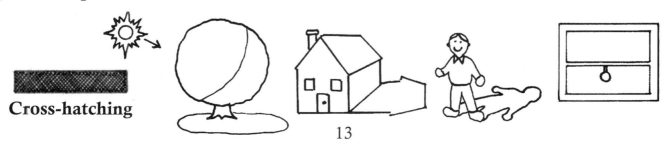

Cross-hatching

13

Lesson #13: The Doodle Page

The *Doodle Page* is like recess. In other words, it's time to have fun. Draw any pictures you like in the figure boxes below. You may want to do some in pencil, colored pencils, or with your black pen. Be creative! Also, do not forget to practice some of the fundamentals of drawing which you have just learned.

Doodle
Doodle
Doodle

God - the Great Creator

Chelsie Werling Age 8 Spencerville, Indiana

....

God - the Great Creator

As every Christian knows, God is an artist. He made man in His own image and likeness. It is also wonderful to know that He made us creative. We are the only living species that has this capacity. Thus, we should learn to understand and appreciate God's artistic abilities and creative nature in order to appreciate art and our own potential. All we need to do is take a walk through the zoo to marvel at God's genius, or look at the way He created the moon and stars. Psalm 8:1,3,4 seems to say it perfectly, *"O Lord, our Lord, how excellent is Your name in all the earth....When I consider Your heavens, the work of Your fingers, the moon and the stars, which You have ordained, what is man that You are mindful of him...?"*

The greatest museum in the world is nature. Our artwork pales in comparison with the Creative Hand of God and the world He has created. One reason God creates is to touch the heart of man. Have you ever seen the bright, vivid colors of autumn? Or pink flamingos in flight? A morning star on the horizon? A sunset over the ocean, or a sunrise over the mountain peaks? Everything that has been created before our eyes is only the beginning of what He has in store for us! It says in I Corinthians 2:9, *"Eye has not seen, nor ear heard, neither has entered into the heart of man the things which God has prepared for those who love Him."* In other words, we have only seen a mere speck of His creative wonders. Can you think of a new color that has never been seen before? It's difficult to imagine, isn't it? But God may have new colors in Heaven! Listen to what He says in Revelations 21:23,24 about Jerusalem: *"And the city had no need of the sun or of the moon to shine in it, for the glory of God illuminated it, and the Lamb is its light. And the nations of those who are saved shall walk in its light, and the kings of the earth bring their glory and honor into it."* You see, we cannot even imagine the breadth and scope of God's creativity. That is why He is the greatest of all artists, worthy to be praised!

Deanna Wong
Age 7
Temple City, Ca

"Love all God's creation, the whole and every grain of sand in it. Love every leaf, every ray of God's light. Love the animals, love the plants, love everything. If you love everything, you will perceive the divine mystery in things. Once you perceive it, you will begin to comprehend it better every day. And you will come at last to love the whole world with an all embracing love."   Dostoyevsky

....

We cannot help but praise God when we see a beautiful autumn landscape or a flock of Canada geese in the morning sky. I wonder how many people really believe God is an artist and the Creator of the universe? How sad it is to realize that most people simply go through life believing everything just happened by accident. Many believe there was a big bang and BOOM! Yet, as Christians, we know the beauty of God's creative hand.

....

"I think that I shall never see, a poem as lovely as a tree." Joyce Kilmer

A.

B.

Lesson #14: *Drawing a tree*

Nature or God's creation, can be a wonderful course of study for any art student. The American poet, Joyce Kilmer, writes his feelings about God's beauty in nature in his poem, *Trees*. For this assignment, go outside and draw a tree from three different perspectives: a branch, one tree, and trees in the woods. First, look at the shape of trees and notice that they come in many different sizes, shapes and forms (A). Then draw a tree in the figure box above (B).

Next, notice that branches become thinner and thinner the farther out they extend (C). Draw a branch below (D) making sure that it becomes thinner as it extends out. It is good to use thick and thin lines when drawing tree limbs and branches by putting more pressure on your pencil for thicker lines and less pressure for thinner lines.

C.

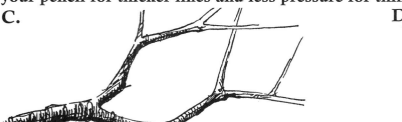

D.

F.

E.

Finally, draw some tree trunks and limbs in the woods. Draw the trunks and limbs lightly, and then darken the foliage and woods behind them with your black pen. Drawing like this will not only create delightful contrast, but will also give softer outlines to the trunks and limbs because you are not outlining them. This is called negative space, or the area that goes around the objects. Notice that some of the limbs in the background have been darkened a little to add more depth. Copy the picture (E) in the figure box to the right (F).

Jehovah-Elohim - *the eternal Creator!*

Jehovah-Tsidkenu *"Jehovah our righteousness"*
Jehovah-M'Kaddesh *"Jehovah who sanctifies"*
Jehovah-Shalom *"Jehovah is peace"*
Jehovah-Shammah *"Jehovah is there"*
Jehovah-Rophe *"Jehovah heals"*
Jehovah-Jireh *"Jehovah provides"*
Jehovah-Nissi *"Jehovah my banner"*
Jehovah-Rohi *"Jehovah my shepherd"*

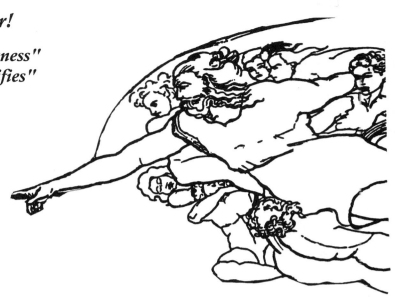

"Creation of Adam" (detail) Michelangelo
copied by Todd Leasure

Did you know that God has many names? He is called our *Heavenly Father, Lord, Almighty, Shield, High Tower, Fortress,* etc. Our God is also Three in One with Jesus Christ and the Holy Spirit. He is also called *Jehovah.* And in that name there are many other titles showing the great and wonderful personality of the Most High God. Remember, the Lord is an all consuming God and as Deuteronomy 6:4 states *"Hear, O Israel, the Lord our God, the Lord is one!"*

One of God's names is *Jehovah Elohim* - the eternal Creator. What a name! It's a name we can call Him as our art teacher or when we are inspired by what He has created. Our God has many names.

Most religions of the past have worshiped many gods and goddesses. Religious idols have been one of the major purposes for art through time. Religions have continually built hundreds and thousands of idols to their gods and goddesses. For example, the ancient Egyptians had Amen-Ra who was their supreme god, their god of life. Then there was his wife whose name was Mut. The Egyptians had the sinister Osiris as the go who presided over the underworld. Isis was the wife of Osiris, and their son Horus was also worshiped as a god. Then their was Bast, the cat goddess. This goddess was sometimes created as an idol with a cat's head and a woman's body. Besides their many gods and goddesses the Egyptians also worshiped animals such as bulls, apes, cats, crocodiles and hippopotamuses. Likewise, certain birds were sacred such as the hawk and the ibis. They even worshiped insects, especially the scarab, or dung beetle.

Gods, goddesses, and more gods! Aren't you glad that we only have one God to worship and that He is the One and only true God? Do you see how pure He is compared to all the other gods and goddesses that man has made for himself over the years?

"Without faith and draftsmanship your paintings will crumble. Faith is needed to keep your subject matter holy, while drawing is a cable that binds one's convictions together."

Tintoretto

Creativity

God tells us of His wonderful creativity throughout the Bible. He states in Job 38:22, *"Have you entered the treasury of snow, or have you seen the treasury of hail?"* Wow! That is remarkable. Have you ever stood in the middle of a snow storm and looked at all the snowflakes? Did you know that no two snowflakes are alike? Can you imagine, no two snowflakes that have ever fallen to the earth have had the exact same pattern or design? Likewise, did you know that no two trees are the same? No two leaves? No two fingerprints? No two voices? God is the great Jehovah Elohim, creating far beyond our imaginations. And we haven't even come close to seeing inside the *"treasury of hail"* that He speaks about. You see, having a better understanding of God not only gives you a better understanding of His personality, but also a much deeper respect for His creative genius.

Our God is so unbelievable in His creativity. And part of that creativity is in the way He has made you, because He has made you *"in His image and likeness."* That is why it is important for you to practice and develop the abilities which God has given to you! Certainly you have the ability to do wonderful things with your hands. Learning to draw and paint takes a good attitude and believing you can do anything you set your heart to. Having *discipline* means being determined to learn the things you need to do in order to become better. Don't give up on yourself, especially in your abilities in art. You never know how much ability God has given you until you really try.

"Noah's Ark" Kimberly Guidroz Age 9 Hammond, La.

Lesson #15: *Creativity*

We are all made in the image and likeness of God. Part of the way He has made us is the ability to be *creative*. Creativity, like everything else in art, should be practiced and nurtured. The more you develop it, the more creative you will be. For this assignment, let's do three creative exercises. First, draw a picture in the figure box (A). You can draw anything you like but try to be creative with your picture by placing a lot of detail in it and a variety of olors with your colored pencils. When you are finished, draw a border around your picture (B) and place interesting designs and colors in your frame. Then do a *contour drawing* in the figure box (C). A contour drawing is when you draw with one continuous line, going in and out, over and under (D). Be creative and carefree! You can do many wonderful pictures in this manner. Start with your orange colored pencil and then add other colors when you are finished. Finally, fill the figure box on the bottom of the page (E) with creative patterns or designs. You can use triangles, wavy lines, leaf patterns or anything else you like (F). Upon completion, color in your designs with a variety of colors.

B.

A. Creative Picture

C. Creative Contour Drawing

D.

E. Creative Patterns & Designs

F.

20

> *"He who works with his hands is a laborer. He who works with his head is a craftsman. He who works with his hands and his head and his heart is an artist."* Francis of Assisi

Artists

"Bethlehem" Erin Kivley Age 15 McHenry, Illinois

Artists

Artist

Do you know what an artist is? Just about everyone has a different opinion as to the definition of an artist. Take a moment and write what you believe the meaning of an artist is, and below that write what you believe is the meaning of art.

"I believe an artist is....."

_____
_____
_____

"I believe that art is...."

_____
_____
_____
_____

Webster's dictionary defines artist as, *"someone who professes (declares) to be an artist and who practices one of the fine arts."* Do you know what the *fine arts* are? They are drawing, painting, sculpture, ceramics, and sometimes architecture. Therefore, with this definition, an artist is someone who both states that he or she is an artist and also a person who practices a great deal. Other definitions of an artist are, *"One who is skilled in the arts, especially the fine arts....one who is creative."* So you see, there are different definitions of an artist.

Likewise, there are many definitions for art. In can mean, *"Sublime, elevating, inspiring, awesome, majestic, and beautiful."* However, *art* means even more than that. Remember, God created the beautiful things around us to touch the heart of man. Thus, there are two parts to the meaning of art - one is that it can be beautiful and secondly, that it should touch our hearts. Take a look at the pictures below of Ruth. The one to the left was done by a professional artist (A). The one to the right was done by a young student (B). However, both pictures bring pleasure to our hearts! So then, are they not both considered to be art?

A.

B.

Danielle Taylor Age 14
Auburn, Ontario

"Charm is deceptive, and beauty is fleeting; but a woman who fears the Lord is to be praised."

Proverbs 31:30

....

Many people believe art has to be beautiful. Even though this is true for most art, it does not necessarily have to be true for all art. For example, Albrecht Durer, the famous German master who lived during the Renaissance did the portrait below of his mother. Albrecht was a devout Christian man who praised his mother. It is said that she continually prayed this blessing over her children, *"Christ be with thee."* Albrecht Durer grew to become the greatest artist in the history of Germany and one of the greatest in all of Europe. However, when we take a look at the portrait he drew of his mother (below), we must honestly think....well, it may be a good drawing but it is certainly not pretty.

"A Proverbs 31 Woman"

As Christians, we should look for spiritual beauty rather than what the rest of the world sees as beautiful. That is how God sees things. Proverbs 31:30 says, *"Charm is deceitful and beauty is vain, but a woman who fears the Lord, she shall be praised."* The Bible states in 1 Samuel 16:7, *"For the Lord does not see as man sees; for man looks at the outward appearance, but the Lord looks at the heart."* Looking at the portrait of Albrecht's mother in this light makes the picture take on a new type of beauty.

"Portrait of Mother" Albrecht Durer

Jean Francois Millet was a French artist who lived during the 1800's. He was a Christian man brought up on the word of God. Millet chose to paint the peasants who were close to the land. Many of his paintings show them in godly settings: praying during their labors, gleaning in the fields (as Ruth did), etc. The artist saw beauty in a different way than the world did. Millet once stated, *"Beauty does not lie in the face....,"* but in other aspects of a person's inner character, like how a mother looks at her child. There are many ways to appreciate beauty but the best way is spiritually - the way God sees things.

"Jesus on the Cross"
Katie Taylor Age 15 Miami, Fl.

"So you shall speak to all who are gifted artisans, whom I have filled with the spirit of wisdom...." Exodus 28:3

Art can be beautiful, yet it doesn't necessarily have to be. Art can evoke emotions, it art can make us feel sad. Look at the drawing of Jesus on the cross by a student. It is undeniably sad. However, in its sadness is beauty. Solomon stated in Ecclesiastes 7:4, *"The heart of the wise is in the house of mourning, but the heart of fools is in the house of mirth."* There is a certain beauty in sorrow, especially in the eyes of God. Therefore, art can be uplifting or it can make us sad. However, above all else, art should touch our hearts.

A term that is relevant both to Christianity and to art is integrity. The Bible tells us about *"walking in our integrity."* Integrity means knowing the difference between right and wrong and living a life with a high code of morals. Webster's states, integrity: *"the quality or state of being of sound moral principle; uprightness, honesty, and sincerity."*

But there is another definition for integrity hidden away in some of the old Webster's dictionaries: *"Having a strict adherence to a code of moral or artistic values."* Artistic values? Does that mean we are to look for integrity in art also? Yes. I believe, in many instances, that an artist should be skilled in his trade, have a strong foundation in the fine arts and be able to apply these masterful skills to his artwork. If you ever have the opportunity to stand before the works of a great master like Rembrandt, you will have a better understanding of what integrity in art is. Rembrandt's ability to draw and his masterful handling of paint and brush are far above the skills of most artists. The great master had integrity because he practiced the fundamentals and became skilled in his profession. Thus, art can mean many things, but art should always touch our hearts.

Artists:
1. States that he or she is an artist.
2. Practices the fundamentals.
3. Should be skillful.
4. Can work in many different areas such as music, dance, writing, and the fine arts.

Art:
1. Can be beautiful.
2. Can be joyful.
3. Can be sad.
4. Does not have to be pretty.
5. Should touch the heart of man.

Colored Pencils

"Joseph's Coat of Many Colors"
Joy Masica Age 12
Rogers, Minnesota

"I want to recapture the freshness of vision which is characteristic of extreme youth when all the world is new."

Henri Matisse

Colored Pencils

"Sharing Five Loaves and Two Fish"
Nicholas Christ Age 7
San Jose, Ca.

Along with studying the great masters of the past, we are also going to learn how to use colored pencils. Colored pencils can be a wonderful tool for the art student. They are both practical and portable - you can take them with you anywhere. In addition, you can learn how to draw *lightly* by starting with a yellow colored pencil and then adding other colors after everything has been drawn correctly. Finally, colored pencils are a great tool for learning drawing and color at the same time. When some students reach a certain age they don't want to color any longer, desiring only to draw. But art students should be *well-rounded,* able to do a lot of things in art, such as drawing, painting, penmanship and understanding color theory.

The term *Renaissance man* comes from Leonardo da Vinci. In his lifetime, he was many things: an inventor, a scientist, an artist, a writer, an architect and even a musician. Da Vinci is a great example of what a person can do by applying himself. Strive to learn as much as you can to the best of your ability.

You will need a set of 12 to 24 colored pencils for these lessons. I prefer the set of 12 because in the beginning it is good for you to learn how to do more with less. Do not forget to sharpen your pencils! I like to sharpen my pencils with an electric pencil sharpener. It gives me a long, sharp point.

Lesson #16: *The Color Wheel*

A.

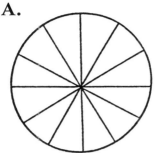

B.

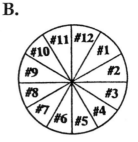

Let's start by coloring the *color wheel*. A color wheel teaches you about color theory. First, we will color in the three primary colors: *yellow, red* and *blue.* Theoretically, you can make every color that exists (except white) by mixing various combinations of these three colors. To begin, color pie shape #1 yellow in the color wheel to the left (A) as shown on the color wheel to the right (B). Then color red in #5 and blue in #9, skipping three pie shapes between each color.

Next, take your colored pencils and drawing paper into the kitchen and draw a picture of what's on the sink or on the kitchen table. Take a few moments to situate everything into a pleasing *composition.* Draw lightly with a light colored pencil like yellow and then color your picture using only the primary colors. You can blend the primary colors together any way you like, but limit yourself to just these three colors. What do you think of coloring with only the primary colors?

Lesson #17: *Secondary Colors*

Secondary colors are colors that are made by mixing or blending two primary colors together. For example, *yellow* and *red* make *orange*; *red* and *blue* make *violet*; *yellow* and *blue* make *green.* However, with some materials, like colored pencils and colored markers, it's not easy to make some of the secondary colors by mixing primary colors together. For the first part of this exercise, see how well you can make the three secondary colors: orange, violet and green by mixing just the primary colors together in the three shapes below (C). Gently lay one layer of color down and then lay the next color over it to make each secondary color. You may want to experiment with different yellow, red and blue colored pencils. For the second part of this exercise take your orange, violet and green colored pencils and color the other objects to the right (D) with these colors.

C. orange violet green

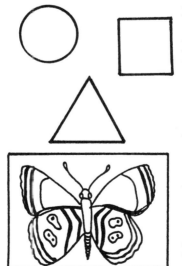

You probably made a nice green by mixing your blue and yellow together, and also a nice orange with yellow and red. However, it may have been difficult to mix a violet with your red and blue pencils.

When you have finished, color in the secondary colors in the color wheel (A) with your orange, violet and green colored pencils. Color orange in pie shape #3, violet in #7 and green in #11. Finally, color the two butterflies (E & F). Color the one to the left (E) with just the secondary colors. Then color the butterfly to the right (F) with the primary and secondary colors.

D. orange violet green

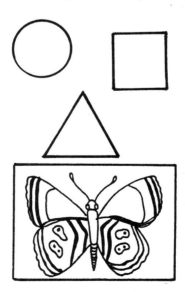

E. Secondary Colors

F. Primary & Secondary Colors

Lesson #18: *Tertiary Colors*

Let's color the remaining pie sections in the color wheel on page 27 with the *tertiary colors*. Tertiary colors are made by mixing a primary and secondary color together. For example, when you blend yellow and orange together you will make the tertiary color *yellow/orange* (for pie section #2). Blend the colors together between red and orange to create *red/orange* (pie section #4). The colors between red and violet will blend together to make *red/violet* (pie section #6). Color in the six tertiary colors on the color wheel, placing each in the correct pie section. Then color in the picture to the left with just tertiary colors. Finally, color the butterflies below (A) using one of the 6 tertiary colors for each.

C. Vertical Lines

A.

Lesson #19: *Coloring with Line*

B.

Analogous colors are colors that are next to each other on the color wheel such as yellow, yellow/orange, and orange. Analogous colors create *harmony* in a picture, singing when they are next to each other. For this assignment, select any 3 colors next to each other on the color wheel, and color the butterfly (B). However, color with *vertical lines*. Vertical lines go up and down (C.). Remember, take your time when coloring with lines and place your lines close together.

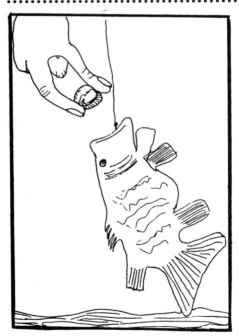

"The Coin in the Mouth of the Fish"
Lisa Myers Age 11
Brazil, Indiana

Many students color the same way as they do with crayons and coloring books, coloring large areas with one solid color. For instance, if a student desires to color a red apple, he would likely take out a red crayon and color it entirely red. There are other ways to color which can be very exciting and colorful. Again, one of the best ways to learn to color is with lines. You have probably noticed that coloring this way can become tedious. However, if you take your time and really put your best effort into it, you will make beautiful colors. Learning to draw and color takes time, effort and discipline. Don't think for one moment that great artists were just born that way. Certainly, some artists are naturally gifted, however, most of the time it takes discipline and determination. Learning the fine arts takes much work and effort, just like anything else in life.

"Moses in the Bulrushes"
Joy Miller
Age 12   Mandeville, La.

Lesson #20: *Complementary Colors*

Let's color another color wheel. However this time we will only color the primary and secondary colors (A). Color the primary colors first, making sure to skip a pie shape in between each. Then take your secondary colors and color the correct one in between the two primary colors which make it. For example, orange would go in between yellow and red.

Complementary colors are colors that are opposite each other on the color wheel. Therefore, green is the complement of red. Looking at your color wheel, write down the complement of each of the colors listed below:

A.

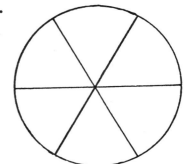

1. The complement of green is "red".
2. The complement of yellow is _____.
3. The complement of orange is _____.
4. The complement of violet is _____.
5. The complement of red is _____.
6. The complement of blue is _____.

. . . .

Next, color the birds and circles using complementary colors (B). First, color the birds with the color printed underneath, and then color the circle behind each with the *complement* of that color. Remember, complementary colors like to be next to each other!

B.

    red   yellow   blue   violet   orange   green

Complementary colors are used for backgrounds, dulling and shading. Suppose you colored an apple and do not know a good color for the background. You can always use its complement which is green. Again, complementary colors sing when they are next to each other. Another way to use complementary colors is for *dulling*. Suppose you just colored an orange balloon but it is too bright. You can dull it by adding a little of its complement, which is blue. Do not add too much of the complement. Complementary colors can overwhelm other colors if you use too much. For the balloon, you may want to first color it with a deep, rich orange. Then, add a very light layer of blue over that and finally, add more orange over it again to give you a very dull, or muted, orange. The third way to use complements is for shading. Suppose you wanted to shade part of a banana. First, color the entire banana with a deep, rich layer of yellow. Then, add a very light layer of violet to the shaded side. Finally, color another rich layer of yellow over the entire banana. Color the apple red (C) and the background with its complement. Color the balloon orange (D) and dull it with a light layer of blue. Color the entire banana with a deep, rich yellow (E) and add a light violet to the shaded side, adding more yellow over the shaded area. Last of all, color the butterfly (F) with any pair of complementary colors you like.

C.   D.   E.   F.

Lesson #21: *Shading with Color*

A.

Most students shade with black. Many times black can be too dark and overbearing for shadows. Students may have better results by using *cool colors* in the shaded areas. The cool colors are *blue, violet* and *green*. Blue and violet are especially good to use in shaded areas just as yellow is good to use in areas where the sun is shining. First, color the shadow behind the flower (A) with blue and violet, using vertical lines. Then color in the shadows on the porch (B) with blues and violets. Finally, color in the other areas with a light layer of yellow to brighten up the picture.

When you are finished, go outside and draw a picture of a plant with a *cast shadow* (C). A cast shadow is simply the shadow that is cast by an object onto the ground or other surface. Draw your picture lightly with your yellow pencil and then add darker colors, making sure to color the shaded areas with violets and blues. Add a lot of yellow to the sunny areas.

B. Shading with Blues & Violets

C. Going Outside

Lesson #22: *Warm Colors*

D.

Warm colors are *yellow, red* and *orange*. There are other warm colors like pink, yellow/orange and red/orange. You can close your eyes and almost feel that a color is warm, just as you can close your eyes and almost feel that a color is cool. Cool colors can create a sad or gloomy mood while warm colors can create a bright or cheerful mood. Color the sunset and its reflection behind the flamingo (D) with yellow and orange. Also, color the sky a bright yellow. Next, color the water with blue, violet and green using short, horizontal strokes. Color the flamingo with pink and a little orange and yellow, blending the colors into his body with your white or light cream colored pencil. Last of all, color the tip of his beak black.

Lesson #23: *Scientific Study*

Art and science are very different. That is why they are considered separate areas of study. However, in some ways art can be very scientific. You will find that many of the great artists of the past were scientific in mixing colors, learning about perspective, and even in the study of anatomy and nature.

For this assignment, we are going to mix colors with our pencils in a scientific manner. See how many new colors you can make by coloring each of the butterflies below. Make some by blending one color over another and others by *blending* several colors together. When blending, place one layer of color over another. See what new colors you can create! (It is always good to lay down the lighter color first.) Print the colors you used underneath each new color you created so that, as a scientist, you will be able to refer to it if you desire to make that color again. For example, if you blended yellow, orange and violet you would print: Y + O + V underneath.

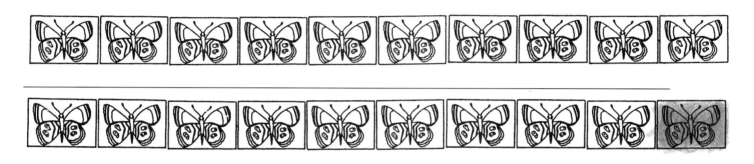

"Jonah at Ninevah"
Richard Reuter
Age 12 Tempe, Arizona

31

"God Almighty first planted a garden; and, indeed, it is the purest of human pleasures."

Francis Bacon

"Let's go outside!"

It is important for us to have a good understanding of who God is before venturing into the fine arts. Appreciating God-the-Artist (Jehovah Elohim), will help us value art more. Remember, no one can surpass God's creative genius. All we can do as mere mortals, is simply imitate the Great Master. We can paint flowers - which He created, or sculpt horses - which He has made, or color a sunrise, which God creates anew every day. We can even draw portraits of people, but alas, man too is another one of God's master-pieces.

One of the best ways to have an understanding of God-the-Artist is by going outside. Unfortunately, many students do not like going outdoors to do artwork. The bugs bite, the wind blows their papers away, it is too hot or too cold and people come by to see what you are drawing.

However, in time you should find "God's Studio" (the outdoors) to be wonderfully inspiring! You will hear the birds singing and feel the cool breeze on your face. The sky will be your ceiling, and you will begin to realize that the people who stop by to see your artwork will only praise the good work you are doing. Likewise, your eyes will begin to see what sunlight does to change colors, and hopefully, you will find a treasure of things to draw and study. Thus, if you stick with it, the day may come whey you return home saying to yourself, *"I like doing my artwork outside."* Here are a few pointers for working out of doors:
A.

1. Take a portable chair to sit on.
2. Bring a hat and something to drink.
3. Clip artwork so it doesn't blow away.
4. Wear the proper clothing.

Lesson #24: *Drawing a Flower*

Take your colored pencils outside and draw and color one flower or a colorful leaf in figure box A. Select a flower with good colors, like an iris or pansy. Start by drawing lightly with your yellow pencil and then adding other colors. Squint your eyes to see how many colors you can see. Place some yellow and blue in your greens to make them more colorful. Color your flower with lines. When you are finished, color a flower on another sheet of paper by blending colors. Which technique do you like best - lines or blending?

32

Leonardo da Vinci was both a scientist and an artist. Like Michelangelo, he was one of the greatest artists of the Italian Renaissance (1400-1600 AD). Did you know that da Vinci invented the ball bearing? He also invented the parachute, the tank, the wheel barrel, and even the handkerchief. Likewise, Leonardo was an architect and a student of *anatomy* (the study of the human figure). However, he was an artist first and foremost and all his other studies revolved around this purpose. One thing da Vinci did was to take his little sketchbook with him everywhere he went to draw and study the things around him, like leaves, acorns, animals, and even facial gestures of people as they talked or argued on the streets of Florence. Below is one of his nature studies. Notice how he drew and shaded with lines.

Nature Study by Leonardo da Vinci

Lesson #25: *Nature Studies*

For this assignment, go outside and do some simple studies from nature such as: an acorn, pinecone, pebbles, a leaf or a flower. Draw your nature studies below. Study each object and see how much color you notice in them.

Lesson #26: Examination #1

Part I: Matching. Find the correct definition for each term and print the letter of the meaning next to the term if defines. 1 point each. (Answers on last page of *God & the History of Art I.*)

_____1. integrity
_____2. humanism
_____3. Renaissance
_____4. tertiary colors
_____5. red & green
_____6. cool colors
_____7. draftsmanship
_____8. secondary colors
_____9. geometric shapes
_____10. discipline
_____11. guidelines
_____12. overlapping
_____13. fundamentals
_____14. primary colors
_____15. color wheel
_____16. warm colors
_____17. Renaissance man
_____18. oval
_____19. Leonardo da Vinci
_____20. vertical lines

a. circles, squares, rectangles, triangles
b. determination to learn in order to become better
c. building blocks in art
d. orange, green, violet
e. light lines used in lettering
f. blue/green
g. a period of time from 1400-1600, means "rebirth"
h. egg-shaped
i. the ability to draw
j. someone who can do many things in a great manner
k. man is the measure of all things
l. placing one object slightly in front of another
m. orange, red, yellow
n. straight up and down
o. red, blue, yellow
p. blue, green, violet
q. adhering to moral or artistic values
r. a "Renaissance man"
s. complementary colors
t. teaches color theory

yellow

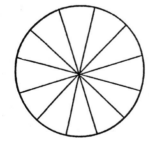

Part II: Complete the color wheel by coloring in each pie shape with the correct primary, secondary, or tertiary color. (Yellow is at the top.) Write the answer to each on the lines provided below. (One point each)
1._____   2._____   3._____   4._____
5._____   6._____   7._____   8._____
9._____   10._____   11._____   12._____

Part III: True or False Answer each of the statements *"true"* or *"false"* by placing either a "T" or an "F" in front of each. (One point each)

_____1. Art is a *"learned discipline."*
_____2. Horizontal lines go straight up and down.
_____3. An ellipse is a circle seen on an angle.
_____4. Michelangelo was an artist who lived during the 18th century.
_____5. Art has to be beautiful.
_____6. A good color to use for a background is its complement.
_____7. The primary colors are orange, violet, and green.
_____8. Jehovah Elohim means God the Creator.

"Then the angel said to them, 'Do not be afraid, for behold, I bring you good tidings of great joy which will be to all people."

Luke 2:10

Great Christian Artists

Rebecca Schluter Age 7
Bartlesville, Oklahoma

Christian Artists

Who were the great Christian artists of the past? Throughout the ages there have been many artists whose desire was to serve God and glorify Him. However, it is rather difficult to know which artists were really committed to serving the Lord, and which were simply working for pay. Let us not forget that artists had to make a living, and in the old days, ordinary people did not purchase artwork to hang in their homes. Religious art was commissioned by the church and, for many years, the church was the greatest *patron* or supporter, of the arts. Thus, artists received commissions to do large religious paintings on the ceilings and walls of the churches, and to do marvelous pieces of sculpture of the disciples and prophets of the Bible.

Before the Renaissance (1400-1600) an artist was not considered to be of any more significance than any other profession. He was a common workman like a butcher, baker, or candlestick maker. There was no personal importance placed upon the work he did, so few artists signed their work or kept any records or journals about their profession. Only with the emergence of the Renaissance, when art achieved great heights, did artists receive recognition and their works became famous. Even so, there is little personal record of the famous artists who lived during and after the Renaissance. Nor do we know about their relationship with God. Fortunately, there have been artists like Leonardo da Vinci, Michelangelo, and Vincent van Gogh, who along with being artists, were prolific writers, allowing us the opportunity to enter into their personal lives.

It is unfortunate that many artists whom we believe to have been Christians were simply artists commissioned to do religious artwork. A prime example of this was the artist Gustave Doré. Look at the print by Doré on the next page of *"Moses Breaking the Tablets of the Law."* It is a powerful illustration of Moses and the Ten Commandments. However, just because Doré created a beautiful religious piece of art does not mean that he was a committed Christian. We must not confuse a great artist who did wonderful religious artwork for pay, with a Christian artist who dedicated, consecrated, and committed his works to God. As the great classical composer Johannas Sebastian Bach would inscribe on his manuscripts, *Solo Deo Gloria (All to the glory of God).*

"Jacob Wrestling with the Angel" Gustave Doré/etching

Gustave Doré (1832-1883)

Gustave Doré (goose-tave door-aye) was born in France in 1832. He was the son of a civil engineer. During his early years he showed much ability in art, but his father tried to discourage this as a profession, insisting that his son remain in school and continue his studies in the academics. Still, every free moment that the young boy had was spent in the Louvre Museum in Paris where he studied the great masters. Gustave had a remarkable memory and was able to retain much of what he observed simply by looking at it.

"Moses Breaking the Tablets of the Law" Gustave Doré

As Gustave became more successful, he was commissioned to illustrate the Bible which became one of his most prosperous endeavors. In these illustrations he strived to be exact with biblical costumes and backgrounds. Doré was very theatrical in his portrayals of stories such as Samson, Moses, the plagues of Egypt and the Ten Commandments (above), revealing a new vitality to these stories from the Old Testament.

Gustave Doré grew to be a famous artist, working very hard and making much money. He was raised a Catholic but professed to having little faith. However, he was warmly embraced by many of the authorities of the church because of his beautiful religious paintings. Doré died in 1883 at the age of 51.

Lesson #27: *Daniel in The Lions' Den*

Notice the etching by Gustave Doré of *Daniel in the Lions' Den* and the detail he placed in his picture. All the shading was done with line. Also, look at the student drawings of *Daniel in the Lions' Den* and notice how different they are. God has made each of us unique and creative in our own way, and you are encouraged to develop the creativity which He has given you. Remember, we are made in His image and likeness, and part of that likeness is the ability to create... a quality that no other living species has.

"Daniel in the Lions' Den" Gustave Doré/etching

"Daniel in the Lions' Den"
Dalton Schmidt, Age 5 Orlando, Fl.

"Daniel in the Lions' Den"
Colette Des Marais, Age 12 Maple Grove, Mn.

For this assignment, do your own drawing of *Daniel in the Lions' Den* in the figure box. Start by drawing with your yellow colored pencil, and then go over it with your black pen.

"I beseech you therefore, brethren, by the mercies of God, that you present your bodies a living sacrifice, holy, acceptable to God, which is your reasonable service." Romans 12:1

Fra Angelico (1387-1455) "The Angelic One"

"Have you considered My servant Job, that there is none like him on the earth, a blameless and upright man, one who fears God and shuns evil?" (Job 1:8). This scripture could possibly have been what God had said about Fra Angelico, the Italian artist, *"...that there is none like him on the earth, a blameless and upright man, one who fears God and shuns evil."*

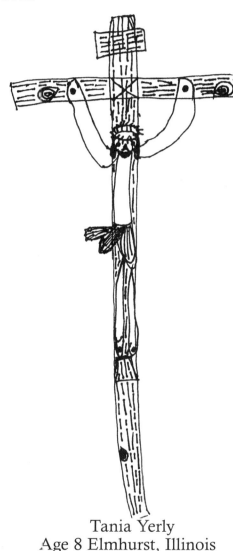

Tania Yerly
Age 8 Elmhurst, Illinois

There is much more to being a Christian than simply being a *Christian,* just like there is more to being in *God's will.* God has several *wills,* one of which is being out of His will. This is where fallen man is, in a world that is void of God and out of His will. Then, there is being in His *permissive will* which means that, even though one may be a Christian, he does not show much love for God as evidenced by his lifestyle. He has established other priorities and has not offered his body up as *"a living sacrifice, holy and acceptable to God."* Finally, there is the third category, God's most pleasing and *perfect will.* This is a much smaller group of Christians, ones who seek God with all their heart, striving to walk in His holiness and righteousness, presenting their bodies as a *living sacrifice.*

Many of the Christian artists of the past were probably in God's *permissive will.* They may have loved and served Him, but when it came to art, they were somewhat polluted by the world's influence, doing what would please others instead of what would please God. This, in part, was out of necessity because artists had to do *commission* work for *patrons.* Throughout the years, patrons have usually been wealthy businessmen who paid artists to create specific artwork for them. This is called *commission* artwork because it is done with another's interest in mind and for pay. Remember, in the past it was difficult for artists to create independently because of financial needs. Thus, out of necessity, there were few artists who could be dedicated, consecrated and committed to serving the Lord in their artwork. However, God always finds a way to make exceptions. Probably the greatest of these was Fra Angelico, the monastic monk who lived in Italy during the 1400s.

Lesson #28: *Drawing Wood*

A.

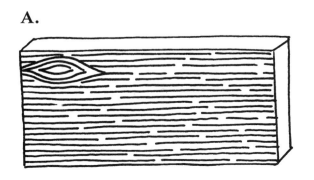

Drawing *texture* is suggesting what the surface of something is like; for example, the surface of a sponge, fur or wood. For this assignment, draw a wooden cross on a plain sheet of paper. One of the best ways to show the texture of wood is with long, broken lines (A). To make a knot on your wood, draw a small candle flame and then draw larger candle flames around it.

"If I honor Myself, My honor is nothing. It is My Father who honors Me."   John 8:54

Giodo di Pietro was born in Italy in 1387. As a youth he worked on *illuminated manuscripts* which were colorful texts that were hand painted and lettered. Through this experience he developed a high degree of elegance and refinement in both line and color. During his youth he was a talented artist but he knew deep down that his main purpose was to serve God. When he was twenty years of age he decided to dedicate his life to Christ by entering the Dominican Convent of Fiesole. Giodo di Pietro was eventually given the name Fra Angelico, *the angelic one.*

After 20 years in the service of the Church, the Dominicans moved to the San Marco Convent in Florence. It was at this new location that Fra Angelico was asked to paint *mural* decorations for the new building. He painted a sacred scene in each of the monk's cells and at the end of each corridor. *Fresco* paintings, which were done on walls and ceilings, were very popular at this time. They were done by applying wet plaster to one portion of a wall and then painting on it while the plaster was still wet. Fra Angelico's mural paintings were done between 1437 and 1446 and are still standing today. These spiritual paintings are a testimony to the pure talents of this godly artist, and a major reason why the building has been turned into a museum.

One of the Bible stories Fra Angelico painted in the San Marco Convent was *The Annunciation* (next page), where the angel Gabriel visits Mary in Nazareth to announce that she is going to give birth to Jesus. What a beautiful story to illustrate! Fra Angelico chose this scene to adorn the front entrance of the convent. It portrays the wonderful visitation of a heavenly messenger kneeling before Mary, bringing the good news.

The 14th century in Italy was a time of much activity because of the Renaissance, but Fra Angelico desired a more simple lifestyle. Except for his early education, he was self-taught in art and his paintings do not show much influence by other artists. The figures in his pictures are rather flat, seemingly frozen in a fixed position. This was a traditional way of painting that had been handed down to artists in the 14th century from the Byzantine period. During the Renaissance, most of the artists were returning to the style of classical art from ancient Greece and Rome. Even though Fra Angelico was in the midst of this great revival in the arts, he remained rather isolated from its influence. Like today, the world was moving at a hectic pace, but this holy artist was seeking after a more peaceful and significant existence with God.

Lesson 29: *Drawing Clothing*

Do you know how to draw clothing? One of the best ways to learn this is by drawing draped material at home. For this assignment, take a beach towel with various patterns and drape it in a nice way. Then, draw it with the designs and folds in the figure box to the left. Try to show different *values* from light, to medium (some shading), to dark (shaded value). Remember, shade with lines. Use your colored pencils for this exercise.

Fra Angelico only painted when he was asked to do so. Before beginning, he would prepare himself with fasting and prayer. It is said that he wept whenever he painted the crucifixion of Christ. Ruskin, the great English art critic of the 19th century, once stated that Fra Angelico's paintings were *"...the most radiant consummation of the pure ideal of Christianity in all art."*

Unlike many artists of his time who were painting scenes from Greek mythology, Fra Angelico only painted religious subject matter. He is best known for his delicate and beautiful colors. Few, if any other artists have expressed the Christian faith with such sweetness and heavenly bliss. The faces Fra Angelico painted seem to capture a certain purity. Simplicity and holiness would best sum up his work. Upon his death, *Beato* (meaning blessed), was added to his name.

··

"The Annunciation"

"Now in the sixth month the angel Gabriel was sent by God to a city of Galilee named Nazareth, to a virgin betrothed to a man whose name was Joseph, of the house of David. The virgin's name was Mary. And having come in, the angel said to her, 'Rejoice, highly favored one, the Lord is with you; blessed are you among women!'

But when she saw him, she was troubled at his saying, and considered what manner of greeting this was. Then the angel said to her, 'Do not be afraid, Mary, for you have found favor with God. And behold, you will conceive in your womb and bring forth a Son, and shall call His name Jesus. He will be great, and will be called the Son of the Highest; and the Lord God will give Him the throne of His father David. And He will reign over the house of Jacob forever, and of His kingdom there will be no end.'"

Luke 1:26-33

··

"The Annunciation" by Todd Leasure
Copied from Fra Angelico's *"Annunciation"* at the San Marco Convent

"Fra Angelico used frequently to say that he who practiced the art of painting had need of quiet, and should live without cares or anxious thoughts; adding that he who would do the work of Christ should perpetually remain in Christ." Vasari

Elias Noatz Age 12 Cannon Falls, Mn.

Felicity Huang Age 12 Ontario

A.

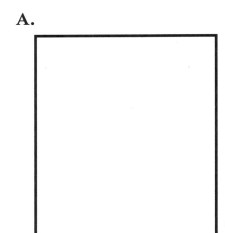

Lesson #30: *Painting a Monastery*

As mentioned, Fra Angelico only painted when he was asked to do so by the church authorities. His first priority was God. Most of Fra Angelico's wonderful paintings still adorn the walls of convents and monasteries in Italy.

For this assignment, let's pretend that you are commissioned to paint a picture from the Gospel on the walls of a monastery. First, draw an angel in the figure box (A) or in a sketchbook. Do you know how to draw an angel? You may want to draw a person with a long robe, and give him wings and a halo. Notice the angel drawn by a student in the upper left as Paul is being freed from prison.

Next, draw a picture for the walls of a monastery on a plain sheet of white paper using your colored pencils. You can choose any story from the Bible that you find to be inspiring. Look at the wonderful picture above of Elizabeth greeting Mary that was done by another student. Do some thumbnail sketches below in the arch frames before you do your final masterpiece.

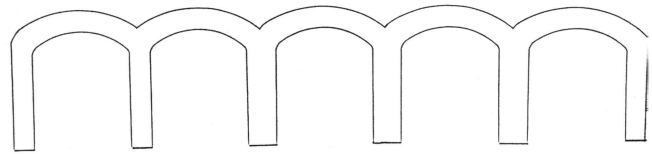

Lesson #31: *Coloring with Symbolism*

During the times of Fra Angelico, color was very symbolic in religious paintings. The three main colors used were gold (yellow), blue and red, as artists like Fra Angelico strived for spiritual meanings more than for realistic ones. For this assignment, draw the picture of Fra Angelico's "Annunciation" (left) in the large figure box below. Then, color it with gold, blue and red. First, see how many "tones" of these three colors you can make. Tone simply means different light or dark variations of one color, from the very lightest to the darkest.

"The Annunciation" by Todd Leasure copied from Fra Angelico

Before beginning, color the balloons with tones from the lightest tone of blue to the darkest blue. For example, start by coloring the first balloon in the blue row a very light blue by adding a lot of white to light blue. Then, add more blue to the second balloon to make it darker. Make a very dark blue by adding black and/or a little red. For gold or deep yellow, you can practice by adding a touch of orange or light brown to yellow. When you are finished, color your picture with a variety of blue, red, and gold tones. Finally, write what you like about your light and dark tones on the lines below. Practicing mixing tones is an excellent exercise.

"And I have filled him with the Spirit of God, in wisdom, in understanding, in knowledge, and in all manner of workmanship, to design artistic works, to work in gold, in silver, in bronze, in cutting jewels for setting, in carving wood, and to work in all manner of workmanship."

Exodus 31:3-5

Albrecht Dürer (1471-1528) *A Man For All Seasons*

Albrecht Dürer (all-breck door-er) lived during the Renaissance in northern Europe. At this time Germany was rather removed from the excitement that was going on in Italy. However, like da Vinci, Dürer was considered a *Renaissance man* because of his unquench-able desire for learning, along with his ability to do many things in a great manner. Certainly Albrecht Dürer, the German artist, was *a man for all seasons.*

"Dürer" Self-Portrait

Albrecht Dürer was born in Germany in 1471, the third of eighteen children. His father was a noted goldsmith, and the young boy was taught his father's trade at an early age. Young Albrecht grew up in a good Christian family, with the fear and admonition of the Lord. This would eventually establish a great purpose for his art. Even though he was much influenced by the spectacular art of the Italian Renaissance, he sought a purer approach to art, especially pertaining to the Bible. He showed such talent for design and draftsmanship that, at the age of 15, young Albrecht was apprenticed to a local painter and wood engraver.

The influence of his parents and his Christian upbringing would leave a lasting impression upon the artist who would one day rise to great acclaim throughout Europe. Of his father, the artist stated, *"My dear father passed his life in great toil and arduous labor, having only what he earned by the sweat of his body to support his family. He experienced many troubles, but he was patient and gentle, at peace with the world and grateful to his Maker."* And of his mother he said, *"She kept us, my brothers and myself, with great care from all sin, and on my coming and going it was her habit to say, 'Christ, bless thee.' I cannot praise enough her good works, the kindness and charity that she showed to all."* As already mentioned, the drawing that Albrecht did of his mother (next page) is not a beautiful picture. She was not an attractive woman, and her son was true to portray her the way she looked. However, as we learn of her godly character, we see another side of the portrait and a fondness is kindled within our hearts. Albrecht Dürer's mother was a *Proverbs 31 woman*.

It was an exciting time for young Albrecht to be an artist. The Renaissance was in full blossom. Europe, like a flower in springtime, was coming out of the winter of the Middle Ages. Man was *enlightened* and free to learn and express himself in the arts. However, there was much turmoil in the air, especially in northern Europe. Along with the revival of the Renaissance, another revival was taking place - the revival of the Church, or the *Reformation*. This was a revolution in religion and was ushered in by another German, the Augustinian friar, Martin Luther. During this time the Roman Catholic Church was the established authority for Christianity, but Luther had many grievances pertaining to its doctrine.

"The Bible is our vineyard, and there we should labor and toil." Martin Luther

Martin Luther became known as *the Great Reformer* and the leader of the Reformation in Germany. Even though he was not an artist, his feelings about man's relationship with God would have much influence on artists in the years to follow, especially those in northern Europe. He believed that the selling of *indulgences* and the church authorities keeping the people from having access to the Word of God were wrong. He professed that everyone should have access to God without needing the intercession of clergy. Luther wrote a thesis with the grievances he had against the Roman Catholic Church and nailed them to the church door in Wittenburg, Germany. Thus, the friar ignited a revolution within the church, and in the process, placed the Bible in the hands of the common people.

He was inspired with new ideas for the Church rejecting the pope's authority and establishing the Bible as the sole source of truth. Luther believed that common people had as much authority as clergy in the kingdom of God. He also denied the necessity of the clergy being celibate, eventually marrying Katherine von Bora and raising six children.

Although the 95 thesis was posted in 1517, it wasn't until 1529 that this religious movement was officially recognized. During a great council of church authorities, the followers of Luther protested against a decree that stated the Roman Catholic Church must be restored as the total source of authority in Christianity. Because of this, Luther and his followers were call *protesters* which eventually led to their name - *Protestants*. Martin Luther and his stance against the Roman Catholic Church was not only the beginning of the Protestant faith, but the first seed planted for many of the modern day Christian denominations such as Baptist, Presbyterian, Mennonite and Calvinist.

Lesson #32: *Drawing a Portrait of Mother*

Notice the drawing below that Albrecht Durer did of his mother. For this assignment, have your mother sit for you and do a portrait of her in the other figure box with your colored pencils.

"Portrait of Mother" by Albrecht Dürer

Over the next several decades there would be war and bloodshed between the Roman Catholic church and many of the northern countries of Europe who were now considered Protestant in faith. Peace treaties followed these religious wars, the most significant being the Peace of Augsburg in 1555, in which the Roman Catholic church finally consented to grant Germany the right to choose whatever religion it so desired.

The religious turmoil of the Reformation was oddly interwoven during the Renaissance. The opposing forces of both a revolution and a period of enlightenment were happening at the same time. The Renaissance was built upon humanistic principles, placing man in the center of everything and believing man could accomplish anything. Artists of the Renaissance sought spectacular art and perfection, and the Roman Catholic church continued to support this style, filling its cathedrals and chapels with works by the great masters. Whereas, the Reformation in northern Europe was establishing a relationship that placed Christ in the center of life. Northern Europe would thus have a much more conservative approach to art. Most northern artists wanted little to do with the spectacular art of the Italian Renaissance. Instead, they focused more on everyday life, concerning themselves with the painting of portraits, landscapes and still lifes moreso than religious subject matter.

During this time, Flemish artists introduced the printmaking technique of woodcarving. With the invention of the Gutenburg press, illustrations for books became a favorite purpose for artists in northern Europe. Engraving, or printmaking, was a *medium* in which many artists could make a living. German craftsmen were, by nature, thorough and patient with every detail and became known as the best engravers in Europe. It was in this atmosphere Albrecht Dürer emerged. Albrecht had been greatly influenced by Martin Luther, who inspired him in his artwork.

Engravings were done by incisions with sharp carving tools into wood or metal. After the picture had been etched out, ink was rolled over the carved out picture and a series of prints were made from the original piece of artwork. This was a wonderful and exciting *medium* for Albrecht to explore and develop. Medium simply means the method or materials used by the artist, i.e. painting, drawing, engraving, etc. Since Albrecht had been raised under the instruction of his father, a goldsmith by trade, it was a wonderful asset for him to learn engraving. Albrecht Dürer was a realist in his artwork and desired to be as true to nature and God's creation as he could. He loved adding every little detail, and with engraving, he found he could put in as much detail as he desired.

The drawing to the left was done in one of his sketchbooks. It shows his studious observations of some of the problems with *foreshortening* in drawing. Foreshortening means that objects seem larger as they come forward and smaller as they go back in the distance, giving the illusion of depth in a picture. In your drawings you can show this by making objects larger than they seem in the foreground and much smaller in the background. This type of exaggeration in art creates the effect of foreshortening. Notice the care Albrecht Durer took with detail.

"The Painter Studying- the Laws of Foreshortening"
by Albrecht Dürer

Notice the engraving by Albrecht Dürer, *St. Michael's Fight Against the Dragon* on page 49. This is a woodcut, carved out of a piece of flat wood and then used for printmaking. Look at the wonderful detail the artist was able to create and how the entire picture was done with lines. Observe how Dürer suggested the sky by meticulously carving out long, horizontal lines. These lines add contrast to the picture, placing light areas against dark areas. To carve such delicate lines Albrecht needed precision tools, a very hard wood and much patience.

St. Michael's Fight Against the Dragon was taken from the book of Revelation and was an immediate success, especially within Germany. The book of Revelation had never been portrayed in such a powerful way, and the picture gave the people a vision of things to come during the times of doomsday. With all the turmoil surrounding the 1500s, many believed that the Second Coming was at hand, Christ was returning to judge mankind and the end was near.

How many angels do you see in the picture? How many demons? What weapons are the angels using? Does this remind you of any scriptures? What about Ephesians 6:12, *"For we do not wrestle against flesh and blood, but against principalities, against powers, against the rulers of the darkness of this age, against spiritual hosts of wickedness in the heavenly places."* Another good scripture that comes to mind might be, *"You shall tread upon the lion and the cobra, the young lion and the serpent you shall trample under foot"* (Psalm 91:13). Or what about, *"Put on the whole armor of God, that you may be able to stand against the wiles of the devil"* (Ephesians 6:11). What armor are the angels using in Dürer's illustration?

Lesson #33: *Drawing Dragons*

Throughout the history of Christianity, dragons have been used to *symbolize,* or represent Satan and his demons. Take another look at the engraving by Dürer and notice how demonic he has made them. Also, notice the dragon that was drawn by Barry Stebbing below and some by students on the top of page 48.

For this assignment, practice drawing demons in the small figure boxes below. These small studies are called *thumbnail sketches* and can help you in formulating your final ideas. You may want to have some pictures of crocodiles and alligators to inspire you for your dragons. Be creative. Give your dragons wings, long tails, fangs and claws. You may even want to make fire-breathing dragons.

Thumbnail Sketches

"Dragon Study"
by Barry Stebbing

47

Joel Nelson Age 12
Brighton, Minnesota

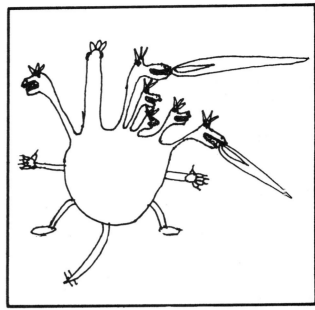

R.J. Dickie Age 9
Strong City, Kansas

Lesson #34: *St. Michael Slaying the Dragon*
Now that you know how to draw a dragon, let's draw the dramatic scene in the Bible from Revelation 12:7. Like Albrecht Dürer, place as much detail in it as you can. Do your picture in the figure box above. Start by drawing lightly, and then go over it with a black marker pen. When you are finished, try to find more scriptures that describe your feelings about what is going on.

"And there was war in heaven: Michael and his angels fought against the dragon; and the dragon fought and his angels, and prevailed not; neither was their place found any more in heaven."

Revelation 12:7,8

"St. Michael's Fight Against the Dragon" Albrecht Dürer

Although the Renaissance was best known in Italy, northern Europe also experienced a *rebirth* in the arts. This was called *the Northern Renaissance,* and Albrecht Dürer was acclaimed as the greatest artist of this period. His position in Nuremberg was equal to that of Michelangelo, da Vinci and Raphael in Italy. Wherever he traveled in northern Europe, he was welcomed with honor by kings and artists alike.

Albrecht Dürer grew to great acclaim all over Europe, especially in Germany. After apprenticing during his teen years, his father allowed him to travel to Venice at the age of 19. The Italians loved the young German artist. Even the great masters were amazed by his talent. He could paint hair with the flick of his brush, capturing detail and variety of color in one quick motion. Dürer loved the warm climate of Italy and the wonderful excitement in the air. The Italians pleaded with him to remain in Italy but his heart was for his homeland. Upon returning north to Germany he sadly stated, *"I shall freeze here, after the sunshine of Italy, but I belong where I began."* Albrecht's artwork was greatly influenced by the Gothic art of the twelfth and thirteenth centuries. It is interesting to contrast his more detailed work with that of the colorful and graceful paintings of the Italian masters of the same period.

Dürer was a handsome man, and painted many self-portraits of himself during his life-time. Like da Vinci, he was continually experimenting with the scientific side of art. He was slow and meticulous with every piece of artwork he did, only completing 50 paintings during his lifetime. Always exploring, always learning, he set out on an expedition during the winter months to study a beached whale. After traversing through cold swamps, he fell ill and never recovered. Albrecht was only 57 years of age when he died.

Lesson #35: *Keeping an Art Journal*

Years ago, many artists kept art journals. Art journals are a combination of a sketch-book and journal. Two of the greatest artists who ever kept art journals were Leonardo da Vinci and Albrecht Dürer. They were scientific in their artistic studies as they searched for answers to their many questions pertaining to nature, anatomy, perspective and much more. Art journals are great to keep for many reasons: they encourage you to draw from *life* (real objects), to be creative and nurture penmanship. Try to keep an art journal. It can be a wonderful source of learning through your own observations.

For this assignment, write and draw about your day below. Draw objects that are around you such as a teapot, a tractor, or a lamp and then write about your day. What is the weather like? How do you feel? What you are learning? What do you like do to in art?

Date: _____

_____
_____
_____
_____
_____
_____
_____
_____
_____
_____
_____
_____
_____
_____
_____
_____
_____
_____
_____

Whereas the paintings done in Italy during the Renaissance were on a large scale, German painting evolved from miniature paintings, the making of stained glass windows and altarpieces for churches.

Around the year 900 A.D., the first *diptych* was created in a monastery near Rabona, Italy. A diptych is a two panel painting, dividing a story into two sections. Notice the diptych of *The Annunciation* (to the left and right) by the Italian Renaissance artist, Fra Filippo Lippi. In this diptych he has placed the angel to the right in one panel, and Mary to the left in the other. There is a certain beauty in this technique of separating a picture into sections. Another popular approach was the *triptych,* or three panels. Artwork like this began to appear in many church altarpieces.

"The Annunciation"
diptych/Fra Filippo Lippi

"The Annunciation"
Fra Filippo Lippi

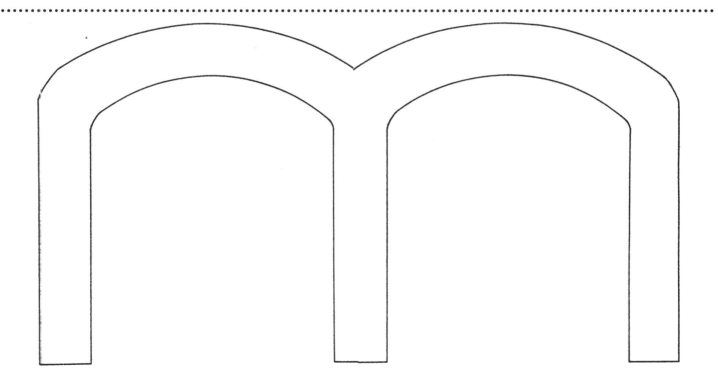

Lesson #36: *Creating a Diptych*   Most diptychs were stories from the Bible and generally created for church altars. Take a story from the Bible and place it in the two panels above. You may want to draw two separate scenes that were going on at the same time, like the birth of Jesus in one and the three wise men in the other. Or, you may want to show the entire picture, part in one panel and part in the other. When finished, place a creative, colorful design in your frame.

"Forest Glade with St. Anthony & St. Paul" Albrecht Durer/Pen & Ink

Lesson #37: *Nature Study with Pen & Ink*

Albrecht Dürer loved to study God's creation and copy it as true to life as possible. The drawing above was done with *pen and ink*, a technique using a black pen. Notice how he shaded the dark areas with a series of lines. In the very dark areas he used *cross-hatching* a series of criss-crossing lines (observe inside the small cave). Notice the way Dürer *suggested* most of the picture, but put more detail in the foreground around the cave and in the distant trees in the upper left. This is called a *focal point,* because it has more detail and contrast and brings the viewer's eye to the area. For this assignment, lightly draw the picture above on a plain sheet of white paper. Then, go over everything with your fine, black pen using lines to create darker values.

Lesson #38:
Objects Around the House

During the 16th century, the artist's of northern Europe, like Germany and Holland, did not do a great deal of religious paintings. They believed that religious artwork could be a form of idol worship. Instead, these artists focused mainly on painting portraits, landscapes and *still lifes*. A still life is a composition of inanimate objects (objects that do not move) like flowers, fruit, books, candlesticks, etc. There are literally hundreds of objects around your home to draw that can be great studies such as: door knobs, pots and pans, tools, lamps, toys, and many more.

Kelly Walsh Age 13 Moon Township, Pa.

A. Notice the student's drawing above. Look at the careful attention she gave to the objects on the shelves. Also, notice that she used *ellipses* to show that the top and bottom of the objects are *round*. Remember, to draw an ellipse simply go around and around with your pencil until you make a perfect pancake shape (A).

For this assignment, search for interesting objects around the house, drawing them in the figure boxes below. Use your black and brown colored pencils for these drawings. This is an old master's technique and can create some interesting effects. Finally, try to have a *light source* which allows you to have a light side and a shaded side to your objects. Do not forget to *shade with lines*.

ellipses

Objects Around the House

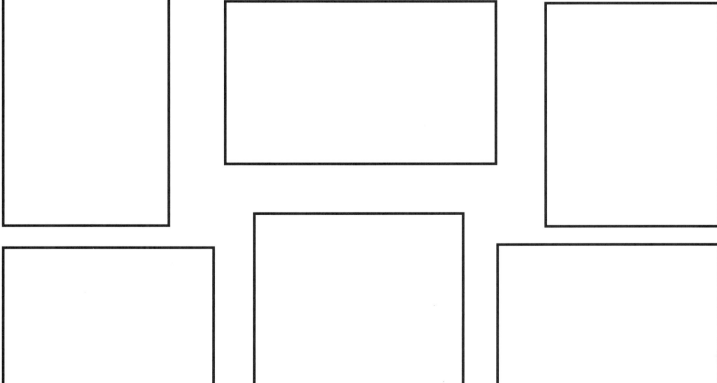

Lesson #39: *Going Outside*

Select from your *picture postcard gallery* the study of the *Stag Beetle* (1505) by Albrecht Dürer. Look at the detail Albrecht placed in the beetle. Also, if you observe carefully, you will see more than black and brown in the beetle. For the first part of this lesson, color the beetle (left) with your orange, brown and black colored pencils. Try adding a little blue to your black areas to make a nice, rich color. Remember to color with vertical lines.

Albrecht Dürer loved to study from nature. Going outside to do your artwork can be a wonderful experience! As a matter of fact, if you stick with it, you may even like working outdoors more than in your own studio. As mentioned, you have the sky for a ceiling, birds in the background, a soft breeze in your face and most importantly, God's creation to study and draw.

When you are finished coloring the stag beetle, go outside and do some more nature studies, drawing each in the figure boxes below with your colored pencils. This time, find an interesting assortment of insects to draw and study, such as butterflies, grasshoppers and caterpillars. Be sure to put a lot of detail and color in your drawings.

Studies from Nature

Beginning Painting 101

Throughout *God & the History of Art* you will be doing many art assignments. There will be lessons in drawing, painting and color theory using colored pencils or colored markers. As you have noticed, the text comes with a set of *paint cards*. These are heavy, index stock cards that are suitable for the painting exercises. In the upper right hand corner of each *paint card* is the page number, showing where you can find the lesson in the text.

Other painting materials needed for this course are: a set of pure pigment acrylic paints (yellow, red, blue and white), brushes, plastic or styrofoam picnic plates, two cups for water and a cloth to clean your brushes. Students should also wear old clothes while painting.

Before painting, shake the containers of paint. Squeeze out about the size of a nickel for each color, placing them at 12 o'clock, 3 o'clock, 6 o'clock and 9 o'clock on the perimeter of the picnic plate (A). This will allow you room for mixing colors.

....

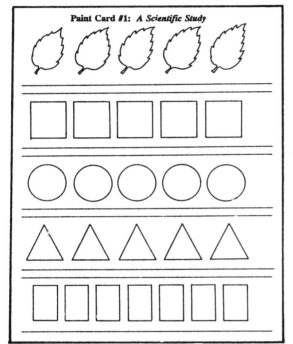

Paint Card #1: *A Scientific Study*

Lesson #40: *A Scientific Study*

Take out *Paint Card #1*, your paints, brushes and a picnic plate (this will be your *palette* for mixing colors). We will start our painting lesson by learning how to mix colors. This is very important and is something you will be doing continually throughout the text. First, pull your white paint out from the side of the puddle with your brush (B). (*It is important to pull your paint away from the puddle, so you don't ruin your puddles with other colors.*) Then, place a *speck* of blue on one or two hairs of your brush and add this to your white to make a delightful *light blue*. Remember, only put a speck of the darker color into the lighter color. *Mixing colors does not take talent, only practice.* Neatly paint the first square on the second row of the *paint card*, painting with *control* by staying in the lines. Make sure you mix enough paint. If you do not have enough paint on your brush, you will have to *scrub* the paint on. This is called *scrub painting*. When you have a lot of paint on your brush, the paint will go on smoothly, like melted butter, making it easier to stay in the lines.

A.

After you have painted the first square a light blue, use a pencil to write the colors you mixed to make the color by printing, *W + B* (white plus blue) on the lines underneath the painted square. Print the color you used most first, and then the color you used least last. This will assist whenever you need to make that color again.

Scrub Painting

B.

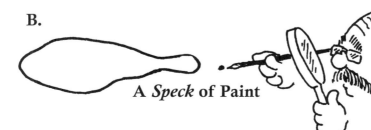

A *Speck* of Paint

55

Whether you are painting or drawing, it is good to hold your brush or pencil back from the tip by at least an inch or two. *Also, never lay your brushes on the table or on your palette!* One of the major reasons why students make a mess when painting is they do not keep the handles of their brushes clean. Have a container, like a jar, to store your brushes in, hairs up. If this is the *only* place you put your brushes, you will cut down on most of the mess in painting. *Keep your brush handles free from paint.*

You should have several brushes for painting: a small, medium, and large. Use your larger brushes for most of the painting. Your smaller brushes are to put details in after you have completed everything else.

Let's mix another color. Add a little yellow to the light blue you just mixed. Notice that you are now creating a light green (you may want to add just a little more blue to this). Carefully paint the first leaf on the top row of the *paint card* and print the colors you used, $W + B + Y$.

Next, pull out some yellow from the side of your yellow puddle and add a little blue to it. Observe that this is a different green because it does not have any white in it. Paint the second leaf and print $Y + B$ underneath. Now, add some more blue to this color to make a darker *blue/green*. Paint in the third leaf and print $B + Y$ underneath (because you have used more blue than yellow). Add a tiny speck of red to this dark green and paint in the next leaf, printing $B + Y + R$ underneath it. Finally, add some more yellow to this color to paint the last leaf, $Y + B + R$.

Store Brushes Hairs Up

Continue mixing colors and add them to the color chart on *Paint Card #1* with an assortment of new colors, painting in the squares, circles, triangles and rectangles. Below are some colors you may want to make:

pink = $W + R$ orange = $Y + R$ flesh tone = $W + O$ *(orange)*
violet = $R + B + W$ brown = $Y + R + B$ black = $B + R + Y$

When you are finished for the day, do not throw away your paints. Since you are using an *acrylic paint* which is water based, you can place them in the freezer of your refrigerator, freezing the colors until another day. Place your wet painting on a shelf to dry (20 minutes) and clean your brushes with warm, soapy water, wiping them dry and storing them hairs up. Make sure to clean your painting area and tightly seal the tops to your paints. We will continue reviewing how to mix colors as the lessons progress. We learned in this lesson:

1. *Pull out the lighter color first.*
2. *Mix a little of the darker color into the lighter color.*
3. *Mix enough paint to paint your areas with fluid strokes.*
4. *Paint with control, staying in the lines.*
5. *Keep your brush handles clean.*
6. *Make sure to clean your area when finished.*

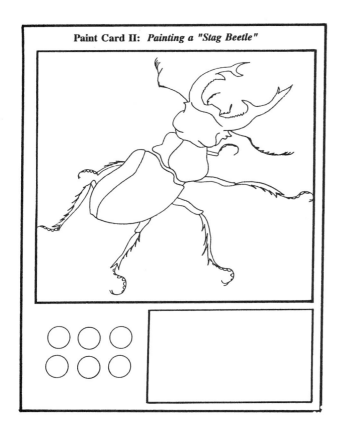

Paint Card II: *Painting a "Stag Beetle"*

Lesson #41: *Painting a Stag Beetle*

Take out *Paint Card #II* and place it in front of you. Also, place the *picture postcard* of the *Stag Beetle* by Albrecht Dürer in front of you. First, mix pale yellow by adding a little yellow to white. Test your color in one of the circles to see if you like it. Then, mix a brown in a separate puddle. Keep your palette neat, mixing your puddles about the size of a quarter. There are many ways to mix brown. One of the easiest ways is by first making a rich orange (yellow and red), and then add just a touch of blue. Again, test your brown in one of the circles. If you add too much blue you will make a slimy green. To make your color browner, simply add some more red to it. Next, take a speck of this brown and add it to the light yellow to dull it down. Test your dull yellow in one of the circles to see if you like it and then paint the entire background behind the stag beetle with your large brush. Paint with control and take your time. You will have to paint over some of the finer areas like the legs, claws and antennas. This is okay as long as you can still see these parts underneath the paint.

Small Medium Large

Many students do all their painting with a small brush. Remember, whenever you have a decision to make as to which brush to use, *always use your larger brushes*. Your small brushes are for putting more details in at the end. After you have painted the background, mix a little of the brown into the orange (Y + R) and paint the larger parts of the body with this color using your medium size brush. Remember, good artwork takes time and patience. Take your time and paint with *control*. The more time you take, the better the results are going to be. If it becomes too tedious for you or you become tired, take a break and return to your painting later. While the brownish/orange of the body is still wet, take some brown and paint over parts of the body, head and claws. Since the paint is still wet, the edges will blend together making them softer. Keep looking at your picture postcard of the *Stag Beetle* and try to mix your colors as precisely as possible.

Finally, make a black by mixing red to blue until it becomes a very dark blue. Then, add just a speck of yellow. This may not look like a black to you, but when you test the color in one of the circles, you will be surprised at how much the color changes. Also, stand at a distance from it and the color should look blacker. Take your medium brush and add some black to the still wet brown edges of the beetle's body. Next, take your small brush and paint the parts of the legs and claws that are thicker. Do not paint the little detail areas though, as we will be doing that when the paint dries.

57

Many students draw their pictures for painting very small. This makes painting in the details frustrating because it is difficult to paint small areas. Make your objects large. Do not forget to use your smallest brush for details and take your time. Have a lot of paint on your brush so you do not have to scrub the paint on, and paint the little areas with fluid strokes and control. Finally, you can wait for the paint to dry and then add the details with a marker or pen.

Painting Details: Painting details is very difficult to do. Most students use too much paint and go out of the lines. Below are three suggestions for painting detail:

1. Do large drawings so your details will not be too small.
2. Use a small brush with a lot of paint on it and take your time.
3. Put the details in with a pen, pencil or marker when your painting is dry.

When your painting has completely dried, take your black pen and carefully add the details to the legs and claws of the stag beetle. Notice the detail that you can place in your painting using this method. Since you are using two or more different art materials (paint and black marker pen), this is called a *mixed medium.*

Finally, notice how Albrecht Dürer signed his name in the bottom right of the picture. Take your light brown colored pencil and sign your name on the bottom of your painting, using your nicest artistic signature.

When you are finished, select your best insect study from Lesson #39 and draw it in the large figure box below with your orange colored pencil. Remember, it is always good to work large. Then, mix some nice colors using your colored pencils and color it in.

Finally, draw this insect again in the figure box on the bottom of your *paint card* and paint it with creative colors. Test your colors in the circles first. This painting will call for a lot of detail. Do not forget, for details, use your small brush or a fine marker pen.

My Insect Study

Tintoretto (1518-1594): The *Thunderbolt* from Venice

Venice is a city located in the northeastern part of Italy and is completely surrounded by shallow waters. There are canals everywhere. This is where the long gondolas travel back and forth along the waterways. Because of its beautiful architecture, its location on the water and its deep appreciation for art, Venice has long been considered the jewel in the crown of cites throughout the world.

When the Roman Empire crumbled in the fifth century after the Huns ravaged and sacked the once powerful empire, a small group of Italian refugees migrated to the marshlands of the Adriatic where there was safety in the many small isolated islands. This is when and where the city of Venice was born. The Italians saw it being birthed like Venus (the fabled goddess of love) and destined to become the cultural center of many worldly pleasures. The Venetians grew to become good businessmen who loved the material things of this world, including the fine arts. They were dedicated to the enjoyment of life and building Venice into a beautiful city of palaces, art, churches and canals. Unlike Florence (its sister city in the arts during the Renaissance), there was peace and security here. Without foreign invaders or civil uprisings, Venice became a wealthy and beautiful city of the waterways.

In most of Italy, religious themes and stories from the Bible were the basis for much of the artwork. Although Venetian artists began to introduce non-religious subject matter into Italian art, they still accepted commissions from the Church and created magnificent paintings. This would be evidenced in Venice's great cathedral, the Church of St. Mark. Venice was also influenced by the Orient, which is obvious in much of the art that adorns the city. While other Italian painters dressed their subject matter in Greek and Roman costumes and placed them in Greek and Roman landscapes, the Venetians donned their figures as citizens of Venice, both in apparel and surroundings.

"And God is able to make all grace abound toward you, that you, always having all sufficiency in all things, have an abundance for every good work."   2 Corinthians 9:8

Some artists throughout history have become very wealthy and famous. There have also been examples of others becoming somewhat greedy. We must remember that art is something that should touch the heart and be shared with others. Have you ever noticed how generous children are with their artwork, desiring to share it with everyone? With this in mind, it is really difficult to put a price tag on a piece of artwork. What better purpose for art than to give it to someone who really appreciates it - from one heart to another. Probably no other artist exemplified this better than the great Venetian artist, Tintoretto.

Tintoretto was born in Venice, Italy in 1518 and was christened Jocopo Robusti. Jocopo's father, known as a *tintore*, tinted fabrics for the Venetian markets. When Jocopo was a young boy, he received the nickname *Tintoretto*, or little dyer, because he adorned his father's shop with large, colorful pictures done with bright dyes. His father, seeing the talent and love that his son had for painting, decided to send him to the great Venetian master, Titian, to be *apprenticed*. There were no art schools during the Renaissance rather, young aspiring students were apprenticed under the masters to learn the trades of the fine arts. These were more like workshops than art schools. The students learned all the basics of the profession, from grinding paint to cleaning the studio.

Unfortunately, Titian saw no worthwhile talent in the young Jocopo and sent him on his way. There would be no further art education for the aspiring artist. He was by nature the captain of his own soul and mastered his profession by working day and night. At 25 he had astounding abilities, and if any single expression could be found to describe his creativity it was *boldness*. Young Jacopo was sensational in his day. The Venetians were amazed by his energy, the large paintings he did, and the amount of work he was able to produce in a very short period of time and gave him another nickname, *the Thunderbolt*. With the exception of the Flemish artist, Peter Paul Rubens, Tintoretto is known for being able to produce more paintings in a shorter period of time than any other artist.

Ann Mossburg Age 7 Markle, Indiana

Tintoretto was also a great *draftsman* with a brilliant sense for color. Draftsmanship is the ability to draw, and he was one of the best. His advice to any student in the arts was, *"One can never do too much drawing."* He cautioned those around him that without faith in God and draftsmanship, their artwork would crumble. Faith was needed to keep the subject matter holy, while drawing was a cable to bind one's convictions together.

Venice was a city dedicated to exciting pastimes, such as parties, fine dining, costumes and social gatherings. However, Tintoretto shunned fashionable living. He was a man of simple tastes, devoted to his family, and very generous with his finances within the community. Often, his favorite daughter Marietta (one of seven children) would assist him in preparing his large canvases for painting.

Story has it that there was an offensive and arrogant businessman in Venice whose name was Arentino. He was known for being a scoundrel, and was feared for his excellent use of a sword. Arentino was also the business manager of Titian, the great master who had rejected Tintoretto as a student. One day he came to the studio of Tintoretto to have his portrait painted. Old *Thunderbolt* casually unsheathed his sword and placed it by his easel, letting Arentino know that he was not afraid of him, nor was he going to take any of his insults. The bully, always boastful of his dueling, was for once meek and silent as Tintoretto quietly completed the portrait.

....

Lesson #42: *Christ at the Sea of Galilee*

Notice the copy of a painting by Tintoretto, *Christ at the Sea of Galilee*. As mentioned, the *Thunderbolt* was not only productive in creating many great pieces of art, but he also worked on a large scale. Do you recognize Christ on the seashore? The men in the boat? The rough sea and swirling clouds? Draw this story from the Bible with your colored pencils on a sheet of white paper. Try to show the storm and the feelings that all the disciples may have had at this time.

"Christ at Sea of Galilee" by Tintoretto

Drawing by Benjamin Iocco   Age 12   Freeport, Michigan

Read Matthew 14:22-33, Mark 6:45-52 and John 6:16-21 to have a better understanding of Jesus walking on water during the storm. Then, notice the way Tintoretto illustrated the story. God has made us all very unique in our own way. That is why we create things differently.

61

Most artwork during the time of Tintoretto was *commissioned* by the church or wealthy businessmen. Many times there would be bidding by artists for a job to be done and the artist bidding the lowest would receive the commission. If there was a job to do, Tintoretto would always bid lower than the other artists. Once, when the Charity School of St. Roch announced it was seeking designs for a ceiling painting, Tintoretto secretly found out what they wanted and came before them with a completed painting before any of the other artists could even bid for the job. The other artists were furious, calling him a cheat. However, the regents of the school accepted his painting. To add to their astonishment, Tintoretto presented this massive painting to the school as a gift on behalf of the Christian saint who cared for the city during the time of the great plague. Then Tintoretto volunteered to decorate the entire school for whatever sum the regents could afford, offering them three paintings a year.

His capacity to work quickly helped him with such massive undertakings. When payments came, he scattered his earnings among the poor and oppressed. Tintoretto was a godly and generous man whose energy and love were directed towards art and family. Often he would make ingenious toys and games for his own children.

At the age of 72 he began to work on one of his last paintings, *The Paradise,* for the Hall of the Grand Council. This painting was a gesture of the good life the Lord had granted him and also to prepare him for the life to come. The great picture was completed and affixed to the wall shortly before he died. It was the largest painting on canvas in existence (74' x 30') with five hundred figures. When asked the price he answered, *"Whatever you think is fair."* The nobles offered a price. *"Too much!"* he replied, and insisted on taking less.

Tintoretto painted many great pictures of scenes from the Bible. He was a man that was as bold as a lion when it came to creating large paintings, yet gentle as a lamb when it came to helping with the poor and needy. I wonder how large the paintings are that he is doing now in *The Heavenly Studio* for the Great Master?

"Jesus Feeding the Five Thousand" Hope Perkins Age 10 Columbiana, Ohio

Tintoretto loved to put a lot of people in his large paintings. People are wonderful to place in your pictures. Keep practicing drawing people. It is not easy, but the more you practice, the better you will become.

Lesson #43: *Drawing People*

For the beginning student, there are many different approaches to drawing the human figure. The first and most basic is the *Stick Figure*. For the first part of this exercise, copy the three stick figures below by drawing them with your drawing pencil next to each example.

Stick Figure Standing   Stick Figure Sitting   Stick Figure Running

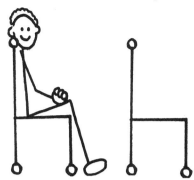

Another way to draw the human figure is a little more sophisticated. This style is called the *Hot Dog Figure* (A). First, lightly draw hot dog shapes around the arms, legs and body of the *Stick Figure* below (B). Then, draw a stick figure in any position (C) and add hot dog shapes to fill out his body.

A.   B.   C.   D.   E.   F.

A third approach in learning to draw the human figure is called the *Rectangular Man.* This time, add thin rectangular shapes for the arms, legs and body instead of hot dog shapes (E). Draw thin, rectangular shapes over the stick figure (F). Then, draw your own rectangular figure, starting with the basic *Stick Figure* and adding thin rectangular shapes over his body in the space provided (D).

G.

Finally, let's see if you can draw some *hot dog* and *rectangular* people in the figure box to the left (G). Draw them in a variety of positions, such as: walking, jumping rope, fishing, sleeping, playing baseball, reading, praying and shooting an arrow.

Lesson #44: *Creating a Massive Picture of People*

Tintoretto created large paintings with many human figures in them. For this lesson, fill the figure box below with human figures. Create a scene from the Bible like *The Transfiguration, The Sermon on the Mount, Moses Parting the Red Sea* or any other story you like that could have a lot of people in it. Use *hot dog* or *rectangular* figures. Draw everything first with a light colored pencil and then color it in. It is best to have a very sharp pencil for details.

Lesson #45: *Making a Larger Picture!*

Now, take a large sheet of white poster board and draw another picture with a lot of people in it. Even though poster board is large, it can really be fun to work with. The key is to take your time and to first draw everything lightly. Poster board has a shiny side and a dull side. You can use either side for your artwork. After you have drawn it lightly, color your picture with markers. Color with lines the same way you learned in earlier colored pencil exercises. If you have large markers and cannot get detail, place the details in with a fine black marker. How do you like working big?

"He has no form or comeliness; and when we shall see Him, there is no beauty that we should desire Him. He is despised and rejected of men; a man of sorrows, and acquainted with grief..."

Isaiah 53:2b,3

Rembrandt van Rijn (1606-1669) *"A Man of Sorrows"*

If art's purpose is to touch the heart of man, then few have surpassed Rembrandt. He is known as one of the greatest engravers and portrait artists who ever lived. He was an outstanding draftsman, one of the very best painters, and is world renowned for his paintings and illustrations of stories from the Bible. It is the heart that is nurtured when one looks at a Rembrandt, by the rich and abundant qualities of his masterful paintings.

I remember when I visited the National Gallery of Art in Washington and saw a self-portrait of Rembrandt. This particular painting was finished when he was 62 years of age, one year before his death, and one year after the death of his only remaining child, a son named Titus. Not only does one see that Rembrandt was highly skilled with the brush, but one's heart can feel the suffering that he endured during his lifetime. One sees the sadness in his eyes and expression, and in the soft, somber colors fading into the dark background. Rarely has a piece of art stirred up such emotions within me, bringing tears to my eyes.

Rembrandt copy by Gregory Iocco Age 14

Rembrandt was born in Leyden, Holland in 1606. He was one of nine children and the son of a miller. The young lad grew up not long after the struggle between the Protestants and the Roman Catholic Church. His family was Calvinist by faith, like many other northern Europeans protesting against the papal authority in Rome at the time. It is said that his mother read the Bible to him continually when he was a boy, and that the Bible was the only book he read throughout his life. Even though his mother recognized his talents and his desire to be an artist, she prayed and pleaded with the young boy to go into a more practical profession. His father even saw fit to have him educated in a very strict Calvinist Latin School. But Rembrandt had his heart set on being an artist, and whenever he had the opportunity he would leave school with his sketchbook in hand to do studies of animals at the zoo or sketches at the docks. Even at an early age he was busy doing portraits, completing nearly a dozen of his father and several delightful portrayals of his mother. His parents finally resigned themselves to the fact that he was going to be an artist and allowed him to study under a local artist, Jacob Swanenburgh.

Lesson #46: *Drawing Rembrandt*

Rembrandt did approximately one hundred self-portraits during his lifetime. Yet, he was a man of plain features with *no form or comeliness*. These self-portraits give us great insight into his soul as we follow the progression of his life throughout the years. For this assignment, take a sharp, dark drawing pencil and copy the self-portrait of Rembrandt (above left) in the figure box to the upper right. Notice all the values he created from light to dark in his drawing. See if you can do the same.

During the time of Rembrandt, many artists traveled to England, France and Switzerland to study the great masters, but most traveled to Italy to see the art that was created during the Renaissance. However, Rembrandt never left Holland. He found enough subject matter in his own city to keep him busy. Even though he was a man of few words and did not like small talk, he loved to study mankind. He had a special fondness for the Jews who lived in the poorer districts and, whenever possible, would go there to draw and paint. These paintings of the Jewish people were remarkable character studies for many of the biblical paintings he was to do throughout his lifetime.

The art world had been going through many drastic changes in the 1600s. The feudal system had ended and there were no kings to paint for. Since the Protestant faith did not have the same views about art as the Roman Catholic Church, there was little demand for religious paintings. Instead, art commissions would come from the wealthy businessmen whose main desire was for portraits. Rembrandt would grow to be one of the greatest portrait artists of all times.

A.

"Casting out the Demons"
Dina Unsead Age 14 Mornton, Illinois

....

Lesson #47: *Appreciating Rembrandt*

Like Albrecht Dürer, Rembrandt was a very successful engraver, considered the greatest etcher of all times. Notice the etching by Rembrandt on the next page *Jesus drives away the Money Changers.* For this assignment, write what you believe is going on in the picture on the lines beneath it. How does Rembrandt bring your eyes to Jesus? If you look closely, you can see the fine lines that Rembrandt used. What do you think of the effect of having some of the people in light and some in dark, or shading? Do you notice that some areas have a lot of detail and others have very little, simply *suggesting* with a few strokes?

When you are finished, draw your own, personal interpretation of *Jesus and the Money Changers* John 2:13-17, in the figure box above (A). Start your drawing with a light pencil. When you have drawn it just the way you like, use your black pen to go over everything. Carefully look at Rembrandt's use of lines, and try to create contrast with light areas against dark areas.

"Rembrandt's temperament was that of a prophet - a God possessed man...and teeming with the future, a future he bore within him as the Hebrew prophets bore within them the coming of the Messiah..."

Andre Malraux

"Jesus Drives Away the Money Changers" Rembrandt John 2:13-25

_____

_____

_____

Rembrandt married Saskia, a Dutch woman whom he dearly loved. For a short period they enjoyed a life of happiness and prosperity and many were acclaiming him to be the greatest artist of the century. But Rembrandt never displayed an exalted opinion of himself, and although a collector of great art and having a luxurious home, he would rather spend his time painting. During these early years of success, he obtained a studio in the ghetto where he spent much of his time painting the impoverished people of Amsterdam. The ghetto was where he found his characters for biblical paintings, such as Abraham, Isaac and many of the old prophets. Meanwhile, Saskia enjoyed the luxury that came with her husband's success. Unfortunately, all this was short lived.

They would have two daughters who died during infancy. Then, there was good news as they gave birth to a healthy son whom they named Titus. Shortly thereafter, Saskia fell ill and died. Rembrandt was greatly grieved by these family losses and never remarried. It wasn't long after these tragedies that he had to declare bankruptcy, losing everything he owned, including his great art collection. All that was spared him were his paints and brushes. Then, one year before his own death, the only remaining member of his family, Titus, died at the age of 27. Isaiah 53:3 seems to describe Rembrandt well, *"a man of sorrows and acquainted with grief."*

Lesson #48: *Pen & Ink*

"The Annunciation" Rembrandt/pen & ink

Truly Rembrandt was a man of sorrows. But none of his emotions or energy went for naught, as he continued to paint with all the fervor of his youth. During his deep moments of suffering, he would always revert back to doing paintings of Jesus Christ. These biblical stories were done more for his own satisfaction, as there were over seventy biblical paintings in his possession just a few years before his death. Notice the pen and ink, *The Annunciation* (left). This was probably a quick study for a future painting, but it has a delightful and fresh beauty of its own in the brevity of lines and simple suggestion.

What do you see different about Rembrandt's *Annunciation* and those of Fra Angelico on page 43 and Fra Fillipo Lippi on the top of page 51? How is the composition different (the way everything is placed in the picture)? What about the motion of the figures and the expressions on their faces? Which is your favorite and why? Write your comments of these *Annunciations* on the lines above. Practice good *penmanship*, using your best handwriting.

Lesson #49: *The Pen & Ink Page*

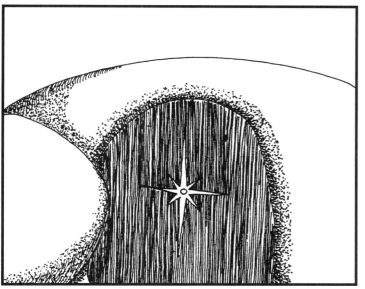

Besides being a renown portrait painter and the world's most prolific artist of stories from the Bible, Rembrandt is considered one of the great masters with pen and ink. *Pen and ink* has been a *medium* used by great masters since the Reformation. A black pen can be great to use in drawing for several reasons. First, it will make your pictures bolder, giving them more *contrast* from light to dark. Secondly, *pen and ink* teaches you some of the basic fundamentals of drawing, like drawing and shading with *line*. Finally, if you ever want to have your work reproduced, *pen and ink* is the most practical for this purpose.

"He is Risen" Dawn Menken Age 15 Rockford, Ill.

All the student artwork done in this book is with a black pen. Notice the example above by a student and how she shaded the dark area in the tomb with nice, controlled *lines*. This not only brings out the brightness of the star, but also gives a wonderful shaded area that is not too dark. Also, notice how the outside of Jesus' tomb is shaded with dots. This is another technique to add values to your drawings. When drawing with a black pen, it may be good to start by drawing your picture lightly in pencil, and then going over it with your black pen. When you are completely finished, you can erase the pencil drawing underneath. For this assignment, practice the shading exercises below with your black pen, completing each drawing by adding darker values with line.

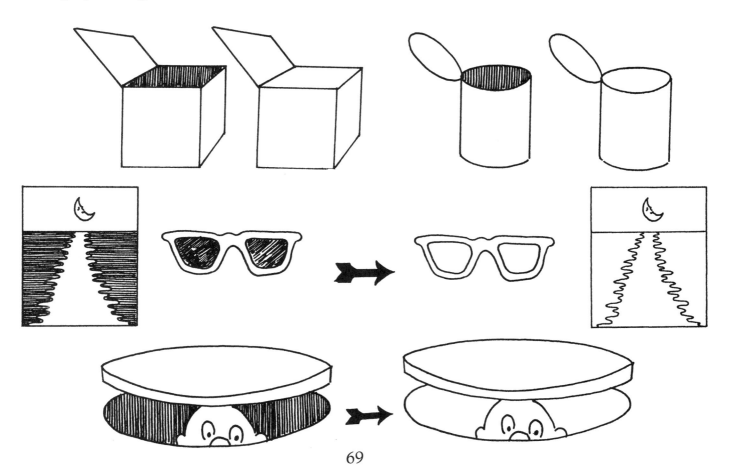

69

Many times I have asked my students, *"How many famous artists do you know?"* Most could not name more than one or two! Some would mention my name, exclaiming *"Professor Solomon is a famous artist!"* Well, I sure do take that as a compliment, but I am certainly not a famous artist.

Let's write each of the famous artist's names ten times on the lines below. This is a very good exercise in helping you remember who they are and how to spell their names correctly. You may be surprised how delightful your dinner conversation with your family will be as you discuss the great masters. Remember, use good penmanship.

Rembrandt van Rijn   **Albrecht Dürer**   **Fra Angelico**

_____
_____
_____
_____
_____
_____
_____
_____
_____
_____

A. horizontal   vertical   diagonal

Lesson #50: *More Lines*

Years ago, many artists worked in *pen and ink*. During those days they used a quill pen and inkwell. Most pen and ink drawings were quick studies for future paintings. Notice the quick strokes Rembrandt used in his sketch *Jesus Saves Peter from Drowning*. Look at the way he simply *suggested* some areas with a flick of his pen. Do you see the back of the boat? Also, notice that all the shading was done with line. There are several ways to shade with line. You can use either *horizontal, vertical,* or *diagonal lines*. Let's practice drawing these lines with our black pen. First, fill in the three shapes (A), using horizontal lines in the triangle, vertical lines in the rectangle, and diagonal lines in the circle. Then, draw your own picture of Jesus saving Peter on another sheet of paper, going over it with your black pen and shading with lines.

"Jesus Saves Peter from Drowning"
Rembrandt (1632) pen & ink

Rembrandt created hundreds of paintings and drawings of stories from the Bible. He loved to study the Jews and their rich biblical history, spending much of his time in the poor Jewish districts of Amsterdam. After his bankruptcy, he moved to the poor district where he had so often painted. Rembrandt spent the remainder of his life there, dying in poverty at the age of 63. It is said that during the funeral procession there were only a few acquaintances present, none of whom were family members since all had died. Thus, Rembrandt died a lonely, poor, old man whose fame and success had seemingly departed from him. Many years later Rembrandt has been acclaimed as one of the greatest artists who ever lived. The Bible states *"Cast thy bread upon the waters, and it shall return to you after many days"* (Ecc. 11:1). Though Rembrandt created these masterpieces many years ago, they have returned to us today as great treasures of art.

"The Prodigal Son as Swineherd"
Rembrandt\etching

"The Return of the Prodigal Son"
Rembrandt\pen & brush drawing

Lesson #51: *Illustrating a Story*

Notice the two quick sketches by Rembrandt (above) of different scenes from the story of *The Prodigal Son*. One is a very simple sketch of the prodigal son in the pig sty, and the other is a bolder illustration of his return to his father. For this assignment, read *The Parable of the Lost Son* (Luke 15: 11-32) and draw two scenes from the story in the figure boxes above. Start your drawings lightly and then go over them with your black pen. Be creative!

"Portrait of the Artist's Son, Titus"

A.

Select from your picture postcard gallery the painting by Rembrandt, *Portrait of the Artist's Son, Titus.* Study it for a moment. This is a portrait Rembrandt painted of his son Titus when he was just a boy. It was a time when there was still prosperity and happiness in the home. Notice the joy that seems to radiate from the painting and the warm colors. Even the browns seem to glow. This great Dutch master used a *limited palette*, meaning he used only a few colors in his paintings. Have you heard the saying, *"less is more?"* This is true with painting, as one can create great harmony in a picture with a limited amount of color. Finally, do you know where the focal point is, or where the eye is directed in the picture? It is led to the head of Titus and his cap with its splash of red feathers. This is where all the color and center of attention is, as the rest seems to fade away.

Rembrandt liked to situate his figures against a dark background, placing a soft, radiant glow upon his model's faces as though a light was coming from above. The light areas gradually fade in with the shaded areas, blending into the rich, dark background. This technique of light against dark in painting is called *chiaroscuro.*

It should be mentioned that, back then, they did not have cameras and pictures to copy from. Thus, this painting was probably done from life, as young Titus patiently posed for his father. Notice that Rembrandt dressed his son in a fine costume for the painting. Do you think that the little boy was excited and proud? And do you think he was curious about how the painting was going to look? Boys generally have a high amount of energy, so either young Titus really tried to hold still for his father as long as he could, or his father had him pose for short periods at a time. A portrait painting such as this one seems to capture much more than a camera ever could, and I am sure that Rembrandt held this portrayal of his son dear to his heart.

Hang the reproduction of young Titus on your refrigerator (or classroom) for a week and view it from time to time. See if there are any other interesting things you notice about the painting. Copy the picture in the figure box above (A) with your colored pencils. How much color can you see, even in the browns and the dark hat? Start off lightly with your yellow pencil. You may want to practice blending some of your colors on a separate sheet of paper. Your picture will not be a masterpiece, as you will probably have problems drawing the face. This is perfectly all right. You will be amazed at how much you can learn when copying a work by a master, even though your finished artwork doesn't look that great!

"As for me, I will see Your face in righteousness; I shall be satisfied when I awake in Your likeness."

Psalm 17:15

Lesson #53: *Drawing Your Self-Portrait* Rembrandt did nearly 100 self-portraits during his lifetime. Just about all the great artists throughout history have done self-portraits. One reason being, you always have your face to study and draw.

A. My First Self-Portrait

Drawing your self-portrait can be both difficult and a lot of fun. For this exercise, draw your face four times. First, draw your self-portrait in the figure box to the left (A). Do this before learning about facial features and proportions in the next few lessons. Then, after the lessons, draw your self-portrait again in the other three figure boxes. Do one self-portrait with a drawing pencil (B), one with colored pencils (C) and one with your black pen (D). All three will be different because you will be using different mediums for each. Make sure to have a good light source on your face for a light side and a shaded side.

B. Self-Portrait/Pencil

C. Self-Portrait/Colored Pencils

Jodi Lyn Swihart Age 11
Quinter, Kansas

Nathan Farley Age 12
Charlotte, North Carolina

D. Self Portrait/Pen & Ink

Levi Unruh Age 11
Greensburg, Kansas

Lesson #54: *A Nose is a Nose is a Nose*

Drawing the human face can be difficult to do. It will require a lot of practice, maybe even drawing hundreds of portraits before you capture a likeness. Don't give up. Portrait drawing can also be lots of fun!

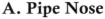
A. Pipe Nose

There are two things you should learn about portraits: one is how to draw *facial features* (the eyes, nose, ears, and mouth), and the other is how to draw with proper *proportions* (placing everything in the right place and the correct size).

Let's start by drawing one of the most difficult facial features - the nose. The nose has caused many a frustration with beginning art students. I have seen all kinds of noses in my years of experience, from a long pipe nose (A), to a triangle nose (B), to a *check mark* nose (C), to a two dots nose (D), to a hog nose (E)!

B.   C.   D.   E.

F.

L.

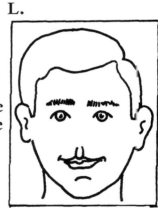

First of all, the nose does not come out of the eyes (F). It comes out of your eyebrows (G). Secondly, you do not need two lines for your nose (pipe nose A). When you draw the face, have a light source and know which direction the light is coming from. This will give you a light side and a shaded side for your face and nose (H). With a light side and a shaded side, you only need one line for the nose (I).

The bottom of the nose is round, or ball shaped. Draw a half circle for the lower part of your nose. Add the two nostrils by drawing an ellipse on either side (J), and then place the flesh over the nostrils (K). Now, that nose should get you by for a couple of years! Practice drawing a nose on the figure above (L).

G.   H.   I.   J.   K.

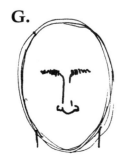 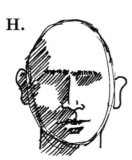 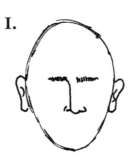 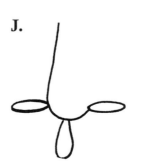 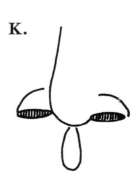

Lesson #55: *Drawing A Self-Portrait with Proportions*

A.

B. No!

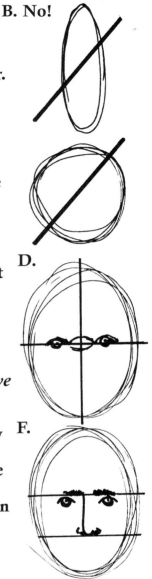

When drawing person's face, or portrait, it is important to learn proportions. Proportions means the size and relationship of one part next to another. For example, how large should the ears be? Where are the eyes located on the head? How wide is the mouth? All these questions can be answered when you learn proportions. It's like putting pieces of a puzzle together. First, the head is an oval shape. Lightly draw an egg shape going around four or five times (A). The human head is not long and skinny or round (B).

C.

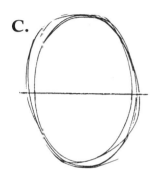

The eyes are located in the middle of the head, not up in the forehead. To place them in the correct position, draw a light, horizontal line through the center of the oval (C). Next, draw a light, straight vertical line down the middle of the head. Since your eyes are one eye apart, draw a light eye in the center of the horizontal and vertical guidelines (D) and then draw an eye to either side of this *middle eye* to have the proper spacing.

D.

E.

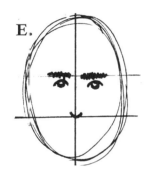

Sketch in the eyebrows above the eyes and draw a horizontal line across the head on this eyebrow line (E). Then, draw a line halfway between the eye line and the bottom of the chin. This is where the bottom of the nose is situated. Draw a half circle on this line and then draw the rest of the nose (F).

F.

Generally speaking, the ears are as long as the eyebrow line to the nose line (G). If you drop a *plumb line* (straight lines used for measurements) down from the center of each eye, you will know how wide the mouth is (H). The neck is not a long thin pipe (I), but is almost as wide as the head. The hair is not pressed down flat (I), but puffed up on the head (J). Draw a face with proper proportions in the figure box (K), and then return to page 73 and draw the rest of your self-portraits using proper proportions.

G.

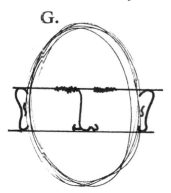

H.

I.

J.

K.

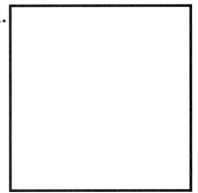

Lesson #56:
Drawing Faces from Pictures:

It is easier to draw a portrait of someone from a picture than from real life. However, practice drawing from *life* as much as possible, by either having some one pose for you, or by drawing your self-portrait in the mirror. Do not forget the basic fundamentals of drawing a face, and use these principles whenever possible.

Let's now draw two faces from pictures. Notice the portrait studies that Rembrandt did below. They look a little comical, don't they? Observe how large and round the eyes of both men are, and that neither one seems to have teeth. You will find that many of Rembrandt's portraits touch your heart with either their beauty or integrity, whereas, some portraits by Rembrandt look quite humorous. Also, notice that the dark values and shaded areas were drawn with lines. There is a wonderful contrast between the dark of the robes and the light of the backgrounds. The lines used for the robes are vertical, and the lines used for the shading behind them are done with cross-hatching, leaving room for a halo, or glow, behind each figure. Do you see how Rembrandt had a light side and a shaded side to each face, and that each nose was drawn with one line instead of two?

Copy the portraits in the small figure boxes above. Draw each portrait as lightly as you can. Then, in the first one, use a black pencil with a sharp point to place in all the darker values. In the second picture, use your black pen for darker values. Remember, do your drawings lightly then, when you add your darker values, you are not as likely to make mistakes.

Portrait Study by Rembrandt

Portrait Study by Rembrandt

"I have reserved for Myself seven thousand men who have not bowed the knee to Baal. Even so then, at this present time there is a remnant according to the election of grace."

Romans 11:4-5

Jean Francois Millet (1814-1874) *"The Salt of the Earth"*

Jean Francois Millet (pronounced mill-lay) was born in Gruchy, a small farming village in Normandy, located in northern France. Millet's family was poor, and their lifestyle was simple and basic. He was raised on a farm with seven brothers and sisters where everyone worked long hours. The children's education came from his uncle, a pastor of a small parish, and his grandmother, a wise and Godly woman. Thus, the young Millet grew up in a poor home of simple means, but with a respect for the land, a yearning for the simple things in life, and a deep reverence for God.

"Old Farmhouse" Millet/pen & ink

Most of Millet's artwork is of simple scenes in the country. Millet loved to draw and paint the common people at work, or everyday scenes and activities. This is called *genre* art. The sketch that he did above of a farmhouse in Vichy, France was probably reminiscent of his home and the way he grew up. The pleasant memories of his youth would remain with him throughout his life, and influenced what he would paint for many years to follow.

Lesson #57: *Genre - An Everyday Scene*

Let's draw two *genre* pictures of ordinary scenes. You may want to draw a picture of your mother doing the dishes, your father working in the yard, or even the mailman delivering mail. Draw anything you like that is a common day occurrence. Place your drawings in the figure boxes on the top of the next page. However, draw one with colored pencils and the other with a black pen. When you are finished, give a description of the ordinary jobs they are doing on the lines below each picture.

77

"Listen, my beloved brethren: Has God not chosen the poor of this world to be rich in faith, and heirs of the kingdom which He promised to those who love Him?"

James 2:5

"Genre" Picture #1

"Genre" Picture #2

_____
_____
_____
_____

"The Loaves & Fish" by Rachel Bell
Age 15 Aledo, Tx.

Even as a boy, Millet's family realized he was different from the rest of their children. Not only did he show a great interest in art, but also great talent. Finally, his father consented to send him to the adjoining town of Cherbourg to enter an art school while his younger brothers continued to work the land. Shortly thereafter his father died, putting a financial burden on the family. However, the town council of Cherbourg recognized young Millet's talents and decided to support him financially, sending him to Paris to further his art education. This was a totally new environment for the farm boy. He had only been accustomed to the simple country life, but now found himself in the center of one of the most metropolitan cities in the world.

Millet found living in the city of Paris to be very difficult, especially after finishing his years in art school. For a long time he struggled making a living by selling portraits on the sidewalks and doing sign paintings. By the time he was 35, he was living a life of hopeless despondency, considering himself a failure.

Self-Portrait by Millet/Pencil

....

Notice the self-portrait of Millet. You can see he was very good at drawing portraits, probably learning much in the art academy, and also from practicing every day on the streets of Paris. Ironically, as Millet progressed as an artist, he revealed less and less of the people's faces he drew and painted. Although the people are the focal point of his works, they carry no great significance, as one only seems to get a glimpse of them. It's as if Millet is saying, *"earth to earth, dust to dust."* Thus, one is not able to see into the person's soul, leaving just an impression of their facial features. This is certainly different from the Age of Enlightenment and the Renaissance where artists placed man on a pedestal, showing every little detail with absolute perfection.

....

Lesson #58: *The Sower*

Millet was a Christian artist who was most concerned with man's relationship to the land. One of the great biblical themes for many artists has been the parable of the sower as told by Jesus. Notice how the English *Pre-Raphaelite* artist, John Everett Millais, portrayed this story below. He shows the sower from a low vantage point, scattering the seed as we are looking up at him. Notice that the birds take up the seed before it can take root. For this assignment, read *"The Parable of the Sower"* in Matthew 13, and do a drawing of it below. Draw it first with your black drawing pen and then color with your colored pencils.

"The Sower" John Everett Millais

"So she stayed close by the young women of Boaz, to glean until the end of the barley and wheat harvest..."

Ruth 2:23

"The Gleaners" Millet

The picture above is a reproduction from one of Millet's most famous paintings, *The Gleaners.* It seems to be right out of the book of Ruth. Do you know the story? How Ruth went to glean in the fields of Boaz for food. *Gleaners*, in the Old Testament, were poor people who gathered the produce that was left in the fields after the harvest. It was common in ancient days for the harvesters to leave ten percent of their crops behind for the poor to glean.

Observe that Millet does not reveal any detail in the faces as he focuses more on the simplicity of this act of labor and the harmony between man and nature. The two figures on the left seem to be a mirror image of each other, while the half standing figure to the right seems to prevent the eye from wandering off the picture.

"Abigail Bringing Food to David" Abigail Gamble   Age 10   Ontario, Canada

80

"Beauty does not lie in the face. It lies in the harmony between man and his industry. Beauty is expression. When I paint a mother, I try to render her beautiful by the mere look she gives her child."
Millet

....

"Study of Mother and Child" Millet/pencil drawing

Look at the picture to the left. It is an ordinary scene of a mother and daughter. Notice the faces are very simple. Again, Millet only *suggests* the features in this touching scene. You can sense the soft light coming in from the window and the peace within the home. Years ago there were no televisions, computers, or even radios. Most of the families spent quality together. The family would work, play, and train together. Certainly Millet was able to capture the heart of this family in a very pure and simple way.

....

Lesson #59: Drawing Light

The soft light coming from the window in Millet's drawing is called the *light source*. The light source lets you know which direction the light is coming from. For this assignment, place a teapot or other object next to a window, and draw it with a light side and a shaded side. Use your drawing pencil and shade with lines. Draw a little sun and arrow to remind you where the light is coming from (A).

A. light source

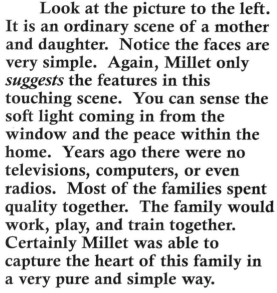

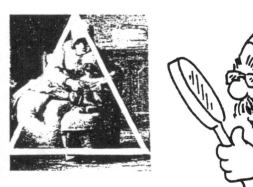

....

Composition means where and how you situate your subject matter for your picture. Notice where the mother and daughter are in the drawing above. They are centrally located. Also, if you observe carefully, you will see that they form a triangle. During the Renaissance, artists discovered that the centrally located triangular shape made for a perfect composition.

81

A.

"The Angelus"
Barry Stebbing/copy from Millet

The drawing to the left (A) was done from one of Millet's most famous paintings, *Angelus.* Another copy from a Millet is of the woman bending over in a garden (B). The viewer has a vague impression of their faces, which is secondary to the message which Millet tries to make. His use of working people, the *"salt of the earth,"* adds a sweet and humble effect to the surroundings he places them in.

In *Angelus,* Millet desires to show the gratitude towards God that the common workers had, being thankful for the work of their hands. During the 1800's, church bells would ring four times a day across the land. At the sound of the bell, the workers would pause from their work to thank God for His many blessings.

The sketch of the woman working in the garden (below) is a study Vincent van Gogh did by copying one of Millet's paintings. Van Gogh was a great admirer of Millet, and often copied his artwork to learn more about his style.

B.

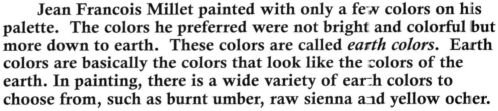

Lesson #60: Earth Colors

Jean Francois Millet painted with only a few colors on his palette. The colors he preferred were not bright and colorful but more down to earth. These colors are called *earth colors*. Earth colors are basically the colors that look like the colors of the earth. In painting, there is a wide variety of earth colors to choose from, such as burnt umber, raw sienna and yellow ocher.

For the first part of this assignment, see how many earth colors you can create with your colored pencils by mixing and blending colors together. There are a wide variety of browns you can make if you experiment. For example: yellow, orange and a little violet make a nice brown, or earth color. You can also try taking brown and adding some yellow and/or orange to it. Experiment in the small stones to the left by coloring them with a variety of browns. Then, color the picture of the workers on the next page with earth colors. Finally, color the picture of the farmhouse on page 77 with an assortment of earth colors and dull greens. One way to dull a green is by adding a little of its complement, red. Add a very light blue to the sky in the background.

_____
_____
_____
_____
_____

Study by Millet

Millet painted in somber *earth colors*. His figures had little expression or identity in their faces, leaving them vague, often in the shadows of a hat. These working people were set against rural backgrounds - woods, farms, cottages, etc. Millet knew the French peasant well, and brought simple beauty to otherwise plain settings of man working in harmony with the land.

What do you think is going on in the picture above? Are the two people going to work or returning home? What do you think they are talking about? What do you think the weather is like? Do you like the drawing? Why? Is there anything else you see in this picture? Write your description of the picture on the bottom of page 82.

"Adopt the pace of nature, her secret is patience." Emerson

"Track Beside a Field" Jean Francois Millet

Lesson #61: *Coloring a Landscape with Earth Colors*

Notice the sketch above by Millet, *Track Beside a Field.* It is of a landscape, and another example of the simplicity of his artwork. He used very little detail and color in both his drawings and paintings. Color *Track Beside a Field* with your colored pencils. See how many greens you can place in the picture. You could have distant green trees, a green hill, light green grass, and larger, dark green trees in the foreground and to the left. If you colored them all the same green, your picture will look rather boring. Remember, Millet used *muted*, or dull, earth colors.

Practice making greens in the circles. You may want to create one by mixing a little brown with yellow and green; another with green, blue and a touch of red; another with green, yellow and a touch of red; and even one with green, yellow, brown and a touch of black. Color at least four different greens in your picture. Then, color the tree trunks and the two narrow paths with a creative brown that you mix on your own. Do you see the house on the top of the hill? Color this with a dull, brownish/red roof, and a dull, yellow/ brown side.

84

Lesson #62: The Refrigerator Gallery

For this assignment, select from your picture *postcard gallery, Man with a Hoe,* by Jean Francois Millet and *The Farewell of Telemachus and Eucharis* by Jacques-Louis David. Place the reproductions in front of you and study them for a few minutes. Then, write your impression of each on the lines below. Are there any similarities? How are they different in style and subject matter? What do you like about each painting? What about the colors and composition? Which is your favorite and why? This is called a *comparative study.*

Comparative Study

_____
_____
_____
_____
_____
_____
_____
_____
_____
_____
_____

During the 18th and 19th century, there was a return to the classical approach to art. This rebirth was called *Neo-Classical,* literally meaning *new classical.* Once again, artists returned to the ways of the ancient Greeks and Romans and to a style that was sublime and perfect. Their desire was to exalt man and show him in a state of perfection. Instead of using stories from the Bible as a source for subject matter, *Neo-Classical* artists reverted to portraying Greek mythological stories. In the painting, *The Farewell of Telemachus and Eucharis,* David depicts a mythological story where a young god and goddess have to bid farewell. As the story tells, Telemachus, the son of Odysseus (one of Homer's heroes), bids farewell to Eucharis before he goes off in search of his father. The artist reveals the pure and perfect ideals of the ancient Greeks. The colors are vivid, and the realism is as perfect as a photograph.

Many Christians believe that art should be realistic since it is a representation of God's creativity and that man's responsibility in art is to interpret God's creation in as realistic a way as possible. However, realism should not be the only concern for Christians appreciating art. Remember, realism was actually birthed in ancient Greece where classical artists glorified man through perfection. Though Millet's style is not realistic like the *Neo-classical* painting, it certainly touches one's heart.

Let's look again at *The Farewell of Telemachus and Eucharis* and *Man with a Hoe.* Both artists were French and lived during the same time. Do you notice the difference in styles? What about the use of color? And what about the story they are telling? Millet was concerned with showing the common working man. As mentioned, this is called *genre* painting. In *Man with a Hoe,* Millet shows a worker in the field, seemingly exhausted and exasperated by the work at hand. The soil needs to be tilled and will take great labors. He seems weary with the task as he hunches over his hoe. In the background is fertile land with crops growing green, preparing for harvest. Possibly, that is the hope of the peasant, as he struggles with what is before him.

"Blessed are the meek, for they shall inherit the earth." Matthew 5:5

Millet did not desire to exalt man, neither was his desire to depict glamorous or romantic scenes from mythology. His heart was with the poor who worked the land. Much of Millet's work is the fruit of his Christian upbringing, exemplifying the word of God in the lives of the meek. His colors are limited and muted (dull), choosing earth colors like reddish/browns and brownish/blacks over the vibrant colors used by the classical artists. He placed very little detail in his work and used large brush strokes. Millet's paintings are not as *linear* as the classicists, as his edges seem softer. Observe the faces on both paintings. There is exact detail in the mythological figures, whereas you can barely see the facial features in Millet's peasant as the detail is not important. Thus, you have a realistic painting exalting humanism and mythology on the one hand, and on the other, a painting that is not nearly as realistic, but praises the humble and strives to touch our hearts with the labors of the poor.

Now compare the two paintings again. Has your opinion changed? Why? One of the reasons we call this *art appreciation* is because it teaches us to appreciate and understand art better. Write any new comments you may have on the paintings below.

A.

Lesson #63:
Copying a Millet

Copy the picture, *Man with a Hoe* from your *picture post card gallery* in the figure box to the left (A). Start by drawing everything in lightly with your yellow or orange pencil, and then color it with muted earth colors. Before beginning, experiment by blending several colors together with your colored pencils. Can you make a very light color for the sky? A light reddish/brown for the distant smokestacks? A pale green for the hills on the horizon? What about colors for the man's shirt and flesh?

Life remained difficult for Millet even after he moved to the country town of Barbizon. Between 1849 and 1855, Millet struggled with poverty and lack of recognition. However, in 1855 *The Gleaners* was exhibited in the *Salon* in Paris, the most prestigious place to show one's artwork in Europe. With this new recognition he received a degree of success. *The Gleaners* sold in 1867 for approximately $400. Just twenty years later it was purchased for $60,000, and now hangs in the Louvre Museum.

Although Millet was a Christian man, he made very few religious paintings. To the upper left and right are pencil studies he did of the crucifixion. True to his style, Millet has managed to make the faces secondary.

Jean Francois Millet spent the rest of his days in Barbizon painting scenes which seemed to capture *the salt of the earth* in the simplicity of their lifestyle. Many other great artists joined him in the country, starting a new type of school whose purpose was to study nature. Corot, Delacroix and Courbet were three of the most prominent to join him. Millet died in 1875, leaving behind him a vast following of patrons whose hearts he had surely touched with paint and brush.

....

"The Last Supper" Meggy Fitzpatrick Age 7 Lowell, Michigan

Lesson #64: Earth Colors

Take out *Paint Card #III* and place it in front of you. Let's see how well you can paint the picture, *Track Beside a Field*. Set up your palette by squeezing out your four colors (see page 55). You should also have a cup of water and a cloth situated on the table. Fill the cup halfway with water to use for cleaning your brushes. A cloth or rag will be used to wipe your brush clean and also to dry it before placing it into another color. It is very important to have clean, dry brushes when painting. Try not to get too much water in your paints. This will allow you to paint thicker. Finally, whenever mixing colors, always add just a touch of the dark color into the lighter color. You can always add more of the darker color if need be. You are a scientist. Mixing colors takes study and practice, not talent.

When painting a landscape, start by painting the background (which would be the sky), and work your way forward. You will be painting the distant hills and trees next as it is much easier to paint over previously painted areas. For example, if you painted a tree and then had to paint the sky, it would be very tedious to paint your sky around all the branches. Whereas, it is a simple matter to paint your branches over the blue sky that has already been painted. Skies are a very light color, generally the lightest color in your picture. Therefore, mix a lot of white with just a tiny speck of blue and paint the sky in the picture on Paint Card #III. Make sure to also paint the sky in the upper left behind the trees.

A.

Next, make some greens. You made greens earlier on Paint Card #I. Many students paint with just one color green, but if you look closely at the colors in nature, you will see a vast assortment of greens across the land. To make green, simply add a little blue to yellow. If it is not green enough, add more blue. A good way to make a dull green is by adding the complement of green. If you refer back to your colored pencil assignments (see page 29), you will see that red is the complement of green. Complementary colors are great for dulling a bright color. However, only add a little speck of red to make a dull green.

B.

C.

D.

Have at least four different greens for your picture: a dull green for the distant trees (A), a slightly brighter green for the distant hill (B), another green for the grass in the foreground (C) and another blue/green for the trees to the left (D). For a brighter, sunny green, add a touch of green to a lot of yellow. If you look closely at nature on a sunny day, you will see that grass, bushes and trees are a very light, bright yellow/green when the sun is shining on them. This color will also brighten up your painting. Paint the distant house with a dull red by adding a touch of green to red, and then paint the track in the field with a light, colorful brown.

"For he will not dwell unduly on the days of his life, because God keeps him busy with the joy of his heart."
Ecclesiastes 5:20

....

Carl Bloch (1834-1890) *The Forgotten One*

Carl Bloch (block) was born in Copenhagen, Denmark in 1834. He was the son of a wealthy, hosiery merchant. Carl's family was large, with six brothers and three sisters. His father, Jorgen Peter Bloch, loved to read the Bible, and brought his children up with the fear of the Lord and a good understanding of the word of God. *"Train up a child in the way he should go, and when he is old he will not depart from it."* Proverbs 22:6.

Carl Bloch

In some ways, Carl Bloch's lifestyle was similar to Rembrandt's. His family was prosperous, they lived in northern Europe and were Protestant by faith. Like Rembrandt, his parents discouraged the young man from becoming an artist, deciding to send him off for an academic education by enrolling him in the naval academy. While there, Carl's only love was in the drawing class he had under a rather well-known portrait and landscape painter, Theodore Restorff. The teacher soon noticed the student's talents and started giving him more difficult assignments than the rest of the students. Carl's focus in art became more intense and he began to spend all his spare time doing artwork, eventually failing his Naval examination. However, this only encouraged him to partake in another career by entering an art academy. In 1852, at the age of 18, Carl was awarded his first medal for a small sketch which he had done.

Carl Bloch would leave Copenhagen at the age of 19 and move to the country where he spent several years struggling to succeed as an artist. During this time, like Millet, he painted a series of *genre* paintings of farmers and fishermen. In 1859, he was awarded a scholarship which allowed him to travel to Rome. On his way to Italy, he visited Holland and other countries where he became inspired by the works of Rembrandt, which had a lasting impression on the paintings he would eventually produce. When Bloch arrived in Rome, he was ambitious to become a portrait artist and genre painter. In time, his desires would change as his interest became more directed towards historical and biblical paintings. While in Italy, he would produce genre paintings of the people working the land. However, because of the great influence of Rembrandt, he would also begin creating biblical paintings, two of which were, *Samson* and *Jairus' Daughter.*

"Mary's Visit to Elizabeth" Carl Bloch copy by Todd Leasure

Lesson #65:
Jairus' Daughter

Do you know the story of *Jairus' Daughter* in the Bible? The picture to the left is from an etching by Carl Bloch. Notice how the artist bathed the daughter of Jairus in light, and that the dark background contrasts the light areas to create a dramatic effect. You can vaguely see the appearance of Jesus on the balcony, about to enter the scene and perform a great miracle.

"Jairus' Daughter"
Carl Bloch etching

Many great masters of the past did preliminary drawings called *cartoons* before beginning their paintings. *Cartooning* refers to a thorough preliminary study. Do not confuse this type of cartooning with what you find in the comic strips. Years ago, artists realized that the more they worked on a preliminary drawing, the more success they would have with the finished product.

Read the story of *Jairus' Daughter* in Mark 5:35-43, and do your own interpretation of it in the figure box on the top of the next page. Before beginning, do a preliminary cartoon drawing in pencil on another sheet of paper. Your cartoon drawing will help you solve any problems or mistakes so you won't make them in your finished picture. Remember, the more you work on your preliminary drawing, the better your finished artwork will be. Try to use light areas against dark areas in your picture to create contrast. You may also want to practice blending your colors in the circles next to the picture before using them. Print the title, your name and date under your picture when finished.

Notice the drawing by a student, *The Empty Tomb* (left). Observe how the student used light against dark areas, very similar to the way Carl Bloch created his picture of *Jairus' Daughter*. Also, notice the use of lines in the dark areas to keep these areas from being too heavy.

"The Empty Tomb" Mark Roddy Kirkland, Washington

90

Title:_____ Name: _____ Date: _____

....

Carl Bloch would spend over ten years in Italy studying the great masters from the Renaissance. In 1868 he met a young lady named Alma Trepka and when he finally returned to Copenhagen, he took her with him and they were married. However, all was not well, as Alma's family was very displeased with their daughter's decision to marry an artist which they considered a relatively unworthy position.

In spite of this, the Danish artist's reputation as a painter continued to grow, especially in his native land of Denmark. Many galleries were purchasing his paintings and he was receiving much recognition. Unfortunately, his larger paintings did not fare well. The public was very critical of them until 1865, when one of his largest paintings was exhibited at the prestigious Copenhagen Museum and received acclaim.

Not long after the exhibition a wealthy man, named J.C. Jacobsen, ordered several paintings to be done for the King of Denmark, King Christian IV. These paintings were to be placed in the chapel at the Frederiksborg Castle. With this great commission from the king, Carl Bloch's reputation was established. During this time, he was also being commissioned to do many large altar pieces for churches throughout the country.

Carl Bloch became ill and passed away in 1890 at the age of 66. He stands as a truly great Danish painter, and one of the greatest religious painters of all times. His altar-pieces have especially brought him fame and recognition, completing over ten of these massive paintings during his lifetime, along with almost 250 other paintings and 75 etchings.

Many have doubted Carl Bloch's sincerity as a Christian man, but his own statements give us no reason to be skeptical. Bloch considered himself a Christian and his Christ-figures underline this clearly. He himself considered the altar paintings to be his most important works. There is no doubt that his own personality is expressed in his paintings, along with a deep reverence for Jesus Christ.

"For every tree is known by its own fruit. For men do not gather figs from thorns, nor do they gather grapes from a bramble bush. A good man out of the good treasure of his heart brings forth good..."
Luke 6:44-45

"Study of Christ" Carl Bloch etching

Many years have passed since Carl Bloch's death and it is difficult to have a sense of what his personality was like. Some of his contemporaries labeled him a *pessimist*. Yet, this negative outlook could have been confused with his frustrations over being an artist. As you study great artists, you will find that many, if not most, became very critical of the work which they did. Thus, this pessimism could have been confused with being self-critical. I am sure you will agree that learning the fundamentals of art such as drawing and painting can be very frustrating.

Another frustration may have been his striving to live up to family expectations. Remember, art was not considered to be a respectable profession during these times. Yet, Carl Bloch's reward has been *the proof in the pudding* - the beautiful paintings of Christ that have touched the hearts of so many.

As far as his faith in Christ was concerned, those close to him believed that he was not only a man of humility, but also very conscientious. His humble character seems to be revealed in the paintings he left behind. Jesus says in Matthew 7:20, *"You will know them by their fruit."*

Have you seen many other paintings and drawings of Jesus Christ? Did you notice that some of them look the way you believe Jesus looked and some do not? Of all the great artists who have done portrayals of Jesus Christ, Carl Bloch reveals Christ's personality in a way that few other great artists have been able to capture. His Jesus is one of beauty, manliness, compassion and purity.

"Peter Denying Christ" Carl Bloch etching

••

   Above is part of an etching done by Carl Bloch. Like Albrecht Dürer and Rembrandt van Rijn, the Danish artist completed many etchings during his lifetime. Remember, years ago etchings were a great way of making prints for books and other publications. The picture above shows Peter after he had denied Jesus three times. Notice the light cast upon Peter against the shaded area of the column. Look at the way the artist has captured the feeling of utter hopelessness in Peter after denying his Lord. Did you also notice the rooster that Carl Bloch placed in the bottom left corner? What does that symbolize?

Lesson #66: Searching for a Lost Artist

Carl Bloch's biblical paintings and portrayals of Jesus Christ are some of the best the world has ever seen. Whereas Rembrandt died in poverty and obscurity, Carl Bloch died with prominence and honor. However, time has all but faded Bloch's name from the list of the great masters. This happens quite often, as tastes change and the world can only acclaim a certain amount of artists to greatness. You will be amazed at how many masterpieces there are in museums and galleries by artists many of us know very little about. Sadly, this must have been the case with Carl Bloch, as today it is difficult to find his name even in the encyclopedia.

Self-portrait of Carl Bloch
by Todd Leasure

A.

For this assignment, research Carl Bloch and see what you can find. If the library does not have anything about him, you may request a book and they will try to obtain it. A wonderful place to find his artwork would be in a very old Bible. Many times these large volumes of God's word contain paintings by other masters like Rembrandt and Titian. Do a review on Carl Bloch's life and artwork, and then write a 150 word essay below. Do you like his paintings? What do you think of the Christ he illustrates? What do you see in the stories he renders? Along with your essay, copy one of his paintings with your colored pencils in the figure box (A).

_____

_____

_____

_____

_____

_____

_____

_____

_____

_____

_____

_____

What did Jesus look like?

It is difficult to say what Jesus really looked like because, for one, he lived so long ago. Also, during the time of Christ, it was the custom of the Jews not to create a likeness of a person in art, whether it be sculpture, drawing or painting, since they believed this to be wrong.

When early Christian art began to appear in the third century A.D., Jesus was first portrayed as a young, beardless man in the setting of a shepherd. Around the fourth century, the Church came to see Jesus the way Isaiah described him in Isaiah 53:2, *"He has no form or comeliness; and when we see Him, there is no beauty..."* Thus, in most early Christian artwork, Jesus is seen as plain, somber looking, clean-shaven and holding a baby lamb.

"Jesus with the Children" Carl Bloch copy by Todd Leasure

During the time of Jesus, there was a written document recording His appearance. The author who attested to this description was Publius Lentulus, a friend of Pilate's. His comments about Jesus were: *"In this time appeared a man endowed with great powers. His name is Jesus, and his disciples call him the Son of God. This Jesus is of noble and well-proportioned stature, with a face full of kindness, and yet firmness, so that beholders both love him and fear him. His hair is the color of wine, straight and without lustre, but from the level of the ears curling and flossy. His forehead is even and smooth, his face without blemish, and enhanced by a tempered bloom, his countenance ingenuous and kind. His nose and mouth are in no way faulty. His beard is full, of the same color as his hair; his eyes blue and extremely brilliant. No one has seen him laugh, but many, on the contrary, to weep. His person is tall, his hands beautiful and straight. In speaking he is deliberate and grave, with little given to loquacity; in beauty surpassing most men."*

"Jesus Walking on Water" Lindsey Fore Age 9 Dave, Iowa

95

Thus, Publius Lentulus agrees with the book of Isaiah that Jesus was a man of sorrows, but also adds that he was a handsome man with striking facial features. This certainly paints another picture of our Messiah, and seems to confirm in many of our hearts, the way we believe Him to look.

Erica Weston Age 7 1/2
Warsaw, Indiana

Katie Peters Age 9
Midlothian, Va.

Early Christian art was influenced by the beauty of ancient Greek and Roman art, and also by the passage in Psalm 45:2, *"You are the fairest of the sons of men."* However, around the fifth Century, Christian leaders came to believe that Jesus was more *comely.* So Jesus began to be portrayed as a masculine, yet kind man, and the unshaven appearance was gone.

Abigail Lisner Age 11
Mahomer, Illinois

When Napoleon Bonaparte was banished in exile to St. Helena island, this is what his thoughts were about Jesus, *"I know men, and I tell you, Jesus is not a man. He commands us to believe, and gives no other reasons than his words, I AM GOD. Philosophers try to solve the mysteries of the universe by their empty dissertations: fools; they are like infants that cry to have the moon for a plaything. Christ never hesitates. He speaks with authority. His religion is a mystery; but it subsists by its own force. He seeks, and absolutely requires, the love of men, the most difficult thing in the world to obtain. Alexander, Caesar, Hannibal conquered the world, but had no friends. I myself am perhaps the only person of my day who loves Alexander, Caeser, and Hannibal. Alexander, Caesar, Charlemagne, and myself founded empires; but upon what? Force. Jesus founded his empire on Love; and at this hour millions would die for him."*

96

Napoleon continued, *"I myself have inspired multitudes with such affection that they would die for me. But my presence was necessary. Now that I am in St. Helena, where are my friends? I am forgotten, soon to return to the earth, and become food for worms. What an abyss between my misery and the eternal kingdom of Christ, who is proclaimed, loved, adored, and which is extending over all the earth. Is this death? I tell you, Jesus Christ is God."*

Tim Mar Age 5
Bellevue, WA.

Melinda Peters
Midlothian, VA.

Josephus (37 A.D.-100 A.D.) Describes Jesus

The best and most accurate accounts of the life of the Jews during the time of Jesus Christ comes from the great historian, Flavius Josephus, whose Hebrew name was Joseph ben Mattathias. A man of immense confidence with a strong instinct for self-preservation during a time of Roman occupation, Josephus survived the troubled times he lived in and wrote two major historical works about Jewish history during his time.

Josephus was born in Jerusalem of a wealthy, priestly family. His native language was Aramaic, but he was also fluent in Greek and Hebrew. During his youth he was a student of the various Jewish sects, and even lived as an ascetic for several years in the desert (an ascetic is someone who isolates himself). In A.D. 64 at the age of 27, he went to Rome to plead the cause of some Jewish priests who had been sent to Emperor Nero for trial. He returned to Judea with a lasting impression of the glory and power of Rome. When the Jews finally rebelled against the Roman Empire, Josephus was placed in command of the Jewish forces in Galilee, eventually to be defeated by the Roman general, Vespasian. Josephus surrendered and with daring presence of mind, predicted that Vespasian would become emperor. When the prediction came true, Josephus' future was secure. He adopted the emperor's family name, Flavius, and was granted the rights of Roman citizenship. After the war he was taken to Rome where he lived out the rest of his life.

Nick Sanders
Terre Haute, Indiana

This great Jewish historian discusses most of the major political figures of the time, including an extensive portrayal of Herod the Great, whom he depicts as both an astute politician and an oppressive tyrant. However, Josephus wrote very little about Jesus as Christianity was still in its infancy at this time.

Here is what we now have about Jesus as written by Josephus, *"Now, there was about this time, Jesus, a wise man, if it is lawful to call Him a man, for He was a doer of wonderful works - a teacher of such men as receive the truth with pleasure. He drew over to Him both many of the Jews, and many of the Gentiles. He was Christ; and when Pilate, at the suggestion of the principal men amongst us, had condemned Him to the cross, those that loved Him at the first did not forsake Him, for He appeared to them alive again the third day, as the divine prophets had foretold these and ten thousand other wonderful things concerning Him; and the tribe of Christians so named from Him, are not extinct at this day."*

"Behold, I stand at the door and knock. If anyone hears My voice and opens the door, I will come in to him, and dine with him, and he with Me." Revelations 3:20
....

"Jesus is Born" Rebecca Rimer Age 9 Roanoke, Virginia

To be sure, all we really know is that Jesus Christ was a Galilean Jew. Thus we can imagine that he wore sandals, a mantle and a tunic just like the other Galilean Jews of the time. Our most perfect picture of Him comes from within our own spirits, nurtured by the word of God and our intimacy with Him.

Lesson #67: The Refrigerator Gallery

Select from your *picture postcard gallery* the painting by the great master Correggio, *Head of Christ.* Place it in front of you and study it for a moment. What do you think of this painting of Jesus? Do you like it? Why? What qualities do you see in Him? Do you see kindness? Compassion?

During the Renaissance there were many great artists like Michelangelo, Leonardo da Vinci and Raphael. Correggio (1489-1534), also known as Antonio Allegri, was also one of the great masters of this time. In this painting, *The Head of Christ*, Correggio is portraying the legendary story of Saint Veronica. It is said that when Jesus fell while carrying the cross on the way to Golgotha, a woman named Veronica wiped His face with her veil. Miraculously, the impression of Jesus' face was imprinted on the cloth. In the painting, Correggio captures the impression of Jesus on her cloth. However, he does it in a way in which the impression comes dramatically to life. If you look carefully, you will notice the white background of the cloth and the fringes of the material in the bottom right corner.

Some Christians believe we should not make any graven images of God or His son Jesus. This is a good point and worthy of prayer and discernment. Again, we must remember what the word of God says in Exodus 20:4, *"You shall not make for yourself any carved image, or any likeness of anything that is in heaven above..."* However, there are also those who believe that through images such as this, Christians can be spiritually edified and inspired. It is up to each of us to decide which is most practical in our faith. For this assignment, write your feelings about the painting of *The Head of Christ* on the lines below.

Ann Reichert Homeschooling Mom
Chesterfield, Virginia

99

Georges Rouault (1871-1958)
Stranger in a Strange Land

Georges Rouault (roo-alt) was born in Paris in 1871, the son of a cabinet maker. His grandfather was a collector of art and had many lithographs (prints) by Honoré Daumier, the famous French artist of the 1800s. Georges Rouault would often comment that Daumier was his first teacher.

Rouault was both a painter and a *graphic artist*. A graphic artist is someone who works with clear, life-like realism. He studied at the Ecole des Beaux Arts, a renown school of fine arts in France, and was a favorite pupil of artist Gustave Moreau.

Georges Rouault's early style was very academic, striving to be realistic in his artwork and learning many of the established traditions in the fine arts. However, he was intrigued by the colorful windows in the old Gothic cathedrals of the 12th and 13th centuries which majestically stood on the streets of Paris. These stained glass church windows were simple, spiritual and colorful, and the young artist's ambition was to return to a style of art that had such simple, spiritual qualities. Therefore, he spent much time studying the designs of these windows which had survived over so many years.

Vincent van Gogh, Gauguin and Cezanne (great Impressionists from the end of the 19th century) also influenced Rouault. The simplicity of their styles and the use of bold colors appealed to him. These influences would also play a major role in developing Rouault's style as he worked with bold primary colors (red, blue and yellow) and black outlines, creating a powerful, yet different effect.

Lesson #68: Creating a Simple & Bold Picture

Look at the picture by Georges Rouault on the next page, *Pensee, profond regard* (Christ on the Cross). Can you see the influence that stained glass had on his artwork both in simplicity and design? What do you think of the picture? Is it realistic? Is it emotional (making you feel a certain way)? Do you find it to be similar to the way a child might portray Jesus on the cross? Write at least 50 words below describing your feelings about the picture.

_____
_____
_____
_____
_____
_____
_____
_____
_____
_____

"Pensee, profond regard." (Christ on the Cross) by Georges Rouault

"Jesus being Baptized"
Cassandra Diehl Age 10 Reading, Pa.

Lesson #69: Christ Crucified

The crucifixion of Jesus is a subject that has inspired many artists. Do you remember the monastic monk from the Early Renaissance, Fra Angelico, and that it was said he often wept when painting Jesus crucified? For this assignment, do your own *Pensee, profond regard* (Christ on the Cross). First, create some thumbnail sketches (A) to better formulate your idea for a finished picture. Like Georges Rouault, keep your picture simple. When you are finished, take your best design and place it in the larger figure box. Start your drawing lightly with your yellow or light cream colored pencil. When you have everything drawn in just the way you like, start adding bolder and brighter colors using only your primary colors. Finally, take your black pencil and place a heavy dark outline around your subject matter. What do you think of this bold effect using just the primary colors and outlining with black?

A. Thumbnail Sketches

B.

"That I may know Him and the power of His resurrection, and the fellowship of His sufferings..."

In 1903, Georges Rouault became a committed Christian. His purpose as an artist was to make personal statements of his devotion to Jesus Christ through his paintings. Even though he was considered a *modern artist*, his roots were established in a deep spiritual faith. He once stated, *"As a Christian in such hazardous times, I believe only in Jesus Christ on the cross. I am a Christian of the olden times."* Besides creating many paintings and illustrations of Christ, he liked to use clowns as a source for subject matter. Some believe the clown could have represented an estranged prophet who was called to plea for the world to repent. Possibly, the clown represented the isolation of the Christian from the rest of the cruel world. Clearly, Rouault's main vision in art was to show man's suffering and redemption through Christ. This relationship between human suffering and Christ's agony was a major theme of the artist throughout his life.

A. *"Vinnie"* the Clown

Lesson #70: *Vinnie* the Clown

Georges Rouault placed a sad clown in some of his paintings to symbolize the sadness of the world without God. For this assignment, draw a picture of a sad clown and let him symbolize how you feel about the world of sin.

Draw a sad clown with everything going in a downward direction to help express a sad mood: the hat slouches, his mouth goes down, his hair sags, the flower droops, even the teardrop trickles down his cheek. Draw a sad clown face in the figure box below (A), and color him with your colored pencils using *cool colors*. Your cool colors are blue, violet, and green. Cool colors will help express a sad mood. You can add a few other colors if you like, but stay mainly with blue and violet. (*When coloring a clown, never color the mask that goes around his mouth. This remains white.*) Color *Vinnie* (A) for practice before beginning.

Finally, draw your sad clown in an everyday situation, like at the park or on a city street. Have him be symbolic for not fitting in with the world around him. Are there any Bible scriptures that could be applied to your picture? Draw your picture in the large figure box below (B).

A.

B.

*"Why should we be in such desperate haste to succeed and in such desperate enterprises?
If a man does not keep pace with his companions, perhaps it is because he hears a
different drummer. Let him step to the music he hears, however measured or far away."*
Thoreau

Georges Rouault was one of the first modern artists. He was often classified with a group of French artists called *Fauvists,* who were given this name for their bold and abstract artwork. During the early 1900s, the art world was still very much established in a classical and realistic approach to art. This new type of *abstract art* was an insult to most. Thus, the title *Fauvists* was given to these modern artists who had broken away from reality. The term means *wild beasts* and was meant as a vulgar insult for the way they painted.

After becoming a Christian, Rouault would often frequent the courts of Paris and observe the treatment of the poor and the sinners. It grieved him to see the wretched state man had fallen to. He also observed the cruelty and heartlessness of the judges who ruled over the common people. These judges would become popular subject matter for many of his paintings. Georges Rouault believed in leading a simple life of little means and solitude and strived to identify with *Christ on the Cross.* He once stated in a letter to a friend, *".... one of the great themes that had always occupied me, the sufferings and death of Christ."*

Even though Rouault was considered a *Fauvist,* his work was different from the other modern artists as there was a moral theme to his paintings. His desire was to show the ways of the good and the bad, the righteous and the sinner, the evil and the godly.

God used Georges Rouault to touch the heart of man in spite of his being an *abstract artist.* We need to remember *not to throw the baby out with the bath water.* Just because a period or style like modern or abstract art is not considered to be worthy, there may be an inspiring message in the midst of it all.

The Bible tells us that the Lord will give His people discernment and wisdom. As you pray, allow God to lead you in what to appreciate in art and what *not* to allow your eyes to fall upon. Psalm 101:3 states, *"I will set no wicked thing before my eyes."* This we should do obediently. But is all modern art wicked? Can God use artists in spite of the times? Christians should have a freer and more relaxed appreciation for the arts. Let the Spirit of God lead you in what to view and what to appreciate of past and present works of art.

"Moses Parting the Red Sea" Jordan Ritz Age 13 Birdsboro, Pa.

"As a Christian I believe only in Jesus Christ on the cross. I am a Christian of olden times."

Georges Rouault

Georges Rouault found himself isolated from other 20th century artists for his unrealistic style which would come to be called *expressionism.* Again, this was considered by most to be a crude, abstract interpretation of reality. However, the artist was also isolated because of his strong faith in Christ. Thus, he stood alone in the art world both for his faith in Christ and for portraying the sufferings of Jesus and the state of fallen man. Notice his portrayal of Jesus to the left. As mentioned, unlike other modern artists, Rouault's artwork had a moral sincerity in the meaning of his paintings. He is considered by many to be the greatest painter of religious themes since Rembrandt.

"Portrait of Christ" Georges Rouault

Rouault's style was bold and simple. His figures have a richness of color, especially with the reds and blues. Even though his paintings look very simple and basic, he often took over 20 years to complete a painting.

Georges Rouault died in Paris in 1958. He was a 20th century artist with a heart for *olden times* and for the things of Christ. He strived to reclaim the excellence of earlier times with spiritual art that would touch the heart of man and his commitment towards the things of God. Although he was emersed in the worldly city of Paris, he continually made bold and powerful statements about the gospel through his paintings. It is important for us, as Christians, to understand how God can use an artist no matter what the period, style or location may be.

"Daniel in the Lion's Den"
Levi Kossow Age 5 Greenville, Wisconsin

A majority of Christians still view *modern art* as a radical break from realism. They believe that God, in His creative genius, has expressed everything the way it is, and that man's part as an artist is to copy creation as realistically as possible. Remember, art does not have to be realistic to touch our hearts, as many great artists have shown us throughout history. For instance, if you look closely at a Rembrandt painting, you will notice that he was not as articulate, or realistic, as many of us imagine. Observe the artwork of children. It is certainly not realistic, but it genuinely touches our hearts. When it comes to art, God has instilled creativity in each one of us, and this expression comes in many different forms .

Lesson #71:
Marker Card "A" - Coloring with Markers

Georges Rouault loved to paint with bold, bright colors. For assignments like this, colored markers are wonderful to use because they are both bright and bold. When using markers, it is good to use a sturdy, durable heavy stock paper so the colors will not *bleed* to the other side. Likewise, heavy paper will not bubble up. An ideal surface for colored markers is either poster board or a heavy *index card stock*. A package of 250 *heavy 110 index stock or bristle board* paper is available at most office supply stores for a reasonable price. Each sheet is 8 1/2" x 11" and is an ideal size for individual pictures.

For this assignment, let's draw and color a Bible story with colored markers. Place *Marker Card "A"* in front of you. There are literally thousands of wonderful stories in God's word to illustrate. As you read the Bible, try to keep notes of stories you would like to illustrate.

Here is a list of several that may be interesting for artwork: Exodus 16:14-17, Daniel 6:16-22, Matthew 3:16, Mark 16:4-5 and John 11:40-44. You may also want to look at student illustrations of Bible stories throughout this text for other ideas. Before beginning, do some thumbnail sketches of Bible stories below.

Next, practice several coloring techniques with your markers before illustrating your own story. To begin, color the pictures in the two figure boxes on the top of your *marker card* with vertical lines. In the happy clown, use only your warm colors (yellow, red and orange). Do not color the mask around the mouth and eyes; these areas should always remain white. In the second figure box, use only your cool colors (blue, violet, and green) to color the sad clown.

In the second row, color the flowers with dots, or *pointillism*, placing the dots close together. In the first flower, color with dots using only the warm colors. In the second flower, use only the cool colors. In the last figure box, color the field with warm and cool colors, filling it with dots of color. However, do not color the sky. When you are finished, it should look like a beautiful field of flowers. Select your best Bible picture from your thumbnail sketches to color in the large figure box with your markers. It is always good to start with your yellow marker. This will keep your drawing light and limit your mistakes. Color your picture with lines, dots and blending.

Last of all, color each of the circles in the bottom left with a different colored marker: color one circle entirely red, another blue, another orange, etc. Now, take your brush and dip it in water. Dip your wet brush in the blue circle and paint the sky above your field of flowers. Dip your wet brush in the other colored circles and paint a light background behind the other pictures on your *marker card*. Your colors will be light and watery, creating a delightful beginning painting lesson. Make sure to keep your brush wet and paint with light and lively colors.

A.   Thumbnail Sketches

"Madonna and Child" Rome and Byzantine Art, 5th to 13th Century
Copy by Benjamin Iocco, Age 12 Freeport, Michigan

Lesson #72: *Early Christian Art*

George Rouault was influenced by Early Christian art and the simplicity and colors of stained glass windows in the old Gothic cathedrals of the 12th and 13th centuries. Look at the reproduction above of a painting done during the Byzantine Period. The figures are simple as the artist was more concerned with a spiritual message than with realism. Rouault used the symbolic colors of red, blue and yellow in his paintings. Early Christians used blue to symbolize heaven; yellow (or gold) to symbolize God, divinity and truth; white to symbolize purity; and purple to symbolize sorrow or penitence. For this assignment, copy the picture above in the open picture frame and color with your colored pencils. Remember, you can mix some of your colors together to make lighter or darker tones. Try to color with colors that have meaning or symbolism.

107

Lesson #73: *Painting with Bold Colors & Outlines*

For this assignment, practice painting with bold colors and outlines, just like Georges Rouault. Place *Paint Card #IV* in front of you. First, we are going to do outlining, or learning to draw with the brush. Mix a black color with your paints by adding red to blue until it is a very dark blue. Then, add a speck of yellow to make black. Be sure to mix a lot of this black color (about the size of a quarter), because you will need a full paintbrush in order to outline. When mixing colors, pull your colors away from the main puddles, mixing them in another area to keep your main puddles free from other colors (A).

A.

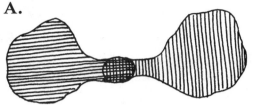

Look at the portrait of Jesus Christ by Georges Rouault on the top of the paint card. Take one of your light colored pencils and copy it in the figure box to the right of the picture. It is always good to lay in a foundation for your picture by drawing it before painting. This will solve many problems and prevent mistakes.

Then, take your thinnest brush and load it with black paint and go carefully over everything. More or less, you are drawing with your brush. Remember, it is important to have a lot of paint on your brush. If you do not, your brush hairs will split apart. Having a lot of paint on your brush will give you a nice point on the end. This is called painting with a *loaded brush.* When outlining, the more pressure you place on your brush, the thicker the lines will be; the less pressure you place on your brush, the thinner the lines will be. Practice some thick and thin brush strokes in the small figure boxes on the bottom of the paint card. Finally, on the bottom right of the paint card, paint over the picture, *Pensee, profond regard*.

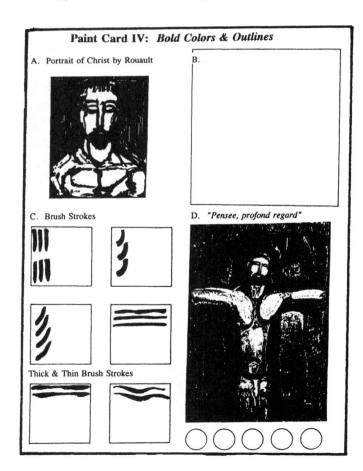

Can you make different tones of red and blue? Tones are simply gradations of one color from light to dark. You can make a red darker by adding a little speck of blue to it. You can make a red lighter by adding some white and yellow. To make a darker blue, add red until it becomes very dark. You can make a light blue by adding a speck of blue to a lot of white. Finally, you can make a duller blue by adding a little of its complement (orange). To make a duller red, add a little bit of its complement (green). Fill the circles with different tones of red and blue before beginning.

Paint the large, dark rectangles (behind the cross) with your blues and greens, blending one color into another. Then, paint the body of Jesus with a very light orange. Make orange by adding red and yellow, and then add a touch of this orange to a lot of white. With a variety of reds and oranges, paint some of the designs that go around the picture. Finally, when everything is dry, take your smallest brush and outline some of the areas with black.

The Nazarenes

The term *Nazarenes* was given to a group of six German Christian artists in the early 1800s. Their desire was to return to a style of art that glorified God, believing that the art of their day had abandoned religious ideals. The Nazarenes yearned to return to a style of painting that was not as mechanical, or classical. They believed that artists were forsaking the true meaning of art by returning to the practice of glorifying man, or *humanism*. The Nazarenes wanted to revert to the methods of the medieval workshops from centuries past, creating art that was simple, pure, and glorified God.

The term *Nazarene*, like many other titles given to movements in art, was intended to be a sarcastic label given to them because of their fondness for biblical dress and style of hair. Nazarene also means, *those who follow the teachings of Christ*. Eventually they were came to be known as the *Brotherhood of St. Luke*, or simply, *the Brethren*. Thus began the first movement against the rigid, established way of painting in Europe.

This small group of artists originally banned together in Germany in 1809. Not long after, they moved to Rome where they obtained an abandoned monastery, St. Isidoro. This old monastic building was used as a studio for painting and also to return to the type of workshops used centuries before. Their desire was to practice a more spiritual, simple approach to art and to revive the art of *fresco* painting. Fresco was a technique used for painting pictures on walls and ceilings of churches in the 14th and 15th centuries.

This group of Christian artists was short-lived and their artwork was not greatly received by the public. The colors used in their paintings were primitive and basic, and their human figures seemed stiff and somewhat unrealistic, similar to the Early Renaissance style. Yet, their belief and purpose came to be a spark of inspiration for another group of artists in the not-to-distant future known as the *Pre-Raphaelites*.

"The Pearl of Great Price"
Anna Marie Rhoades Age 13
Gainesville, Virginia

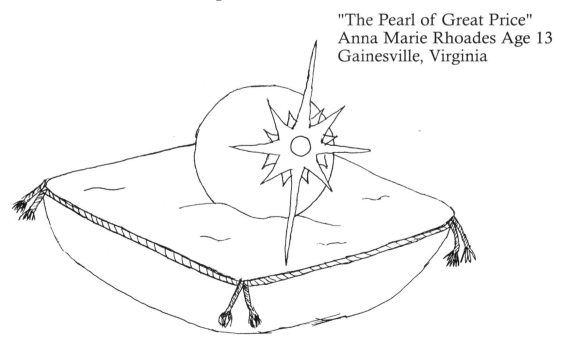

The Pre-Raphaelites

Another *brotherhood* came forth several generations after the Nazarenes. This group of artists blossomed in England in 1848, and eventually came to be known as the *Pre-Raphaelites.* Three artists started this *brotherhood*, but it soon grew in number. All were under the age of 25 when they first banded together. Their names were: John Everett Millais, William Holman Hunt, Dante Gabriel Rossetti, William Dyce, Burne Jones, James Collison, F.G. Stephens, Thomas Woolner and Ford Madox Brown. The group had two basic desires: like the Nazarenes, they wanted to show deep religious feelings in their paintings; secondly, they desired to return to an art that was more spiritual. They were called *Pre-Raphaelites,* because their desire was to return to a style of art that was before the time of the great Renaissance artist, Raphael. They believed that Raphael and the art that followed him was too perfect, too articulate and too beautiful. Art was becoming spectacular and drifting away from its main purpose. Their desire was to return to a style that was more basic - once again reverting to early Christianity. Many people from the established school would condemn their paintings. However, there was a renown English art critic, John Ruskin, who greatly supported and endorsed their approach and style to art.

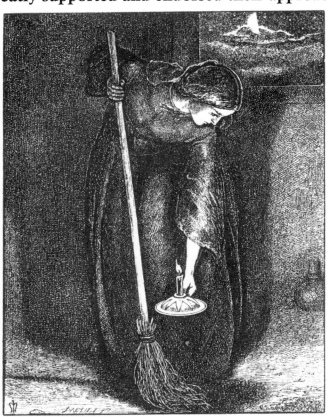

"The Lost Piece of Silver" John Everett Millais

The group had their first exhibit in 1850, two years after uniting. Desiring to remain anonymous, at first they simply signed their paintings, *PRB (Pre-Raphaelite Brotherhood).* Soon their identity was revealed. The majority of people in the art world criticized their style because it went against the classical philosophies in art which were being taught in the academies, such as the Royal Academy in England. They were also rebuked for their down-to-earth interpretations of stories from the Bible and for not doing their paintings in the grandiose style of the classical artists. Contemporaries believed religious art should be spectacular, since that is what had adorned the Churches since the 15th century. A nearly perfect and beautiful approach to Christ and the Church had been the rule for many years. However, the Pre-Raphaelites approached religious painting with a more realistic point of view, returning to the earlier style of simplicity.

The Pre-Raphaelites placed a great amount of detail in their artwork and strived to be as true to nature as possible. Much of their work was done outdoors, copying nature with exactness. There is much vitality and freshness through their use of vivid colors, and Pre-Rahpaelite paintings would come to truly touch the heart of man.

"Who exchanged the truth of God for the lie, and worshiped and served the creature rather than the Creator, who is blessed for ever."   Romans 1:25

....

Like the Nazarenes, the Pre-Raphaelites active life as a group was short-lived, less than ten years in all. Yet they would have a great impact on the art of England, especially in the area of decorative art. The high level of *design* they incorporated in their paintings by use of flat, decorative colors was similar to the earlier style of the Byzantine period.

As mentioned, the basic belief of the Pre-Raphaelites was to return to painting that would glorify God. Although many of their religious paintings are inspiring and touching, their stance concerning spiritual matters was not strong. Most of the members of this group were also writers and poets, and in time, the group became more focused on *Romanticism* than with godly aspirations and purposes. Thus, the Pre-Raphaelites would eventually concern themselves more with the perishable passions of this life and nature as a god, rather than the Creator.

"David & Goliath" Joshua Havenschild
Age 13 Coraopolis, Pa.

John Everett Millais is a good example of this change in purpose. Take a look at the back cover of *God & the History of Art II* and the painting of *Christ in the House of His Parents* (1850). This was one of his early Pre-Raphaelite paintings of the young Jesus. Millais would gradually shift philosophies and in time, abandon biblical paintings.

Romanticism should be viewed by Christians with curious interest. Many of the Romantic paintings are beautiful and touch our hearts, but its philosophy can lead one to focus their attention on beauty, passion and self-centered emotionalism. Simply put, Romanticism believes that nature is as a god to worship, and that man's existence, at least while he is young, should be one of passion and vibrance. Like the flower, these passions eventually wither away with age. However, our faith is in a living God, and our lives should be selfless in Jesus Christ. We encourage you to enjoy the beauty of Romanticism, but not become carried away with worldly emotions.

As time passed, most of the Pre-Raphaelites leaned more towards Romanticism and less towards glorifying God in their paintings. Holmon Hunt was the only exception, striving to glorify God in his artwork for the remainder of his life.

"If My people, who are called by My name, will humble themselves, and pray, and seek My face, and turn from their wicked ways; then I will hear from heaven, and will forgive their sin, and will heal their land."

II Chronicles 7:14

"The Hidden Treasure" John Everett Millais

Lesson #74: *Studying the Romantics: "Ask Me No More"*

For this lesson, place the *picture postcard* by Alma-Tadema, *Ask Me No More,* in front of you and look at the artwork. It is certainly a beautiful picture isn't it? Before continuing, write how you feel about it on the lines below.

_____

_____

_____

_____

Alma-Tadema was influenced by the classical works of the ancient Greeks and Romans. However, like the Pre-Raphaelites, he was also influenced by the Romantics of the 18th century.

Observe the reproduction of the painting again. Can you see that he was a master at both painting and creating his composition? *Composition* is the way you plan your picture. Did you know that artwork, like the written word, is supposed to read from left to right? That the eye should be led into the art from the left side of the picture? Observe how Alma-Tadema masterfully has accomplished this, as the young man bows gracefully into the scene by embracing the extended hand of the fair young lady. Then, her right arm subtly leads us to her as she becomes the focal point of the painting. Notice also, that her eyes look to the right and, along with her other arm, continue to lead us across the setting from left to right. Finally, the bouquet of flowers, like a period at the end of a sentence, stops the eye. It is a delightful job of planning a pleasing composition.

Likewise, notice the colors. What is the main color used? Blue! It is everywhere: the distant sky and water, the apparel of the young man and lady and, if you observe closely, even the marble is permeated with a soft blue. The cool colors set a calm, subtle message in the painting along with the title, *Ask Me No More.* Remember, warm colors (red, yellow and orange) create a bright and cheerful atmosphere, whereas cool colors may be used for a more sedate or melancholy message. Alma-Tadema accentuates the painting with warm flesh tones and a note of warm colors in the flowers.

The figures are both young and attractive. The artwork is sublime and heavenly. A note of love plays throughout the painting. Everything is in perfect order. However, Romanticism often seems to have a sad note, or an unhappy ending. The ideals of life, love and youth age like flowers. Love ends on a sad note, youth and beauty wither with age, and life is an ending story. Ah, but we have the word of God which says, *"The grass withers, and the flower fades, but the word of our God stands forever."* (Isaiah 40:8)

Now take a look at the *picture postcard* by Edgar Degas, *Dancers in Pink.* Degas was also a master of composition. What do you think of the way he planned his picture? Where is the eye led? What do you think of the colors? Which painting do you like best? Write your comments below.

_____

_____

_____

_____

_____

_____

_____

Lesson #75: *Holmon Hunt*

Holmon Hunt/portrait by Sir Richmond

Sadly, it is difficult to find books on Holmon Hunt. Just like Carl Bloch and the Nazarenes, art history has not been gracious to him. For this assignment, go to the library and research the Pre-Raphaelites. (You may have to look in an art history book or ask your librarian.) Study the artist, Holmon Hunt and his paintings. Then, draw one of his paintings in the figure box below with your colored pencils. Start your drawing lightly with a yellow pencil and, when you have it drawn in correctly, go over your picture with darker colors.

Finally, write an essay about Holmon Hunt on the lines below. What do you think of his paintings? Do you think his artwork is realistic? Do you like his colors? Do you see any symbolism in his artwork?

Lesson #76:
Nature Studies-Green, Green, Green!

Not only did the Pre-Raphaelites strive to return to a style of art less grandiose and spectacular than that of the Renaissance, but they also wanted to copy nature as closely as possible. Let's now study some of the greens which are found outdoors.

Two difficult studies for the young art student are learning to both see and create the many various greens in nature. Many students simply take one green colored pencil and color everything the same green! It is said that Vincent van Gogh knew over one hundred different greens he could create for his paintings when he was painting outdoors.

Let's make a variety of greens with our colored pencils. Remember, you can make delightful colors by mixing other colors together. Learning to mix colors takes no talent and is really a scientific endeavor. Take your yellow pencil and color all of the first five trees below. Then, go over *Tree #2* with your blue pencil to make a green. Next, go over *Tree #3* with your green pencil to make a yellow/green. Go over *Tree #4* with both your blue and green to make another tone of green. You can also add a little red to green (its complement) to make a dull green. Keep experimenting and see if you can make other interesting greens for *Tree #6, Tree #7* and *Tree #8*. When you are finished, print the colors you used to make each green next to the tree, starting with the color you used most. For example: *Y+B+G* means yellow plus some blue and a little green. Notice that we left the first tree yellow. Many times it is good to use yellow to show an area where the sun is shining on grass, bushes, or trees. Last of all, color the entire picture below with an assortment of the different greens.

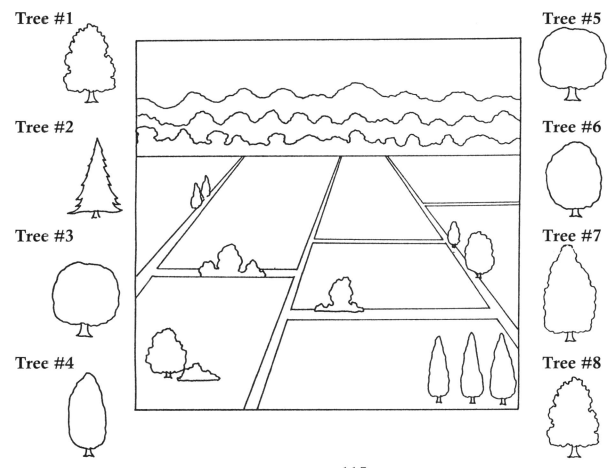

Tree #1   Tree #5

Tree #2   Tree #6

Tree #3   Tree #7

Tree #4   Tree #8

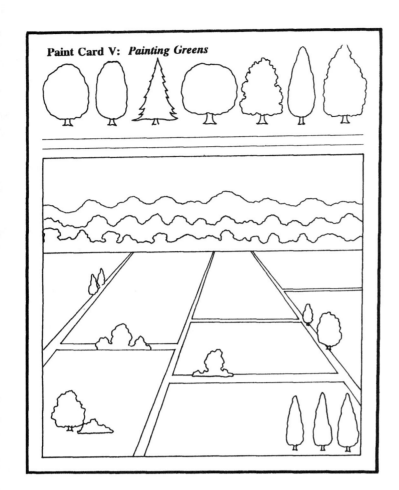

Paint Card V: *Painting Greens*

Lesson #77: *Painting Greens*

Place *Paint Card #V* in front of you. In previous painting assignments we experimented with mixing greens and creating a variety of tones. Green is such an important color because God has placed so many tones of green in nature. Let's make some various tones of green again, adding more tones of green to our collection. First, mix yellow with a very small speck of blue to make a light green. Remember, *always start with the lighter color and add a little of the darker color to the lighter color.* By adding only a speck of blue to yellow, you will make a very light *yellow/green.* It is much easier to make a darker green by adding more blue than it is to make a lighter green by adding more yellow. Paint in the first tree at the top of your paint card with this light yellow/green. Print underneath it the colors you used, starting with the color you used most: Y + B (yellow + blue). This will assist you in making that color again.

Paint the next tree by adding a little more blue to your light yellow/green. Finally, see how many different greens you can make, painting each of the trees with a different tone. You may want to add white to green to make a light lime green. Add a speck of green's complement (red) to make a dull green. Add more blue to make a dark blue/green. When you have finished, paint the picture on the bottom of *Paint Card #V* with an assortment of greens. Keep some of your greens very light. Start by making a very light blue to paint your sky, and then work your way forward by starting with the distant trees. To make a brown for your tree trunks, mix yellow and red together to make orange, and then add a speck of blue. Let's paint the pathways pink by adding a speck of red and yellow to white.

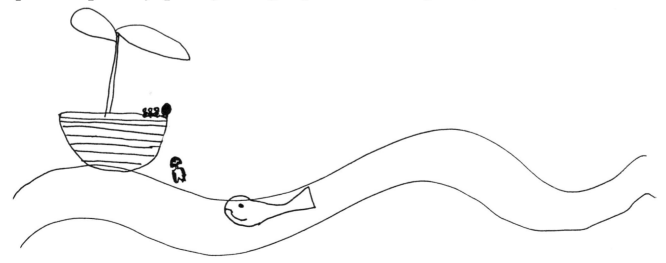

"Jonah & the Whale" Heidi Jenkins Age 9 Ceres, California

116

....

Art Historians

Georgio Vasari (1511-1574)

Georgio Vasari is known as the first true art historian and has been called *the father of art history and criticism.* He was born in the Italian town of Arezzo and received his first art lessons from a cousin of his grandfather, Luca Signorelli. When he was 13 years of age, he went to Florence and apprenticed under the great Italian master, Andrea del Sarto. While still a young student of the arts he met Michelangelo. His encounter with this great master would leave a strong impression on him for the remainder of his life. This was also the time when Raphael and Leonardo da Vinci were living. Thus, the young Georgio Vasari was not only alive during the tremendous artistic revival of the Renaissance, but also lived where three of the greatest masters of all time were working.

"Noah's Ark" Dallas Tucker Age 12 Martinsburg, W.Va.

Even though the Renaissance was from 1400-1600 A.D., the period of time from 1500 to 1520 came to be known as the *High Renaissance.* All three of the great masters were living during this brief span, with art reaching insurmountable heights of perfection.

Although Vasari spent many years as a student of the fine arts, he is best known for his works in the field of architecture and the writing of books about art and the great masters. One of his greatest feats as an architect was in designing the Uffizi in Florence. This beautiful building was commissioned in 1560 by the Medicis, a very wealthy and powerful Italian family.

However, Vasari is even more renown for his writings about the history of art. *Lives of the Most Eminent Painters, Sculptors and Architects* was first written in 1550, and a second, revised edition was published in 1568. Some art historians have claimed that it is the most important book on the history of art ever written. Vasari, like most of the Italians during the Renaissance, believed that the artwork produced during the Medieval Period (500 A.D. to 1200 A.D.) was an inferior style. He stated that it was strongly influenced by the Dark Ages (500 A.D. to 1000 A.D.) when tribes of barbarians ravaged the civilized world of Europe. It would not be until the Renaissance, that the greatest art ever created would be by the Italian masters who embraced the classical art of the ancient Greeks and Romans.

Vasari's emphatic support for the Renaissance style in painting and sculpture was a *humanistic* approach to art. Remember, the art of ancient Greece was the birthing place of humanism - placing man in the center of importance instead of God. As the Italians began to dig up the classical art of the ancient Greeks, they revitalized the age-old belief that, through his accomplishments, man was great. Vasari also believed that art's main purpose was to copy nature precisely, and that the artist should interpret everything as realistically as possible.

"I believe in Michelangelo, Valasquez, and Rembrandt; in the might of design, the mystery of color, the redemption of all things by beauty everlasting, and the message of art that has made these hands blessed."
George Bernard Shaw

In Vasari's first edition of his book published in 1550, he concentrated on the revival of the arts in Italy during the Renaissance. This *revival* started with the great Italian artist, Giotto, in the early 1300s, and ended with Michelangelo during the latter part of the 1500s. Regretfully, Giotto and Michelangelo were the only artists mentioned in his first book. Fortunately, he wrote a revised edition which included biographies of many other artists who were living during his time, along with his own biography. Georgio Vasari's writing is simple and easy to follow, and his understanding of the arts agrees with much of what modern day art historians have to say. Yet Vasari is noted for placing many of his own opinions in his books in areas where he did not have proper facts or information. Even so, much of his writing affords us the opportunity to learn about the lifestyles of the artists during the Renaissance.

Before the time of Vasari's art history books, artists struggled with the acceptance of their profession. For many years people did not believe that being an artist was a worthy occupation. Vasari's books did much in making the artist's life worthy of praise in society. Thus, he promoted the artist to a higher level of acceptance. In his writings, there are guidelines for how an artist should lead his life. Among other things, Vasari mentions that artists should insure their hands against damage or disability.

"Elijah being Translated" Ruth Kitchen Age 9 Ajax, Ontario

"Now as soon as the lad had gone, David arose from a place toward the south, fell on his face to the ground, and bowed down three times. And they kissed one another, and they wept together, but David more so."

I Samuel 20:41

Lesson #78: *Brotherly Love*

Vasari believed that most artists should not marry. During the Renaissance, artists were very committed to their work and diligently created their masterpieces day and night. Simply put, marriage was something that many artists did not have time for, and only about half of them ever married. Thus, there were many that led a single lifestyle.

Men in past centuries had more endearing friendships with other men. It was not uncommon for men, as friends, to hug each other and spend time together. Since many artists did not have time for marriage, their friendships with other men were special, enduring and much deeper than most male friendships today. Friends were greatly embraced. However, this behavior should in no way demean the character or integrity of these men. Just as the friendship between Jonathan and David was endearing and loving, the friendships of the men of the past were also respectable.

"Moses" Sarah Losinger Age 9 1/2
Marietta, Georgia

A.

Michelangelo, da Vinci and Raphael never married. They were too committed to their life's work. Even though relationships were different many years ago, this choice of artists is no reason to slander their character by believing they may have engaged in an alternate lifestyle.

In 1564 (the same year as Michelangelo's death), an authority of the Roman Catholic church, Scipione Ammirati, wrote and documented this statement pertaining to the personal character of Michelangelo, *"Bounarotti having lived for ninety years, there was never found through all this length of time, and with all the liberty to sin, any who could with right and justice impute to him a taint or any ugliness of manners."* In other words, most of these great masters had good reputations. When studying history there are some things we need to discover on our own or decide for ourselves, not always believing everything we hear or that is written.

Notice the student drawings on page 121 of a loving relationship. Then, read the story of the friendship between David and Jonathan (I Samuel 20), and draw a picture from the story in figure box A. Draw your picture with a light colored pencil and then go over it with darker colors. You may want to do some research, finding pictures of buildings, scenery and clothing from ancient times to place in your picture.

"When you're alone, everything belongs to you." Leonardo da Vinci
....

John Ruskin (1819-1900)

John Ruskin was born in London, England in 1819 of Scottish heritage. Young John was homeschooled by his mother and several tutors. His early years were invested in learning many languages, along with the academics, music, drawing and an extensive understanding of the Bible. During this time, his parents realized he was of great genius and strived to shelter him from the world with a rather protective lifestyle. His father, James Ruskin, a successful wine merchant, relocated the family outside the city while John was still a boy. The Dulwich College Picture Gallery was located close to their new home and the paintings that hung in the gallery had a profound influence on him. This gallery, along with the drawing lessons he received and the encouragement from his parents, would have much bearing on the direction he would take when he was older.

"Moses" Christina Fries Age 11 Satellite Beach, Fl.

John Ruskin's later years of education were spent at Oxford, but his heart was not into serious academic study. At the age of 20, he won the Newdigate prize for poetry. With this and the help of his father, he was able to start an art collection of works by the great English artist, J.M. Turner.

In his early twenties he accompanied his parents to Italy. Given to a thorough study of the Italian masters, he was able to have a clearer understanding of what great art really was. While traveling home he visited Venice and Switzerland, and was inspired by what he saw both in museums and nature. It was during these travels that John Ruskin began to see the beautiful spectrum of nature, from a wide mountain range to a solitary flower. These new inspirations were noted with great skill in his early writings.

When Ruskin returned to England, he finished his formal education and graduated from Oxford in 1842. He immediately set upon the task of writing *Modern Painters,* which defended the works of Turner (whom many scoffed at, considering the artist's works too abstract). Ruskin would also write about other landscape painters, experiences in Italy and his deep feelings about nature. The book was published in 1843 and was a success. The young author was only 24.

Like Visari (the art historian of the Renaissance), John Ruskin desired to add to his first volume by completing a second volume of *Modern Painters,* published in 1846. Not long afterward he began to write about Gothic architecture. This style greatly moved him; thus, he would have much influence on England's return to this grandiose style, especially in its buildings. His book, *The Seven Lamps of Architecture,* was completed in 1849. This was another well-written book pertaining to art and art history. (Do you think that John Ruskin may have been influenced by the Bible in selecting that title for his book?)

During this time, several other things happened to John Ruskin. He married a young Scottish woman named Effie Gray. Her family was friends with the Ruskin family and the marriage was arranged in 1848. A new group of artists called the *Pre-Raphaelites* had formed, whom the young art historian and critic supported wholeheartedly. This handful of young English artists had banned together in defiance of the teachings of the Royal Academy's academic methods of teaching art. Among the Pre-Raphaelites that Ruskin supported, he especially befriended Dante Gabriel Rossetti, Edward Burne-Jones and John Everett Millais. Unfortunately, Millais fell in love with the young and beautiful wife of Ruskin. It wasn't long after this that Millais' success was established as a painter, at which time Effie left her husband and married the artist.

Ironically, the success of the Pre-Raphaelites was due in no small way to the loyal support of the renown Ruskin. Even after his wife's departure, John Ruskin still stood behind his support of Millais, continuing to promote his work along with the other Pre-Raphaelites. It is difficult to imagine the pain and rejection that Ruskin experienced during this time, but the godly integrity that had been instilled in him as a child allowed him to continue on as a professional, praising the artwork of Millais without allowing personal feelings to interfere.

"The Good Samaritan"
Erin Davis   Age 12
Antioch, California

Christine Baskin   Age 14
Niagara Falls, Ontario

Lesson #79: Examination #II

I. Matching: Match each definition with the correct term by printing the letter next to the number in the left column: 3 points each. (Answers on last page of *God & the History of Art I.*)

1. integrity
2. Martin Luther
3. Fra Angelico
4. illuminated manuscript
5. humanism
6. Nazarene
7. apprentice
8. Protestants
9. commission
10. Vasari
11. indulgences
12. Renaissance
13. the "Thunderbolt"
14. diptych
15. Josephus

a. Jewish historian
b. glorifying man
c. the father of art history
d. Tintoretto
e. having a strict adherence to a code of artistic values
f. the "angelic one"
g. "rebirth" in art (1400-1600)
h. money payment for penitence of sin
i. a student who studies under a master
j. colorful painted texts that were hand-lettered
k. artwork done for pay and for a patron
l. "the great reformer"
m. one who follows the teachings of Christ
n. a two paneled painting
o. "protesters" against the Catholic Church

II. Fill in the blanks. Write the correct word in the blanks to complete each statement: 2 points each.

1. A _____ artist is one who works with detailed, life-like realism.
2. The _____ was a period of time when the Christians of Northern Europe revolted against the authority of the Roman Catholic Church.
3. One of the great leaders of the Reformation was _____.
4. A triptych is _____ pictures that are placed side by side.
5. "The Gleaners" was painted by Jean Francois _____.

III. True or False. Place a "T" or "F" next to each statement if it is true or false: 3 points each.

1. _____ Talented boys studied under the great masters in workshops during the Renaissance.
2. _____ "Genre" paintings are pictures of people in common, everyday occurrences.
3. _____ Landscape paintings are paintings of oceans and seas.
4. _____ "Composition" is how you situate your subject matter in your picture.
5. _____ "Chiaroscuro" is the use of light areas against dark areas in paintings.
6. _____ "Foreshortening" means placing one color over another.
7. _____ A "palette" is a brush cleaner.
8. _____ The "focal point" is an "X" marked on the horizon line in perspective.
9. _____ Small studies for a final picture are called "thumbnail sketches."
10. _____ "Draftsmanship" is the ability to "draft" a piece of sculpture from a painting.
11. _____ "Fresco" paintings were wall paintings done on wet plaster.
12. _____ A "patron" is someone who pats clay and sculpts from it.
13. _____ "Tones" are colors that are opposite each other on the color wheel.
14. _____ Fra Angelico's nickname was "Thunderbolt."
15. _____ "Medium" means a method or material used by an artist.

Ancient Egypt

"Tower of Babel" Colleen O'Hara Age 11 Slidell, Louisiana

"Then the Egyptians shall know that I am the Lord, when I have gained honor for Myself over Pharaoh, his chariots, and his horsemen." Exodus 14:18

Ancient Egypt

Man has been on this earth for thousands of years, and ever since his beginning, he has been creating in one form or another. God created man in His own image and likeness, and part of this *image and likeness* is our ability to create. The student of the arts needs to think of God as a Creator who has given this gift of creativity to each and every one of us. We are the only living species with the ability to be creative. Granted, many living forms innately construct, like the spider weaving a web, a beaver making a dam, or a bird building a nest. However, the definition of *creativity* is the ability to create, an ability exclusive to man.

Do you know where Egypt is located on the map? At one time it was the most powerful country in the world. The Egyptians were one of the earliest societies to develop their creative skills. The Egyptians inhabited a long, thin country stretching along both sides of the river Nile. The land was kept fertile by the annual flooding of the river. The Nile was also a great means for communication and transportation throughout the country. The deserts that surrounded Egypt provided a natural barrier against invading armies. Thus, ancient Egypt was a protected and prosperous country. It was also a country that had much to do with Moses and the ancient Jews thousands of years ago.

"The Plague of the Flies"
Haley Harned Age 9
Lansing, Michigan

Throughout the ages there have been many reasons, or purposes, for art. Art was used by some cultures for beautiful decorations; by others to worship idols or gods, to tell a story, or to make a strong statement. The ancient Egyptians, Greeks and Romans created much of their art to worship their gods and goddesses. However, like the artists during the Middle Ages, the ancient Egyptians also created art to tell a story, many times showing the military exploits of their kings. Accordingly, art has been used during various periods of time to support a philosophy or belief.

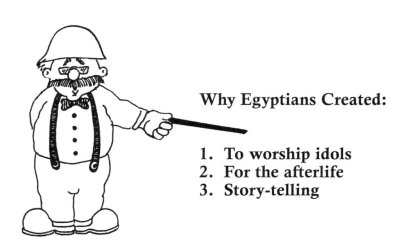

Why Egyptians Created:

1. To worship idols
2. For the afterlife
3. Story-telling

Lesson #80: *Geometric Shapes*

    Geometry in ancient times meant *measurements of the earth*. The Egyptian farmers had to know the shape and size of their land because markers would sometimes disappear when the Nile River overflowed. Thus, some of their land was square, rectangular, or triangular in shape.

    How many of the geometric shapes can you identify below? (Answers appear on the bottom of the page.) Connect the correct name with each shape by drawing a line from the term to the object, using a different colored pencil for each. Then, see if you can draw each of the shapes *freehand* on the bottom of the page and print the name of each underneath. Freehand means without the use of a ruler or other technical devices.

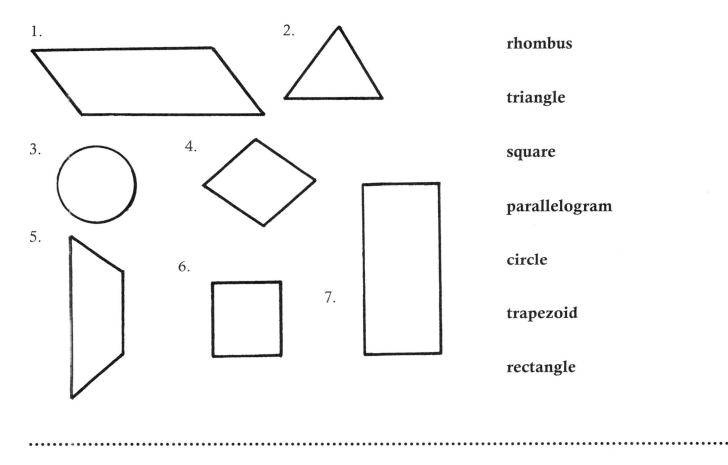

1.   2.

         rhombus

         triangle

3.   4.

         square

         parallelogram

5.   6.

         circle

      7.

         trapezoid

         rectangle

1. parallelogram 2. triangle 3. circle 4. rhombus 5. trapezoid 6. square 7. rectangle

"They lavish gold out of the bag, and weigh silver on the scales; they hire a goldsmith, and he makes it a god; they prostrate themselves, yes, they worship. They bear it on the shoulder, they carry it and set it in its place, and it stands; though one cries out to it, yet it cannot answer nor save him out of his trouble." Isaiah 46:6,7

....

As mentioned, the Egyptians had many gods and goddesses to dedicate their artwork to. They had a supreme god named Amen-Ra. He was usually shown with the horns of a ram. His wife's name was Mut (meaning mother). Then there was the god of the underworld, Osiris, his wife, Isis, and their son named Horus. But the Egyptians didn't stop there. The sun and the Nile were also worshiped as gods. The ancient Egyptians imagined that supernatural beetles, or scarabs, pushed the sun across the sky. The king of Egypt was called *Pharaoh,* and was treated as a semi-god and intermediary between man and the various gods. When he died, his body and spirit were supplied with all necessities to enter paradise. The walls of the great pharaohs' tombs were covered with paintings of them and their queens, along with strange, part-animal gods whose supernatural powers the kings claimed to share. It seemed as if they had a god or goddess for every thing and occasion under the sun. How wonderful that we, as Christians, worship and honor only one God: *the One and only true God.*

The ancient Egyptians were very skilled artists, but their purpose for art was different than how we perceive it today. Many of us expect art to be beautiful, realistic, or filled with details. The ancient Egyptians created artwork to be both simple and practical. Art was used for decorative designs around the tombs of the pharaohs and other great structures, or it was used to tell stories. They believed the more simple the pictures, the easier the story was to tell.

Egyptian artists had a different way of representing real life. They were not concerned with beauty, but committed to preserving the style of earlier artists as clearly as possible. Neither did they try to do their artwork realistically. Instead, they drew from memory, according to strict rules that were set down by the artists before them.

The ancient Egyptians did an extensive amount of wall paintings. They were not interested in showing *perspective*, or depth, in these pictures, and we find everything that was illustrated to be flat. The scenes of animal and human figures did not show movement, but were one dimensional and motionless. They did not use *overlapping* (the placing of one object slightly in front of another), so man, animal and object were seen above, below, or next to each other in the wall paintings.

"Moses in the Bulrushes"
Angela Gross Age 11
Cape Coral, Fla.

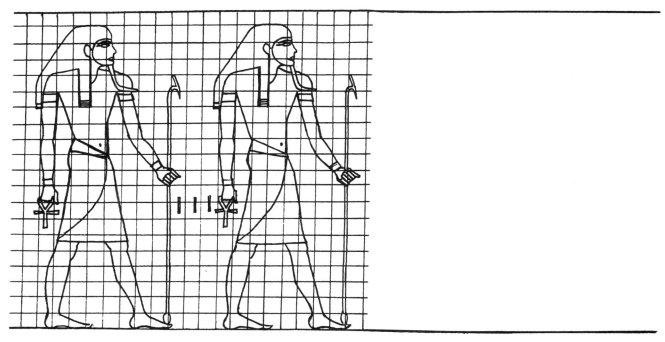

The ancient Egyptians drew and painted all their figures in *profile,* meaning the side-view. The head and feet were seen from this vantage point, but the shoulders were shown from a front-view position. It is as if the person were walking in one direction, but the shoulders and upper body were twisted and facing another direction. Another peculiar thing about figures in Egyptian art was that they were always illustrated with two left or right feet, with both feet being drawn identically.

These ancient Egyptian artists tried to make their figures look like people at their best, leaving out any imperfections. Maybe the Egyptians were vain or detested the thought of growing old, because they never made a statue or created a painting of an old person. Neither did they illustrate an overweight person. Thus, wrinkles and obesity were omitted. They also painted the skin lighter for women and much darker for men. Finally, the people of nobility were illustrated larger than the servants or workmen that surrounded them. This was to show their importance.

"Moses in the Bulrushes"
Sarah Newstead Age 14
Vancouver, Washington

Lesson #81: *Drawing an Egyptian*

Study the drawings on the top of pages 127 and 129. Notice that while the head and feet of the figures are seen in profile, the shoulders are in the front-view position, as if the bodies were twisted towards the viewer. Have you noticed that the figures have the big toes on the same side of the feet?

The artwork done by the ancient Egyptians was very methodical and technical, done precisely to rules and regulations that were handed down from generation to generation. One way was by using *grids*. A grid is a series of lines going both horizontally and vertically to create small squares of equal proportions. A picture would then be copied onto the grid by carefully copying each little square, or part of the picture, as exactly as possible. This enabled the artisans to make their picture just like the picture they were copying. They also used grids in making proper *proportions*. Proportion means placing everything in its correct size. Incomplete artwork has been found in some of the pharaohs' tombs showing this concept, with the grid lines still evident on the unfinished pictures.

For this assignment, take a ruler and pencil and continue drawing the grid on the top of page 127. Then, lightly draw one of the two Egyptian figures as exact as you can by copying it, square by square, onto your grid. You may want to lightly number the squares so it will be easier for you to copy each square precisely. Start your drawing with a very light pencil. Then, when you have copied it exactly, go over it with your black pen.

"Walk Like an Egyptian" Sylvia Beard (Homeschool Mom) Coldwater, Ontario

A.

Notice the picture of the Egyptian man fishing (A). He is seen in profile with two right feet and the side-view of his head. However, his shoulders are seen in the front-view (wide across). Also, notice how large he is in comparison to the other Egyptians in the picture. Making him larger symbolized his importance in society. Finally, look how dark the artist made the flesh of the figures. This symbolized that they were men. Maybe this was done because they spent a great deal of time in the sun fishing and hunting in the sun.

Next, look at the design quality of the picture, especially the row of fish merrily swimming beneath the boat. Notice the delightful array of birds in the upper left corner. Observe how the artist composed the picture by placing the man of importance a little *off-center* to the right, and balanced the scene with birds, an intricate building design and perches to the left. The stylized hieroglyphics to the top of the picture seems to balance out the frolicking fish on the bottom. (Did you notice the cat in the far left corner keeping an alert eye on the fish?)

B.

Lesson #82: *Copying a Picture*

For this assignment, copy the picture above (A) in the figure box (B). Start your drawing with a light colored pencil. Then, color your picture with bright and vivid colors. You may want to review the exercises on colored pencils and use some of those methods. Finally, see if you can make a dark color for the skin by mixing colors together without using black. You may want to try blue, red and brown, or yellow, red and blue, or any other combination of colors to make a dark color. Practice blending your colors before using them in the picture.

Lesson #83: *Drawing the Eye*

The eye has also gone through many changes throughout the centuries. In illustrations done by the Egyptians, it was shown very much like the figure by drawing the front view of the eye even though the head was seen in profile.

In the beginning, the eye was drawn in a circular manner with the pupil as a smaller circle within (A). The outline of the eye then became more like an *ellipse*, with the shape becoming much thinner at each side, and the top part being identical to the bottom (B). The eyelids eventually began to separate and the pupil was placed more within the lids. As the lids began to open, the inner circle (the pupil and iris) became larger (C).

A.   B.   C.

Let's draw an eye. A simple way to do this is to first draw the lids. The top lid is darker and has an arch that is highest near the side of the nose. The bottom lid is much lighter and has its lowest point away from the nose (D). The iris is a large circle that sits on the bottom lid, and the pupil is a smaller circle in the center of the larger circle. Leave a little pie shape in the pupil for a highlight, and then darken the pupil with your black pencil. The pupil is always the darkest part of the eye (E). With your brown pencil, draw *wagon wheel spokes* close together around the pupil. However, leave a pie shape opening in the same place as the highlight in the pupil (F). Copy the eye (F) in the figure box below (G). Next, look in the mirror and draw your eye close up in figure box H. Then, find a photo of a face in *profile*, cut out the eye, and glue it in the figure box (I). Finally, draw the eye from that position by copying the eye you just placed in figure box I.

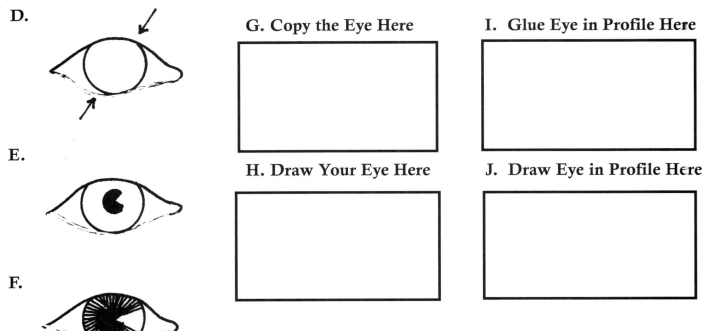

D.

E.

F.

G. Copy the Eye Here

H. Draw Your Eye Here

I. Glue Eye in Profile Here

J. Draw Eye in Profile Here

130

The history of Egyptian civilization began approximately five thousand years ago. King Menes united the many small kingdoms that lived along the Nile valley and became the first of a long line of rulers known as the *first dynasty*. There were 31 such *dynasties* which ruled Egypt in ancient times. The kings of Egypt were called *pharaohs* and were treated as semi-gods throughout their lives. After their deaths, they were buried with magnificent rituals in large tombs.

The first known artwork that came out of Egypt was from *The Old Kingdom* (4500 BC until 2475 BC). It was rather peculiar that the Egyptians believed a man's soul would continue to live after his death, but only if the body was preserved with statues of his likeness to accompany him into the hereafter. This was the main purpose of the *pyramid* - to entomb, protect and prepare the pharaoh for the next world. These pyramids also stored, protected and preserved many artifacts from this time. Today there is so much ancient Egyptian artwork to look at because the Egyptians were masters at creating massive protective tombs for their deceased kings. These enormous stone structures took many years to build and the labor of thousands of slaves. So fervent was the belief that the deceased pharaoh needed protection for his future life, that much of the great wealth of Egypt was given to build these monuments. Wealthy people also had pyramids built to protect them, but not nearly to the size or proportion of the great pharaohs. Pyramids are still the largest stone buildings ever made by man.

"Egyptian Taskmaster" Kelsey Klopfenstein Age 9 Peopria, Illinois

"Those who make a graven image, all of them are useless, and their precious things shall not profit."

Isaiah 44:9

....

Lesson #84: *Finding King Tut*

Almost 80 pyramids still survive to this day. Sadly, throughout the ages robbers have managed to enter and rob nearly all the great tombs, taking the wealth of artwork and belongings that were meant to escort the kings into the next world. However, in 1922 a young king's tomb was excavated and found to still be completely in tact after nearly 3,000 years! This was the tomb of King Tutankhamen, better known as King Tut. King Tut was a minor pharaoh who died at the age of 19. When the contents of the young pharaoh's tomb finally went on display, it attracted more attention than any other art exhibit in the history of mankind.

A.

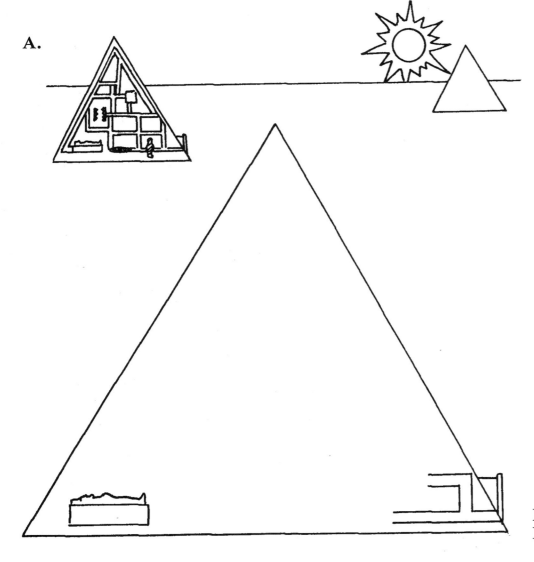

In the pyramid to the left, let's create a difficult maze leading to King Tut's burial place and the inner room of treasures. Use a ruler to create your maze and draw it with one of your light colored pencils. Have some of your passages blocked by walls, fake mummies, traps and ditches (A). When you are finished, go over the entire drawing with your black colored pencil. You may want to make some copies of your maze and challenge your friends. Time them to see if they can find King Tut's grave in 20 seconds or less.

Enter
Here

Obstacles: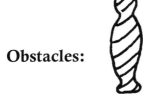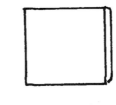

132

"I am the Lord, that is My name; and My glory I will not give to another, nor My praise to graven images."

Isaiah 42:8

Inside the great tombs, wall paintings and hieroglyphics told the story of the deceased person's life in great detail. The pictures reveal servants doing the labors they did thousands of years ago, harvesting crops, fishing and hunting. There are illustrations of bakers kneading bread and weavers working at the loom. We also see them at their leisure - dancing and playing sports. Some of the wall paintings show miniature seamen waiting by their boat to take the pharaoh on his journey to the next land, while others do chores which they will continue to do for the king after his death.

Amanda Flynn Age 9
Plainville, Mass

Jeanna Quant
Shoreview, Minnesota

Lesson #85: *Creating Hieroglyphics*

Hieroglyphics was a style of writing used by the ancient Egyptians. This type of writing was prominent from about 2800 B.C. to 300 A.D., and was for inscribing decorative writing onto stone monuments and wall paintings (notice the hieroglyphics in the picture of the fisherman on page 129). The same artist who did the artwork also did the lettering, or hieroglyphics. It was beautifully written on the walls of the tombs of the nobility, giving a detailed description of their lives. Hieroglyphics has been a great asset in learning how the Egyptians lived many thousands of years ago.

Hieroglyphics was used only as decorative writing, and was unsuitable for everyday purposes. For popular use, hieroglyphics was done in a simple and abbreviated form of picture symbols, and was written with a pen on a smooth paper called *papyrus*.

For this assignment, create your own hieroglyphics by drawing symbols to represent words like the examples below. When you are finished, write a story on the wall below using your hieroglyphics and see if one of your friends can decode the message. Take your time. Make each letter, or symbol, as decorative and colorful as you can.

CAN

I

SAW

BEE

GLAD

WARM

133

"To whom then will you liken God? Or what likeness will you compare to Him? The workman molds a graven image, the goldsmith overspreads it with gold, and the silversmith casts silver chains. Whoever is too impoverished for such a contribution chooses a tree that will not rot; he seeks for himself a skillful workman to prepare a carved image that will not totter." Isaiah 40:18-20

The Egyptians were also sculptors, with much of their work being carved out of stone in *relief*. Relief is simply having a raised surface. It is done by carving out areas around an object so it becomes raised above the surface, giving it a three-dimensional appearance. A good example of relief is a coin. Close your eyes and feel the figure carved on a coin.

Most of the relief art during the times of ancient Egypt was barely carved out and could almost be considered painting instead of sculpture. This is called low-relief. After carving out a picture, the artists would paint in the various areas. Many of the rooms within the great tombs of the pharaohs were adorned with relief artwork showing everyday life and telling stories.

"Egyptian Grape Pickers" Levi Unruh Age 9 Greensburg, Ks.

In many ways, the artwork of ancient Egypt seems childlike. However, these artists were very skilled in what they did, learning how to do their art from generations of artisans before them. There were strict rules set down for the artists which spanned hundreds and even thousands of years. These techniques showed the artist everything from how to draw the figure to how to paint the skin. Remember, during this time an artist's skills were not measured by how creative he was, but rather by how perfectly he could copy the art from previous generations. There was no purpose for self-expression. So, in the course of nearly 3,000 years, the art of ancient Egypt changed very little.

Nyssa Dhillon Age 11 Oxbridge, Ontario

Lesson #86: *Mural of My Life*

A *mural* is a wall painting. For this assignment, do a mural of your life below. Draw yourself the way the Egyptians did, in profile and with full shoulders. Then, illustrate all the things you like to do. Have a nice design for your picture. (Look at the Egyptian fishing in the picture with the birds and fish on page 129.) Start your drawing with a light colored pencil, and then darken with other colors.

A.

B.

Lesson #87: *Designing an Obelisk*

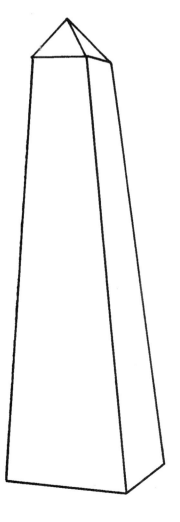

An *obelisk* is a large, tapered stone pillar. It is designed to have either a square or rectangular base, becoming thinner, or tapered, as it rises upward. These Egyptian monuments were made out of one solid piece of red granite and weighed hundreds of tons. Hieroglyphics were inscribed on all four sides, usually in honor of some pharaoh or one of their gods. In a way, they look like a giant needle. One was actually named *Cleopatra's Needle*. Obelisks are known to have existed as early as 2500 years before Christ, and it is still difficult for modern technology to figure out how they were cut, transported and lifted up to stand perfectly erect. The Washington Monument (in Washington, D.C.) is a contemporary example of an obelisk. For this assignment, draw the obelisk (A) in the space to the right (B). You may use a ruler for this exercise. Make sure to start your drawing lightly. Shade the shaded side of your obelisk with diagonal lines when finished.

"...and I will give him a white stone, and on the stone a new name written which no one knows except him who receives it."
Revelation 2:17

The Old Kingdom was followed by another period called, *The Middle Kingdom* (2160 B.C. to 1090 B.C.). During this time, the pharaohs no longer built huge pyramids to house their bodies after death. Instead, they began creating lavishly decorated tombs and palaces for their ceremonious departure from this world. The tombs were being built on the sides of cliffs in the south of Thebes known as *The Valley of the Tombs.*

During the Middle Kingdom, the Egyptians strived even harder to protect their kings in the tombs. They began creating massive pieces of sculpture of their gods and goddesses *in the round*, placing them in front of the tombs for protection. In the round means that the entire figure was carved out, and could be seen from all sides.

Painting also changed. Instead of carving out low relief on the walls and painting on it, they began painting directly on the walls. This new style had to be done because the tombs were on the sides of cliffs, and the walls were too rough for carving.

Egypt was a country built and established on tradition. Art continued to be steeped in tradition as the artist continued to copy the style handed down to him for thousands of years. However, there was one king, or pharaoh, who wanted to change this. This was a young pharaoh named Akhenaten who ruled during the 18th Dynasty. He was the son of the great warrior Amenhotep III. One of the young ruler's main desires was to have art that was more true to life, or realistic, than the traditional style of art that had been handed down for so many years. After his death, the Egyptians once again returned to their traditional style of artwork.

Lesson #88: *Painting a Stone*

For this assignment, let's paint a stone using acrylic paint. Try to use pure pigment acrylic paints which have several wonderful qualities. First, the *pigments*, or colors, are pure, making it easy to mix other colors with just the primary colors and white. Secondly, they are a *water base* paint, meaning you can clean them with water (before they dry), and you can use water to mix your colors. Finally, you can paint on many different surfaces: canvas, poster board, metal, wood, or even stones!

Go outside and find a smooth stone with a nice shape. We are going to paint the rabbit to the left, so find a stone that you believe would be good for this subject. It may take a little while to find just the right one. Draw the rabbit on the stone with a black pencil. Practice drawing your rabbit on a piece of paper first to make sure you can draw it correctly. If you like, you can draw another simple animal figure like the ones on *Paint Card #XVIII.*

Paint the rabbit brown by mixing yellow with red to make orange, and then adding a speck of blue (adding too much blue will make a slimy green). If this happens, add a little more red to your color. Use your color chart to select other nice colors. For example, make a light pink for the rabbit's nose and inside the ears. The pupil of his eye is black and the iris of the eye is a light brown. Add a little white highlight to each eye and to the tail. Finally, take a small, thin brush and add whiskers to each side of the nose with white paint. You may want to practice painting your rabbit on another sheet of paper before painting your stone.

"...that they may add sin to sin; who walk to go down to Egypt, and have not asked My advice, to strengthen themselves in the strength of Pharaoh..." Isaiah 30:1,2

"The Columns in the Court of the Temple in Luxor, South of Thebes"
Levi Unruh Age 9 Greensburg, Kansas

The culture of Egypt was based on immortality. Much of the artwork and architecture was especially created to accompany the pharaoh's spirit as he entered eternity. The Egyptians gave a great deal of attention to the idea of death, and well stocked the graves (pyramids) with treasures for him to take into the next world.

The Book of the Dead contained a collection of magical spells intended to guide the soul of the deceased safely through the realm of the gods. This book was written by the ancient Egyptians on *papyrus* scrolls, a type of paper used for writing made from the papyrus plant. The Book of the Dead included pictures of their gods. Some had heads of animals who held scales in which to balance the heart of the deceased with a feather, which was the symbol of truth. If the scales balanced, the spirit could enter the next world in peace.

The ancient Egyptians also mastered the science of *embalming* by preserving the body against decay. In the 19th century one such *mummy* was excavated. It was Ramses II, supposedly a pharaoh who lived during the time of Moses. Throughout his lifetime, Ramses was a very powerful king who ruled over a mighty nation. However, when someone recently viewed his embalmed body, the person commented that the king looked like a *dry fish*.

Sharon Age 14 Fowlerville, Michigan

Jeanne Sasser Age 11 Ft Wayne, In.

"Do not lay up for yourselves treasures on earth, where moth and rust destroy and where thieves break in and steal; but lay up for yourselves treasures in heaven..."

Matthew 6:19-20

Sad, isn't it? Man strives for such greatness, and through all the worldly treasures and power still becomes no more than mere bones. But our hope, as Christians, is in the resurrected Christ and not in earthly treasures. Paul states in I Corinthians 15:17,20, *"And if Christ is not risen, your faith is futile...but now Christ is risen from the dead, and has become the firstfruits of those who have fallen asleep."*

So we see that the great pharaohs, with all their power, wealth, gods, goddesses, embalming and the Book of the Dead, still wind up as *dead fish.*

Unlike the Egyptians, Christians have a more pure and simple entrance into *the next life.* I Corinthians 15:42-44 goes on to state, *"So also is the resurrection of the dead. The body is sown in corruption, it is raised in incorruption. It is sown in dishonor, it is raised in glory. It is sown in weakness, it is raised in power. It is sown a natural body, it is raised a spiritual body. There is a natural body, and there is a spiritual body."* The Christian does not need to be embalmed, nor does he need to store up his treasures on earth to escort him into the next world. I Corinthians 15:54 goes on to state, *"So when this corruptible has put on incorruption, and this mortal has put on immortality, then shall be brought to pass the saying that is written: Death, where is your sting? O Hades, where is your victory?"*

"The Empty Tomb" Jessica Dopler Age 14 Davenport, Iowa

Ancient Greece

"The Warrior's Leavetaking" Greek Pottery (510-500 B.C.)
Benjamin Iocco Age 12 Freeport, Michigan

Ancient Greece

One ingredient that makes for a great civilization is its art. Art is much more than paintings that hang on walls, the architecture of buildings, or the sculpture which surrounds such structures. It is a physical, creative product which reveals the way each civilization lives and breathes. Art takes on the personality of its people and becomes their philosophy about life, their purpose and their religious beliefs. Throughout the ages, many great civilizations have stepped forward and greatly influenced the rest of the world's appreciation of art. For example, thousands of years later we are still greatly influenced by the artwork done by the ancient Greek civilization.

Just like a wave that crashes to shore and then ebbs, so too have the great civilizations followed each other. As the great Egyptian empire began to ebb, another began to flow - that of the ancient Greeks. While the power and splendor of one great civilization was fading, the beauty and strength of another was blossoming.

Greece is a beautiful land surrounded by sparkling blue water and dappled by many islands. The country is filled with grand valleys, mountain peaks, and many marble quarries (marble being a wonderful stone for sculpting). It was the perfect place for a new beginning in art.

The Greek culture actually evolved from an earlier *Mycenaean* civilization. Mycenae was located in the southern part of the country. The Mycenaeans were a very artistic and creative people who lived around 1,000 B.C. As the Mycenaeans faded from existence, a period of several hundred years followed which historians know little about (800 B.C. to 600 B.C.). These 200 years were considered a cultural transition period and has come to be known as the *Dark Ages* of ancient Greek history. It is believed that, after this, Greece was invaded by a tribe of people from the north known as the Dorians. The Dorians brought with them a simple artistic style that included wall paintings and relief sculpture done with clay, stone and an assortment of metals.

"Zacchaeus"
Matthew Polley Age 12
Albion, Indiana

Sculpture

Greece was very different from the civilizations that preceded it. There was no ruling central government, king or pharaoh. Instead, Greece was made up of many *city-states* which were independent of each other and self-governing, much like the states in America.

In the beginning, Greek artists copied the very flat and simple style of Egyptian art in their paintings and sculptures of human figures. This was approximately 2500 years ago. However, because paintings deteriorate as they age, very few examples still exist for us to study. Names of only two of the most famous Greek painters have survived over the years - Plygnotus and Apelles. Yet, even these artists may be legend since none of their original artwork is known to be in existence.

"The Discus Thrower" Ancient Greece (Myron 400 B.C.)

Even though there is little to study in the way of ancient Greek painting, the works of quite a few sculptors, such as Praxiteles and Phidias, have endured throughout the ages. It may be that sculpture was more popular than painting or that it was more durable, able to withstand the wear and tear of many centuries. In any case, much more sculpture has withstood time than paintings.

In the earliest Greek sculptures carved out of stone, the human figures were stiffly posed with arms positioned straight down at the sides. The hair looked very artificial, more like a wig than hair. As the years passed, the Greeks began to improvise, becoming more creative. The artisans simply were not satisfied with copying the old, tested ways. They wanted to explore, recreate and add to these old styles. Thus, the Greeks became more interested in portraying things the way they really were instead of the simple style of the ancient Egyptians. Improvisation and creativity were a new approach to art, very different from the traditional techniques handed down from one generation to another.

For example, the Greeks strived to show the bones and muscles of the human figures beneath the clothing in a more realistic manner. They even went a step further and began to *glorify* man, sculpting and painting the human figure in a perfect manner and, like the Egyptians, all the wrinkles and imperfections were taken out. Rather than creating an ordinary man, the human figure was given a divine form. These artisans did not have a person to model, or pose for them. They drew from their imagination, striving to make their human figures as ideal and perfect as possible. The term *classic profile* comes from the ancient Greeks because of the perfect, classic expression of modeling the head. This type of art has come to be known as *idealization,* and the ancient Greeks were masters in this field.

Lesson #89: *Studies from Sculpture*

Thumb through your *picture postcard gallery* and place the picture of the head and bust of *Caligula* in front of you. Notice the perfection of the head. The artist was careful to omit any blemishes in the figure, leaving it in a perfect and *sublime* state. It is difficult to imagine that this was carved out of stone with a hammer and chisel. Though this is a piece of Roman sculpture, the style was influenced by the Greeks. Many believe that the sculpture created in ancient Greece has never been surpassed in the history of mankind.

A.

Value Study

Most of the great traditional art schools have their students draw from *cast model*s, or pieces of sculpture, like that which is shown in this picture. Drawing and studying in such a way is considered to be a great discipline as students learn to see values from light to dark. For this assignment, copy the picture of the bust of *Caligula* in figure box (A). Use only a pencil for this, and see if you can place four or more values in your drawing. You may want to do a value study in the circles above before beginning, starting with your lightest value (which would be the white of the paper), and gradually becoming darker and darker. Lay in each with lines. The closer you place the lines, the darker the value will be.

Lesson #90: *Drawing Objects Around the House*

C. Looking Up

D. Eye Level

Drawing from *life*, or objects that are okay in front of you, is a wonderful teaching tool; learning to see correctly. For this assignment, find a toy and place it in front of you. Then, draw it from three different vantage points, or angles. Draw your subject in the small figure boxes below: looking up at it (C), having it at eye level (D) and looking down at it (E).

E. Looking Down

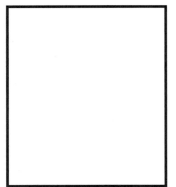

The ancient Greeks were the first civilization to express nudity in art. As mentioned, they placed man upon a pedestal and showed him in all his splendor and perfection. The ancient Greeks seemed to have had a sense of self-admiration, or vanity as they created man in the light of strength, beauty and perfection.

The term *narcissism* comes from ancient Greek mythology. It derives from the story of a young man named *Narcissus*. Narcissus was a handsome youth who refused to love a nymph named Echo. As punishment, the goddess Aphrodite condemned him to fall in love with his own image. Forced to gaze constantly at his own reflection in a clear pool, Narcissus pined away and died. In pity, the gods turned him into a beautiful flower, bending his head over the water. Today narcissism means to be in love with oneself. Do you think that vanity is the same today as it was with the ancient Greeks?

Since the ancient Greeks have been a model of perfection in the arts, many societies and artists have strived to *emulate,* or copy them. Not only were later periods of art influenced by *humanism*, but the naked form also became praised. The ancient Romans were the first to be inspired by the Greek's approach to art. After Rome had become an empire and had conquered much of the civilized world including Palestine, they brought with them the great influences from the Greek culture. Most of the mixed peoples of the Holy Land loved to watch the thrilling and dangerous chariot races, which were sometimes bloody and cruel. However, such events were offensive to the religious Jewish groups who refrained from such entertainment. But, most offensive to the Jewish population were activities which took place in the large amphitheaters. Here athletes took part in foot races, wrestling matches and other events in the Greek manner - in the nude. Even though the Romans were world conquerors and the Greeks had become the artistic inspiration for the civilized world, the Jewish people had the spirit of God to lead them in discerning what was right and wrong. God states through Isaiah 47:3 that *your nakedness is your shame,* and Psalm 101:3 proclaims, *"I will set nothing wicked before my eyes."* Thus, the righteous Jews in Israel took no part in attending the Roman games in the amphitheaters.

Still, the Romans would not be the only civilization influenced by this Greek philosophy of humanism. The Renaissance (rebirth) in Italy was also inspired by the ancient Greek arts and their Age of Enlightenment, or humanism. So were the Romantic and Neo-Classical artists that came out of France during the Age of Reason in the 18th century. So too, the 20th century has hoisted its flag of humanism, once again glorifying man, his body, and his accomplishments.

"Building the Temple"
Sean White Age 13
Maple Grove, Mn.

"Pass by in naked shame, you inhabitant of Shaphir." Micah 1:11

Nudity

Well, um, let's see...how do we discuss, hm-m-m nudity in art? This is a most sensitive area for Christians, and we have many different feelings concerning nudity. Some Christians accept the nudes of Michelangelo that adorn the ceiling of the Sistine Chapel. Others accept paintings of nude baby cherubs, or the infant Jesus by Raphael. Then there are the works of Renoir, the great French Impressionist who painted many nude figures on his canvases. And so on, and so on....

As Christians first, and then as students of the arts, it seems the best approach to this sensitive concern might be in understanding how God feels about it. There are many verses throughout the Bible that indicate a man's nakedness is his *shame*. Nudity is a complex and delicate subject for many Christians, and the body of Christ has diverse opinions about whether or not one should look at nudes in art. Yet, it seems as if nudity goes hand-in-hand with *humanism*, as artists have strived to show the beauty of the human form ever since the times of ancient Greece.

However, I would urge you not to throw the baby out with the bath water. Although an artist has painted nudes in some of his artwork, you can still appreciate other great works by the master and forego the ones which are offensive.

"Then the eyes of both of them were opened, and they knew that they were naked; and they sewed fig leaves together and made themselves coverings." Genesis 3:7

As we grow in the things of God, He will reveal to us the truths regarding nudity. When we begin to realize that nakedness does grieve God, we will refrain from compromising by viewing nudity.

Amanda Blume
Age 15
Ft. Wayne, Indiana

Lesson #91: *How Much to Reveal*

How much can and should an artist reveal of the human figure in his artwork? As you study art, you cannot help but notice that many artists have painted, sculpted, or drawn the nude figure. But this is not what God wants His people to partake in. The question is, what is considered nudity and where do we draw the line? For this assignment, take from your *picture postcard gallery*: William Bouguereau's, *Le premier baiser;* Raphael's, *Sistine Madonna* (detail); and *Madonna and Child with Book;* and Giovanni Battista Gaulli's, *Saint Joseph and the Infant Christ.*

These are all pictures that deal with a suggestion of nudity, but each artist strived to deal with it in an artistic manner that would not be offensive. This is called *artistic discretion,* meaning that an artist has the liberty to change things to make a more pleasing composition. Artists may situate the body or clothing in such a way that the naked figure is not revealed. After looking at the artwork, write your feelings about each on the lines below. Is each picture an honorable and godly representation of art? Do you like the pictures? Why? Are any offensive to you? Remember, you and your faith in Christ should set the guidelines for what to appreciate in art.

_____

_____

_____

_____

_____

_____

"Jesus on the Cross"
John Stahel Age 11 Plymouth, Mn.

The ancient Greeks excelled in their artwork, and historians have noted it to be some of the greatest ever created by man. Unfortunately, most of their paintings, sculpture and buildings have perished. They were either destroyed during times of war or, in many instances, demolished by the Christian church because such art was looked upon as idol worshipping or offensive. These gifted artists spent most of their creative energies exalting man or edifying their many gods and goddesses. The Lord says, *"You shall not make for yourself a carved image, or any likeness of any thing that is in heaven above, or that is in the earth beneath, or that is in the water under the earth; you shall not bow down to them nor serve them."* (Exodus 20:4-5). Many of the famous statues of ancient Greece perished because, after the rise of Christianity, it was considered a pious duty to smash artwork that was dedicated to heathen gods or exalted man.

Lesson #92: *Clothing a Baby*

For this lesson, let's put clothing on a baby. First, using your yellow pencil, lightly draw an infant's body by making a large oval (A). An oval is egg-shaped and not as round as a circle. Then, draw a circle for the head (B). Keep in mind that infant's heads are larger in proportion to the rest of their body unlike older children and adults. For the arms and legs, use two plump hot dog shapes for each (C). Draw a fat hot dog shape for each foot and a circle for the hands (D). Add small circles for the toes and longer and thinner hot dog shapes for the fingers and thumbs (E). For the eyes, you can either make them round and large, or draw a short, curved line to show they are closed (F). When finished, use darker colors and wrap the baby in a swath of clothing (G). Draw a baby in the figure box (H).

A. B. C. D.

E.

F.

G.

H.

"Jesus and the Children"
Estie Brodwater Age 10
Jane Lew, West Virginia

146

"Men of Athens, I perceive that in all things you are very religious; for as I was passing through and considering the objects of your worship, I even found an altar with this inscription: To The Unknown God. Therefore, the One whom you worship without knowing, Him I proclaim to you."

Acts 17:22-23

....

The Greeks, like the Egyptians, had a whole family of gods and goddesses. Their gods lived in Mount Olympus, eating godly food called *ambrosia* and drinking nectar. Zeus was their paramount god. His wife's name was Hera. And, like the Egyptians, the Greeks seemed to have a god or goddess for every occasion. However, where many of the Egyptian gods were represented by animals, the Greek gods took on human-like form. They were characterized with supernatural qualities, such as being able to move with great speed or to see great distances.

Greek gods & goddesses

Zeus	the hurler of thunderbolts
Hera	wife of Zeus
Appolo	god of divine distance
Artemis (Diana)	goddess of marriage
Athena	wisdom, war & peace
Demeter & Persephone	goddesses of the harvest
Dionysus (Bacchus)	god of wine and drama
Poseidon	god of the sea and rivers
Hermes	the messenger god
Pan	lord of the woodlands
Pluto	god of the underworld

"Athena" (4th century B.C.)
Greek goddess of wisdom, war, and peace
drawing by Gregory Iocco Age 14 Freeport, Mi.

"Then certain Epicurean and Stoic philosophers encountered him. And some said, 'What does this babbler want to say?' Others said, 'He seems to be a proclaimer of foreign gods, because he preached to them Jesus and the resurrection.'" Acts 17:18

···

Epicureanism

To better understand a people, it is good to understand their *philosophy*, or what they believe life is all about. Ancient Greece had many philosophers and thinkers, such as Aristotle, Plato and Socrates. Each professed that he knew the true meaning of life. However, there was another philosopher named Epicurus whose beliefs probably best summed up the philosophy of his time, giving us a better idea of how the ancient Greek's (over 2,000 years ago) truly lived.

Epicurus (341-270 B.C.) believed that freedom from pain in the body and a trouble free mind were the keys to a happy life. *Epicureanism* was a devotion to pleasure, comfort and a high style of living. Their desire was to eat, drink and treat their flesh to all the comforts life had to afford. That is why today we call people who like fine dining, *epicureans.* Like the *narcissist* (lover of self), it seems as if modern man has also embraced the philosophy, *eat, drink and be merry.*

However, the beliefs of the epicureans were far more reaching than fine dining, comfort and pleasures of the flesh. Their concepts were based on man's ability to understand the natural world around him in addition to the relationship between body and soul. Epicurus felt that as long as the human soul existed within the body, it was capable of reporting everything through the senses. If one kept the senses comfortable with good things, life would be good! Once the body stopped receiving stimulation through the senses, it dulled and ultimately broke down into nothingness, ending life totally. Thus, epicureanism was the beginning of *atheism*, a total disbelief in any supreme being and the hopelessness of death.

Isn't it peculiar how a society's beliefs filter through its artwork? Like the lifestyle which Epicurus professed, the art of the ancient Greeks had to be pure, perfect and pleasing to the senses. There were no wrinkles or aged people, only perfection. One wonders how the ancient Greeks treated their elderly when they became incapable of enjoying the pleasures of life.

"Noah's Ark" Stephen Krason Age 10 Steubenville, Ohio

148

"No great thing is created suddenly, anymore than a bunch of grapes or a fig. If you tell me that you desire a fig, I answer you that there must be time. Let it first blossom, then bear fruit, then ripen."
Epictetus

Throughout history, being an artist has not been considered a profession worthy of respect by society. Even in ancient Greece, the wealthy and powerful who managed the affairs of the city-states looked down on artists. Although the art that came forth during this time reached new heights of perfection and beauty, it was still a difficult time for artists. For one thing, art was not purchased for the home, but was created solely to immortalize the gods and goddesses and to glorify or exalt man. Although creativity was being encouraged as it had never been before, an artist would still be severely condemned by the state if he did not stay in certain guidelines. For example, if an artist was guilty of introducing politics, propaganda, or too much personal sentiment into his artwork, he would often be given hemlock (a poison) and erased from society. It is quite a paradox that this ancient society which was steeped in the arts and so advanced, could also be so cruel in other ways. Thus, as enriched as the Greeks were in the arts and as sophisticated as their civilization had become, they were still barbaric in many ways.

Family life, as we know it today, was non-existent. The Greek family sent their children away to public nurseries to be educated by the state. They had a low opinion of women, whose main duties were in the kitchen. Most of them dressed alike in pleated robes.

Through it all, Greece was still a very cultured society that cherished the arts. A truly great awakening occurred between the years 520 B.C. and 420 B.C. which has come to be known as *The Golden Age*. The period was also known as *The Age of Pericles*. It was named after the great leader from Athens who inspired free thinking and a democratic government. The Greeks loved beauty and desired to surround themselves with it. Besides sculptures of the gods, monuments were erected for the athletes who honored their cities by winning games played during the famous Olympics, which were started 776 B.C. and held every four years.

During this period, artists strived to show the true form of man and nature by realistically interpreting them. This was also a time when the Greek people began to question the old traditions and legends about the gods and goddesses, seeking to learn the true nature of things. It was a time when science, philosophy and theater came to life. Thus, a society was coming forth that generated free thinking and encouraged those involved in the arts to venture into creatively unknown areas in their artwork.

One of the greatest artist of this time was the sculptor and architect, Phidias, who was selected to restore the Acropolis which had been destroyed by the Persian army. Phidias' fame rests solely upon the stories of the Greeks, since not one piece of his original artwork is still in existence.

Samuel Winstead   Age 8   Atlanta, Ga.   Jennifer Vargas   Age 16   LaHabra, Ca.

"Beauty, as expressed in the fine arts, helps to purify the soul, making it harmonious, good, and beautiful .... and that the contemplation of beautiful works of art is extremely helpful .... in restoring the body to health."   Pythagoras

A.

Lesson #93:
Drawing Samson

The ancient Greeks were very interested in showing every muscle in man. Can you draw muscles? For this lesson, let's draw *Samson* from the Bible. First, read about his life in chapters 13 through 16 in the Book of Judges, and then draw him in the figure box (A). Use your drawing pencil, and then go over it with your black pen.
"Samson"
Patrick Bennett
Age 11 Troutville, Va.

Lesson #94: *Story of Samson*

The ancient Egyptians always illustrated man in profile, showing little action. One of the innovations of the Greeks was *contrapasto*, or showing the human form in motion, balanced on one foot and at different angles. Let's draw Samson again, but this time put him in a different setting. See if you can be like the ancient Greeks and show contrapasto in Samson's action. Before beginning, practice an action position for Samson using contrapasto in the smaller figure box below. You may want to start with a stick figure and then draw over that. Finally, do your finished drawing in the large figure box below using your colored pencils.

By the fifth century, Greek culture had reached its height of acclaim in the city-state of Athens under the leadership of Pericles. It was during this time that one of the greatest events in the history of mankind took place which would impact the future glory of Greece. The Persian Empire was to the east of Greece, located in a place called Asia Minor. Just as during the time of Christ the Jews had an historian named Josephus, the ancient Greeks had an historian named Herodotus who graphically wrote about the times. There was much rivalry and contention between the two powerful nations. The Persians relentlessly sent great armies against Greece to conquer them, each time being defeated. Finally, the son of Darius, King Xerxes (who was married to Ester in the Bible), decided to once again invade Greece, advancing with an army of over one million men. To transport his vast army across the waters, King Xerxes built large ships. His army destroyed everything in its wake, even the Acropolis which was a sacred hilltop fortress with beautiful buildings and pieces of sculpture. It was the highest part of the city of Athens and personified their greatest works in architecture and sculpture. However, the brave Greeks never gave up and finally defeated King Xerxes and his great navy at the Battle of Salamis in 480 B.C., totally devastating the Persian army and saving the Greek civilization.

After the victory, Greece entered into its most glorious period known as *The Golden Age*. In the next fifty years, Greek art reached a height of perfection and splendor which many believe has never been equaled. Plato summed up the Greek approach to art when he said, *"Art has no end but its own perfection."* It was an era given to the gaining of knowledge in such academics as history, philosophy and mathematics. Likewise, there was a great outpouring of creativity in sculpture, architecture, drama and poetry.

It was during this time that the Parthenon was built. The Parthenon was a beautiful temple built atop Acropolis in Athens to house the goddess Athena. Even though this grandiose structure still stands today, much of it was destroyed by a Turkish shell during the 1660s when the Turks invaded Greece. The temple not only has great architectural design, but is also filled with beautifully sculpted marble statues of the gods and goddesses. The years have bleached away the bright and lively colors that were painted on these figures during this glorious *Golden Age*.

"The Parthenon" Athens, Greece (5th century B.C.)
Gregory Iocco Age 14 Freeport, Michigan

A. Doric Column
(capitol)

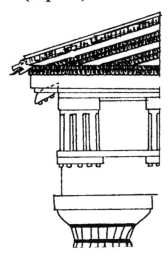

B. Ionic
(capitol)

The ancient Greeks were not only outstanding sculptors and painters, they were also creative when it came to architecture. Their building styles would later influence the Romans who, in turn, would influence the modern architecture of the Western world. Observe some of the old stone banks and capital buildings in your town or city and you will see the influence of ancient Greek architecture.

Notice the columns on page 154. The buildings created by the Greeks consisted of many separate parts. They used *columns,* or long shafts, to support the upper part of the building, known as the *entablature.* The columns consisted of vertical, ribbed sections called *flutes.*

Lesson #95: *Drawing Columns*

For this assignment, complete the two columns in the space provided to the left and right (A & B). The *Doric Column* was both subtle and simple and stands directly on the base or *stylobate.* It has the least amount of flutes and bows out slightly. The *Ionic column* flutes are vertical (see page 154). See if you can draw the flutes (grooves) freehand for the Doric and Ionic columns in the space provided. *Freehand* means without the use of a ruler. This is a good exercise for learning to draw controlled lines. Remember, learning to draw lines is one of the best disciplines in drawing. There is a mark at the top and bottom of each column to show where to connect your lines. You may want to turn your paper sideways in order to have a better angle for drawing. Draw lightly with your yellow pencil and go over with your black pen. Then, erase the pencil lines and letter the style of column on the lines below.

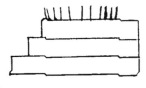

(base/*stylobate*)

(base/*stylobate*)

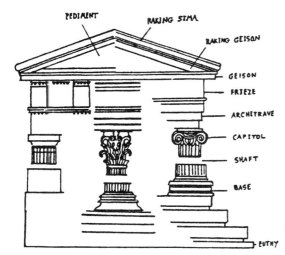

PEDIMENT
RAKING SIMA
RAKING GEISON
GEISON
FRIEZE
ARCHITRAVE
CAPITOL
SHAFT
BASE
EUTHY

Order is a term used to describe a certain style of Greek architecture. The Doric Order refers to the Dorians who were early inhabitants of Greece. Thus, *Doric* would seem to be a good title to give to any architecture that was very Greek in style. In the Doric style, the frieze section was simple in design. Broken into three sections called a *triglyph*, the middle section, or *metope*, was left either plain or contained carved relief sculpture of figures or designs.

The *Ionic Order* was another style of Greek architecture. Whereas, the Doric Order was developed in Greece, the Ionic style was developed in Asia Minor. Both styles reached their peak of perfection in the building of the Parthenon.

Lesson #96: *Drawing A Greek Building*

For this assignment, connect the top (*capitol*) of the Greek column with the bottom (*base*) by completing the middle section (*shafts*) and label the parts as shown above. Complete the rest of the columns to the left with your "HB" pencil, and then go over them with your black pen. Notice that you have a different *order,* or style, for each of the capitols. Then, draw your own Greek building on another sheet of paper. Finally, write the three orders below. Which style do you like best? Why?

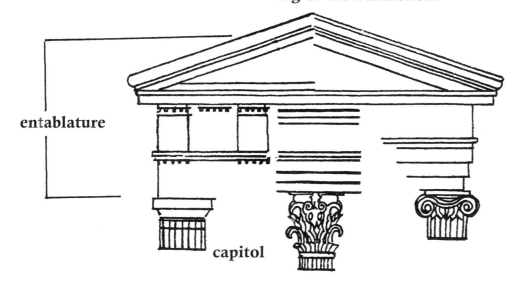

entablature

capitol

base

_____

_____

153

The most prominent styles of architecture in ancient Greece were the Doric Order and the Ionic Order. A third style, the *Corinthian Order*, was very similar to the Ionic Order. The main difference between the two was the *capital* (the top decoration of the columns). The Corinthian Order was more decorative with its leaf patterns. Years later, the Corinthian Order became a favorite of the Roman Empire and appeared in much of the ancient Roman architecture.

A good way to remember the main styles is: the more the progress in the columns, the more syllables there are in the order. The first, Dor-ic (two syllables), the second, I-on-ic (three syllables), and the third and most sophisticated order, Cor-in-thi-an (four syllables).

Corinthian Order

Lesson #97: *The Greek Orders of Architecture*

In the last assignment you drew flutes on the two styles of Greek columns. For this assignment, draw the entire column from top to bottom by copying the examples below. Notice that the Doric column, or shaft, bows out. This creates an illusion of being straight when standing in front of the temple and looking up. See if you can draw this column freehand. However, use a ruler for the Ionic column which is much straighter. Start by drawing lightly with your drawing pencil, and then go over it with your black pen.

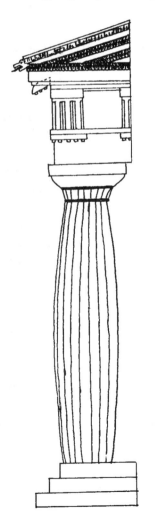

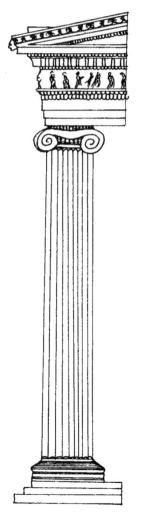

The Doric Order   Drawings by Gregory Iocco Age 14 Freeport, Mi.   The Ionic Order

154

The Hellenistic Period

In 431 B.C., not even 50 years after the Battle of Salamis, the powerful military city-state of Sparta went to war against the equally powerful city-state of Athens. This clash lasted for 27 years and is known as the *Peloponnesian War*. By the end of the century, the once spectacular city of Athens was totally devastated and would never again return to her former glory. This disastrous war left Greece drained of its resources and the other city-states competing for supreme power. For brief periods, Sparta and then Thebes took hold of the leadership of Greece, but both were unsuccessful for any extended period of time.

It was during the fourth century B.C. that Philip of Macedonia gained power. Macedonia was a region to the north of Greece, and Philip, playing upon mutual jealousies of the city-states, was able to unite all the Greek city-states under his rule. In time, Philip's son Alexander became king. With a united Greece, Alexander proved to be one of the greatest military leaders in the history of mankind. He was responsible for conquering many of the Oriental armies in the East and creating a vast Greek empire. Unfortunately, *Alexander the Great* as he came to be known, died at the young age of 32. After his death, the generals of his armies began to rule over many of the conquered kingdoms. As Greece expanded its empire to other lands, it brought along its style of art. The Greeks called their people *Hellenes* and, since their influence was everywhere, this style of art came to be known as *Hellenistic art*. The Greek Jews of this time were also called *Hellenists* (as mentioned in the Book of Acts in the Bible).

The Greek culture also influenced the rest of the world through trade - specifically with pottery. There is still much of this pottery in existence today, giving us wonderful examples of the way these artisans created and painted. One reason so much pottery still exists is that these containers were produced in great abundance to serve many practical purposes. Large vessels were used for storing wine and water, and smaller ones were used for ointments, oils and perfumes. Another reason they have long-endured is that the clay was *fired* in a brick oven, becoming hard and very durable.

Pottery is made on a *potter's wheel* - a round, flat disc that spins around, similar to a lazy susan. The potter places a wet slab of clay on this surface and spins the wheel. As the wheel spins around and around, the potter's hands form the clay into a smooth round object. This is a technique still used today.

The earliest Greek pottery was influenced by the Mycenaeans who placed intricate patterns and designs on their vessels, such as triangles, checkers and herringbone (A, B & C). Gradually, beautiful pictures were painted on these containers that included mythological stories, scenes from everyday life, and stories of military conquest. At first the figures were painted in profile with little *perspective*, or depth. These figures were painted in black on red earthenware, and then the details were scratched, or *etched*, into the dark figures. Eventually Greek potters, especially in Athens, began to paint the human figures a reddish-orange color on a black surface.

....

Lesson #98: *Drawing Designs*

Early Greek pottery had designs like: triangles (A), checkers (B) and herringbone (C). For this exercise, place some nice designs on the two vessels below (D).

A. Triangles   B. Checkers   C. Herringbone   D. Your Designs

"Bring me a denarius that I may see it. So they brought it. And He said to them, 'Whose image and inscription is this?' And they said to him, 'Caesar's.'" Mark 12:15-16

....

Even though all the Greek paintings and most of the architecture and sculpture have been destroyed, we still have a wealth of pottery as a testimony to their artistic abilities. The ancient Greeks also made statuettes out of molded red clay which was baked much like the pottery. This form of sculpting from red clay and baking was called *teracotta*. The Greeks used *kilns*, or ovens, for baking the once soft clay after it had dried and hardened. The kilns were very large, made out of firebrick, heated with wood and used for baking both pottery and small clay sculptures. Coins are another form of art that has revealed a great deal about the Greek artisans. Designed with a high degree of skill, these coins are a portrait gallery of ancient gods and heroes.

....

"Then one poor widow came and threw in two mites, which make a quadrans." Mark 12:42

....

Lesson #99: *Designing Coins*

By viewing and studying the many coins that survived from ancient Greece, we have been able to learn a great deal about the artisans of that time. Did you know that the *two mites* the widow donated were small, copper Greek coins worth a fraction of a penny? For this assignment, place a quarter, dime, nickel and penny in front of you and draw the front and back of each in the circles provided. In the final two circles design your own coin. Use an "HB" pencil and make sure your pencil is sharpened to allow you to put in all the details.

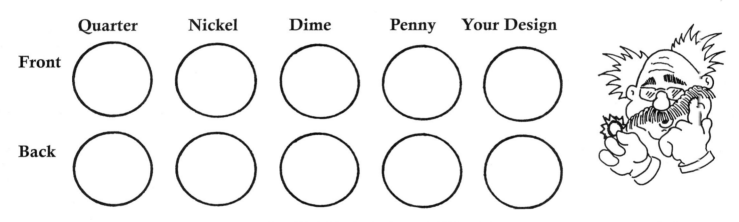

	Quarter	Nickel	Dime	Penny	Your Design
Front	◯	◯	◯	◯	◯
Back	◯	◯	◯	◯	◯

....

"Queen Ester" by Joni Hunt Age 12
Malabar, Florida

Amy Peters Age 7
Midlothian, Va.

A.

After the Mycenaean period of pottery with its intricate patterns, the *geometric style* became popular. This style used geometric designs and simple forms of human figures and animals. Like the Egyptians before them, the Greeks represented these figures from the side view, or profile. The artwork was *symmetric*, or balanced. In other words, if a man was placed on one side of the picture, an animal might be placed on the other side to give it *balance*. These pictures and designs generally went around the pot within large bands or stripes (A). This was a time when Greek artists began painting the *silhouette* figures, painted black against a light surface to emphasize their outline.

With the expanse of trade, the Greeks produced even greater amounts of pottery. Their style soon became influenced by the art of the Orient, which they had encountered during their exploits. Oriental, or *Eastern art,* was more *curvilinear* than the art of the Greeks. Whereas the Greek artists were using geometric shapes with straight lines and angles, the Oriental style was more curved.

During the sixth century B.C., Athens became the center for producing quality vessels of pottery. At this time artists began to sign their work. Throughout the ages there have been few periods when artists signed what they created, leaving most artists in obscurity. A possible reason these ancient Greek artists signed their work is because they were receiving acclaim and becoming very successful. The artist's signature identified the piece of work with the individual.

···

Lesson #100: *Greek Pottery & Creative Designs*

The Greek pottery which has been preserved gives us a wonderful example of the way the ancient Greeks painted. Their pottery was produced in great abundance and used for storing wine, water, ointments, oils and perfumes.

For this assignment, place a nice design on each of the vessels below. You may want to place designs like triangles, checkers or herringbone on them just as the Myceanaeans did, or you can create your own designs. Practice on the smaller vases before beginning on the larger ones. Start with a light pencil, and when you have finished each, outline them with your fine black pen.

"The precious sons of Zion, valuable as fine gold, how they are regarded as clay pots, the work of the hands of the potter."

Lamentations 4:2

A.

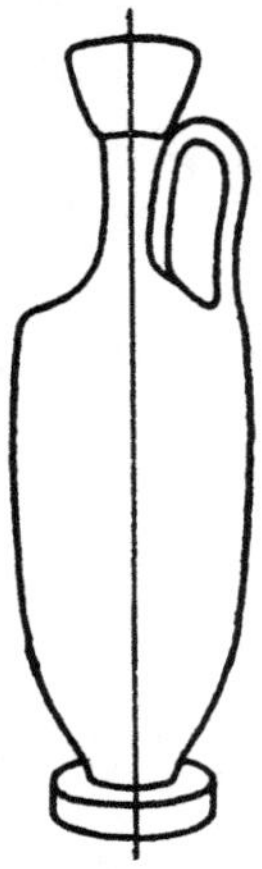

Greek pottery was created in many different sizes and forms and served many different needs. The Greek artisans became masters at making a variety of pots and vases for all occasions, trading their beautiful merchandise throughout the Mediterranean. Below are just a few varieties. See if you can draw each in the figure boxes. Use a light axis line for balance, and ellipses to show the form (A). Start lightly, and then go over each with your black colored pencil.

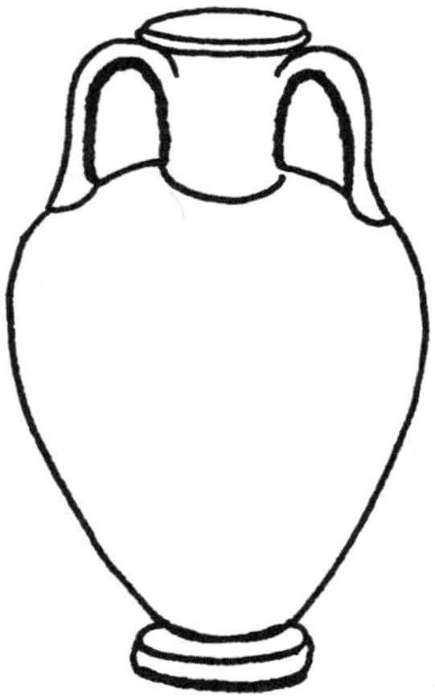

The Amphora

Since it had 2 handles it was meant to be carried on both sides. The opening at the top was large enough for a ladle, and there was usually a top to cover it with after use.

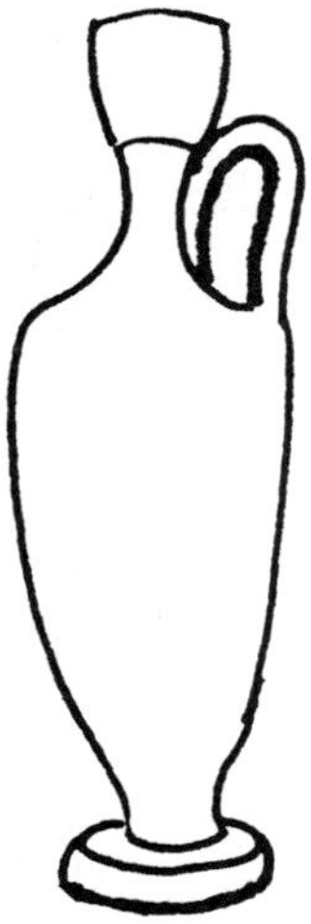

The Lecythos

(Meaning oil flask). This vessel had a long, narrow neck, and was good for pouring slowly. The *Lecythos* was used mainly during funeral services.

The Hydria

(From the Greek word meaning *water*). The main purpose of this vessel was for carrying water from the local springs.

The Crater

(Derived from the Greek word meaning *to mix*). This vessel was used for mixing wine with water, which was the most common drink for the Greeks. The jar had a large mouth, making it easy to use for this purpose.

The Cylix

The name *Cylix*, from the Greek and meaning *to roll*, was given to this vessel because of the way it was turned or rolled on the potter's wheel when it was being created.

Liberty Wiggers Age 17 Kentucky

159

"So Jesus came to a city of Samaria which is called Sychar, near the plot of ground that Jacob gave to his son Joseph. Now Jacob's well was there. Jesus therefore, being wearied from His journey, sat thus by the well. It was about the sixth hour. A woman of Samaria came to draw water. Jesus said to her, 'Give Me a drink.'" John 4:5-7

Lesson #101: *"The Woman at the Well"*

During the time of Jesus, Greek merchants and their pottery were everywhere, and there seemed to be a beautiful vessel for every occasion. Do you think the woman at the well whom Jesus met was carrying one of these Greek vases? If so, which type do you believe she was carrying? Was it the *lecythos, the amphora, the hydria, the crater or the cylix?*

For this assignment, read the story about the woman at the well (John 4:5-7), and draw the scene below. Be creative with your picture. You may want to research the style of clothing worn, the architecture and even the land during the time of Christ. When you draw the vessel that the woman carried, try to imagine that it was made by the Greeks. Start by drawing your picture lightly, and color with colored pencils when finished.

Rebekkah Roddy Age 15 Kirkland, Washington

Lesson #102: *"Light against Dark & Dark against Light"*

Around 530 B.C., the artists of Athens began a new approach to painting called *red-figure* pottery - illustrating the figures with a light *reddish/orange* color against a black background. This was the opposite of *black-figure* painting which was dark against light. The figures were now becoming more realistic than the old black figure technique, as the light *reddish/orange* color for the figures represented the bronzed skin of the Greeks. During this time, the Greek artists began to show the human figure in positions other than the profile. They also started using foreshortening and overlapping in the pictures on their vases.

For this assignment, draw two pictures on the Greek vases below. You may want to look at the *picture postcard* of a Greek vase, *Black-Figured Neck Amphora*, and copy that design on one of your vases. Then, draw any picture or design you like on the other. For the first vessel (A), color your figures black. Make your black by mixing your dark blue, dark red, and a touch of yellow together in one of the circles between the vases. Try mixing various combinations of these colors until you create a rich, dark color similar to black. If this color is still too light, add some of your black to make it darker.

For the second vessel (B), color the background with your dark color. Then, mix a light reddish/orange by mixing a little red with orange. Practice mixing this color in the circles first. You may want to add a light brown to dull the orange. Continue to practice mixing colors in the circles until you find a nice reddish/brown or reddish/orange to color your figures. You may even want to add a touch of blue (the complement of orange), yellow, or white to your orange. When finished, color the figures on the vase (B), and also the background on the other vase (A). Remember, the black-figure technique is a reddish/orange vase with black figures (A), and the red-figure pottery is a black vase with reddish/orange figures (B). Finally, print the type of vessel it is on the line above each piece of pottery.

A. Vessel: _____   B. Vessel: _____

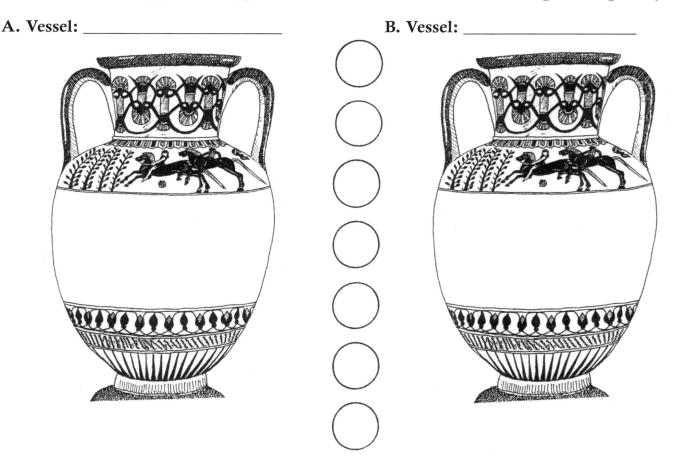

"Black-Figured Amphora"   Gregory Iocco Age 14 Freeport, Michigan

161

Lesson #103: *Painting Black-Figured & Red-Figured Amphora*

For this assignment, take out *Paint Card #VI* and place it in front of you. Today we are going to paint pottery with the techniques of the ancient Greeks. One vase will be the *Black-Figure* technique with black figures on a red/orange background (A), and the other will be the *Red-Figure* technique with red/orange figures on a black background. First, mix a black by adding red to blue (making a very dark blue), and then add a speck of yellow. Mix a lot of this dark color because you will be using it for the figures on the first vase and the background of the second vase (a puddle about the size of a quarter should do). It is important to test your colors in the circles before you actually start to paint. You will be surprised how much a color will change when you see it applied to paper. Your black may look a little bluish, however when you hold it at a distance, it should appear black. Refrain from mixing water in with your paint; this will make your paint too thin. You want to paint with nice, fluid strokes - as if you were painting with melted butter. After you have mixed your dark color, paint the second vessel black (B) and let it dry. Take your time in painting around the figures. If you lose any of your design, you can copy from the picture below. Make sure you have enough black paint left for painting the figures on the first vessel (A).

Next, mix a reddish/orange. First, mix yellow and red to make an orange. Then, add a little more red to make a more reddish color. Make sure to mix a lot of this color. If you would like to dull this color down, you may want to add a very tiny speck of blue. After you have mixed a nice reddish/orange, paint the entire vessel (A). Likewise, paint the figures a reddish/orange in the second vessel (B) when the black has dried. This is the *red-figure* technique. Take your time, use a lot of paint on your brush, and paint with control - staying in the lines. Finally, using your fine brush, paint the figures on the first vessel black (A). This is similar to the method used by the ancient Greeks called the *black-figure* technique. You can also use your black pen for the little details in both vases when the paint is dry.

A. "*Black-Figure*" Neck Amphora (540 BC)
Gregory Iocco Age 14 Freeport, Mi.

B. "*Red-Figure*" Neck Amphora (510 B.C.)
Benjamin Iocco Age 12 Freeport, Mi.

162

Lesson #104: Examination #III

I. **Matching:** Match each definition with the correct term by printing the letter next to the number in the left column: 4 points each.
(Answers on last page of *God & the History of Art I.*)

____1.	perspective	a. a style of Greek architecture
____2.	grid	b. a type of paper
____3.	Pharaohs	c. a sacred hilltop fortress
____4.	pigments	d. having a raised surface
____5.	papyrus	e. vertical, ribbed sections of columns
____6.	humanism	f. a great awakening in art
____7.	the Golden Age	g. showing depth in pictures
____8.	contrapasto	i. colors of paint
____9.	Herodotus	i. showing the human form in motion
___10.	Order	j. a design on Greek pottery
___11.	flute	k. small equal squares used to make proper proportions
___12.	Hellenes	l. a type of Greek vase
___13.	herringbone	m. showing man in all his splendor & glory
___14.	Amphora	n. Greek historian
___15.	relief	o. devotion to pleasure and comfort
___16.	Epicureanism	p. Greek people
___17.	Acropolis	q. ancient kings of Egypt

II. **Fill in the blanks:** Write the correct word in the blanks to complete each statement: 2 points each.
1. Greece was made up of many _____ -states.
2. The Bible says your nakedness is your _____.
3. An _____ has a total disbelief in any supreme being.
4. The _____ was the top decoration of the Greek column.
5. The term "classic profile" comes from ancient _____.
6. Sculpting and baking red clay was called _____.
7. _____ means placing everything in correct size to other parts.

III. **True or False:** Place a "T" or "F" next to each statement if it is true or false: 2 points each.
1.____ Ancient Egyptian figures were drawn and painted in profile.
2.____ Hieroglyphics were a system of mathematics.
3.____ The ancient Greeks used models to pose for them.
4.____ Values are shades from light to dark.
5.____ A narcissist loves nature.
6.____ In Egyptian art, making figures larger symbolized importance in society.
7.____ The ancient Greeks have been a model of perfection in the arts.
8.____ Art expresses a civilization's philosophy about life.
9.____ Many ancient statues were destroyed as idols by Christians.

Doodle Page

"And God spoke all these words, saying: 'I am the Lord your God, who brought you out of the house of bondage. You shall have no other gods before Me. You shall not make for yourself any carved image, or any likeness of anything that is in heaven above, or that is in the earth beneath, or that is in the water under the earth; you shall not bow down to them nor serve them.'"

Exodus 20:1-5

Ancient Rome
&
Early Christian Art

"Christ Washing the Apostles Feet" (1000 A.D.)
copied by Gregory Iocco Age 14 Freeport, Michigan

Ancient Rome

Every great civilization goes through a period of growth before it reaches its height of glory, and then finally fades from power. As Greece passed through this last cycle, Rome took its place as the foremost world power. Many centuries earlier, when Greece was in the midst of its *Age of Enlightenment*, another people known as the Etruscans ruled in Italy. Like the Dorians in Greece, not much was known about them until recently when weapons, armor and jewelry were unearthed. These artifacts tell us that they were both fierce warriors and skilled metal workers.

The Etruscans were intensely religious and worshiped many different gods. Like the Egyptians, they furnished their tombs with material things that would be needed for the next life. The walls of their tombs were painted with scenes that portrayed daily life. We have learned from these tomb paintings that music and dance were important to their lifestyle.

The city of Rome is located in Italy, a country in Western Europe which is basically a large peninsula. Legend has it that Rome was organized as an Etruscan city-state in 753 B.C. on a site where a pair of abandoned twins, Romulus and Remus, were raised by a she-wolf. Around 400 B.C., the Etruscan rulers were overthrown and a Roman republic was established. As the republic gained wealth and power it conquered the rest of Italy, Sicily and Carthage, and then marched eastward defeating the Macedonians and adding Greece to its empire. Though a political victory, it would not be a cultural one, as the Grecian *Hellenistic* style continued to greatly influence the cultures of both the Eastern and Western parts of the civilized world.

During this time, the Roman army conquered much of the Western hemisphere, becoming the most organized, well-equipped and disciplined in the world. The average Roman soldier was not only skilled in conquering, but constructing as well. These soldiers possessed the engineering tools and abilities to build magnificent roadways, bridges and aqueducts in the vanquished lands, many of which still stand today.

Thus, it was now Rome's time to influence the world with its might, engineering abilities, culture and religions. Its battle-honed armies continued to expand its borders on the Mediterranean by conquering Asia Minor and Syria. Egypt also became an independent vassal of the growing Roman empire. Then in 63 B.C., the renown Roman general Pompey set his sights on Jerusalem. After a three month siege, he marched victoriously into the holy city and placed Herod the Great on the throne of Palestine. Unlike the conquering armies before him, Pompey did not sack the Holy Temple which housed the *Holy of Holies,* the most sacred place in Jerusalem. However, in the eyes of the Jews, he committed a grievous sin by simply walking in the hallowed Temple curious to see who this *God* was that the Jews so fervently worshiped. The Romans would make their grand entrance just before the life of Jesus Christ and Christianity began.

The Romans not only brought their culture with them, but also their many gods and goddesses. Like the Greeks and Egyptians, the Romans had a god for every occasion, many being imported from other cultures rather than passed down in tradition. Some of these were: Isis, the goddess of love (borrowed from Egypt); Magna Mater, the great mother of the gods (imported from Asia Minor); Sol, the sun god (Syria); Adonis and Atargatis (Greece); and Jupiter (similar to the Greek god Zeus). There were also Apollo, Aseanius, Attis, Bellona, Bona Dea, Venus, Vulcan, Psyche, Vesta and many others. Hence, the Romans were no different than the great civilizations before them in the way they set up various graven images to worship.

"I will hand them over to trouble, to all kingdoms of the earth."   Jeremiah 15:4

The Jewish Culture: The *Diaspora*

There are several reasons why it is important for Christians to understand Jewish culture. For one, we should know how the influences of other cultures not only impact the world, but our faith as well. God continually warns His people to be separated from worldly influences and their polluting effects in order to remain holy. Much of the Jewish lifestyle has been imparted to us through the word of God, which we have gained access to by being grafted into the same vine. Spiritually, their inheritance is our inheritance, allowing us to have a deeper and more significant appreciation of art through a relationship with God and an understanding of His word.

It is important to study the Jewish culture during ancient times to see not only what their lifestyle was like, but also how they were affected by the different cultures that ruled over them. Sadly, despite God's warning, the Jewish culture would continually be influenced by the rest of the world. Whenever the Jews were taken into captivity by nations like Rome, Egypt or Babylon, they would be changed by the conquering culture.

The introduction of Roman rule to Palestine would begin another long and painful period for the Jewish people. Although the Romans brought law and order, a mastery of engineering, and a structured trade system with the rest of the world, they also exiled thousands of Jewish war prisoners by shipping them to Rome. Like so many times before, God was removing His people from the Holy Land and dispersing them to foreign lands. This dispersion came to be known as the *diaspora*. Ever since the first great dispersion of the Jews in 586 B.C. by Babylon, the Jewish people would be continually relocated by conquering nations.

Jan Clapp Palm Bay, Fl.

Gentile is a term derived from the Roman word for races, and was a title given by the Jews to all non-Jews, such as Romans and Greeks. The Jews who remained in Palestine under *gentile rule* were governed with an iron hand by the Roman Empire. However, in many instances, the Jews refused to bow down in submission to this new government. Because of this, the government was forced to create unique exceptions for those religious zealots. For example, Jews did not believe in carrying weapons on the Sabbath, and were therefore exempt from serving in the military. Also, the Romans had to exempt the Jews from paying reverence to the Roman Emperor as a god because the Jews would rather die than worship any other gods. Jewish law also restricted them from intermingling with other races, or gentiles, who tried to taint their pure standing before God. Even though the Jewish people were ruled by one godless nation after another and were influenced by their various cultures, they still maintained a strong sense of spiritual preservation.

"Woman, believe Me, the hour is coming when you will neither on this mountain, nor in Jerusalem, worship the Father." John 4:21

The Hellenist Jews

During the time of Jesus there were many various sects of the Jewish faith. They spoke different languages such as Aramaic, Greek and Hebrew. One such was the Greek-speaking *Hellenist* Jews who lived in the scattered colonies known as the *diaspora*. This dispersion of the Jewish people was so prevalent that nearly five million Jews lived outside of their beloved Palestine during the first century.

However, there was a major difference between the Hellenist Jews and the Jews of Palestine that went far deeper than language alone. Jerusalem was the center of Jewish life and the Temple was the physical rock of their faith. It stood for everything that set them apart from the rest of the world. The Jews in the Holy Land were close enough to Jerusalem and the Temple to feel a sense of security even when other cultures and empires ruled over them. The Hellenist Jews who had been separated throughout other lands did not have that advantage.

The Hellenist Jews who were removed from the Holy Land set up *synagogues* which were a place of worship and a local community hall where they met for legal matters, schooling and various debates. The word of God instructed the Jewish family that their children were gifts from God and schooling was very important. Traditionally, a child's upbringing was an important part of Jewish life. It was generally the family's responsibility to educate their own children, much like homeschooling today. The girls and young boys were taught at home by their mothers while the older boys were educated in the synagogues by their fathers and *rabbis*, or teachers. These students were trained to take care of the elderly, the homeless, and the poor, and to look for God's will in every aspect of their lives. All instruction was based on scripture and teachers emphasized history, religious ethics and the law.

After the Jewish people settled in the Promised Land, education became more specialized. Having been inspired by the writing techniques of the Phoenicians, students who excelled in writing became known as *scribes*. Charged with writing legal documents and other important business affairs, their profession became one of prestige, and they were called to copy the Holy Scriptures in Hebrew during a time when Greek and Aramaic were becoming the main languages.

"Mary Washing the Feet of Jesus"
Whitney Age 7 Lincoln, Va.

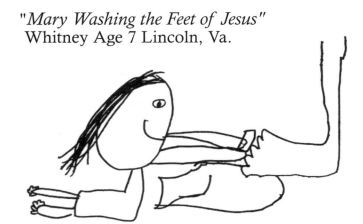

However, Jewish education was weak in the sciences and the fine arts. They did not encourage their young men in drawing, painting and sculpture, which accounts for the lack of artwork in the synagogues. It was also against their belief to create a likeness of anyone. That is why it is difficult to know what Jesus looked like. As a result, except for the building of the Temple, there was little artistic creativity in the Jewish culture.

Lesson #105: *Penmanship*

Jewish students may have lacked an education in the fine arts but many excelled with the pen. Penmanship is an integral part of the arts and should be highly regarded in the education of our students today. Penmanship should be practiced and developed just as it was in ancient Israel. Like drawing, it is an art and skill learned through discipline and practice.

For this lesson, let's practice penmanship. Similar to drawing, students must practice control with the pen in the same way they practice control with a pencil. Control creates beautiful strokes for your letters, just as it forms beautiful lines for objects you draw.

Notice the strokes on the *guidelines* below. Guidelines are light lines used to assist in making each letter the same size as well as keeping your lines straight. For this assignment, practice each stroke four times using a different colored pencil for each series of strokes. Make sure all your letters are at the same slant, or angle. When practicing penmanship, go from top to bottom with your strokes. If you like exercises like this, you may want to go to the library and obtain a book on *calligraphy*, the art of beautiful handwriting. The purchase of a special calligraphy pen is recommended. Continue to practice your basic strokes. The more you practice, the quicker you will achieve good penmanship.

After you have finished, place *Marker Card "B"* in front of you and practice the strokes again, but this time with markers. Markers will give you bolder strokes and are good for learning the art of lettering. Use a different colored marker and copy each letter three times on the top of your *Marker Card*. When you are finished, copy the alphabet with your markers on the bottom of the *Marker Card* using your best penmanship.

The Romans loved the entertainment provided in the open air arenas called *amphitheaters*. Events such as the dangerous chariot races were always well attended. Charioteers pulled by as many as four pairs of horses, would race furiously around the track using any tactic imaginable to gain victory over their opponents. There were also gladiatorial events where men would fight wild beasts - or each other - to the death. The Romans also had foot races, wrestling matches and other events that were performed the Greek way - in the nude. This viciousness and nudity of Roman entertainment was very offensive to the religious Jews and they refused to be entertained in such a pagan manner.

During the time of Christ, Herod constructed a huge amphitheater. This was a spectacular structure both in its Greek style and size. It was decorated with marble inlays and imported materials from around the Mediterranean and was designed mainly for musical and dramatic performances. Most of the performances were of Greek dramas that celebrated the exploits of their gods and goddesses, or comedies which were too crude for the taste of the Jewish people.

Even though the Jews shared in the main beliefs and customs of their faith, there was still much quarreling among them. Various Jewish sects had their own interpretation of doctrine, like the *Hasidim*, the *Essenes* and the *Pharisees*. There were also the *Zealots* and the *Sadducees*. These groups constantly argued with each other and against the Roman rule. The contentiousness, the pagan gods and goddesses of the Romans, and the heathen forms of entertainment would cause much turmoil in the Holy Land during this time.

Roman gods & goddesses

Isis (Egyptian):	goddess of love
Attis:	a consort of Magna Mater
Mithra (Persian):	god of light
Jupiter (Syria):	a sky god
Adonis (Greek):	god of vegetation
Atargatis (Greek):	female partner of Adonis
Sol (Syria):	sun god
Juno:	goddess of women & marriage
Minerva:	goddess of the arts and war
Magna Mater:	great mother of the gods
(Asia Minor)	

"Emperor Augustus"
drawing by Gregory Iocco Age 14
Freeport, Michigan

170

You have learned that the Romans were a practical and industrious people who excelled in building and engineering, along with being brilliant planners of war, law and urban design. Unfortunately, their contributions in the fine arts were secondary. The Romans were, in most aspects, imitators of those around them. They incorporated the gods and goddesses from other countries, and the art and artisans as well. You have heard the old saying, *When in Rome, do as the Romans do.* Ironically, much of the artwork that was completed during the glorious days of ancient Rome was actually done by Greek artists who had been enslaved and placed in Roman households.

"Roman Bust" Benjamin Iocco
Age 12 Freeport, Michigan

Roman painting, for the most part, was merely an imitation of colorful Greek paintings. The wealthy Romans were fond of adorning their homes and estates with realistic wall paintings of animals, landscapes, still lifes and religious icons. Like the paintings of the ancient Greeks, very few paintings from Roman times have survived. Ironically, due to a catastrophe in 79 A.D. when Mt. Vesuvius erupted and destroyed the prosperous Roman village of Pompey, we now have a good idea of what the painting style of this time looked like. Miraculously, the volcanic ash preserved everything in the town exactly as it was almost 2,000 years ago, including the paintings on the walls.

The Romans also adopted the Greek style of architecture but made it more grandiose. One significant contribution of the Romans was the arch which was used repeatedly in many of their stone structures. The Roman Colosseum is a perfect example of the use of arches. After nearly two thousand years, this massive structure is still standing and is used as a model for modern stadiums. Additionally, the *medium* of sculpture would become prominent and well-defined by the Roman artistic style. Although sculptures of the *bust* (head and shoulders) of a person were first created by the ancient Greeks, the Romans perfected this form of art. In their sculpted portraits, they departed from the idealistic style of the Greeks and portrayed man in a more realistic manner. The Romans preferred to create a true like-ness, complete with wrinkles, baldness and other blemishes rather than a glorified portrait.

Lesson #106: *Into the Picture Gallery - Portrait of Caligula*

For this assignment, select *Portrait of Caligula* from your *picture postcard gallery* and place it in front of you. This is a sculpted portrait of *Caligula* (the third Roman Emperor of Rome who ruled from 37 A.D. to 41 A.D.). His real name was Gaius Julius Caesar, but he was given the name *Caligula* early in his boyhood because his parents dressed him up as a Roman soldier, including the footgear, known as *caligae*, meaning *little boots*. Caligula became emperor of Rome at the age of 25. His rule was so ruthless and tyrannical that he was assassinated just four years later. Because of his cruelty and unpopularity, most of his portraits were destroyed. This sculpted portrait is one of the few pieces that have survive.

What do you think of the portrait? Remember, this was carved out of stone and the Romans, unlike the Greeks, strived to make their portraits as realistic as possible. What do you think of the hair and eyes? Do you think it is a realistic depiction of a man? Write a fifty word essay describing your thoughts on this piece of artwork.

Lesson #107: *Drawing Arches*

The Romans used the arch in many of their architectural designs for large buildings, bridges and monuments. Arches are enjoyable to draw, especially old stone arches, because they are *aesthetically* pleasing to the eye. For this assignment, draw a stone bridge with an arch underneath as shown below (A). First, using your yellow pencil, draw a hill on both sides of your bridge in the large figure box below.

"The Colosseum at Rome" Gregory Iocco
Age 14 Freeport, Michigan

Then, draw a straight horizontal line for the top of your bridge connecting the two hills, and draw a half-circle for the arch. Since we will be looking under the bridge, draw another half-arch under the right side of the arch. Shade the bottom arch of your bridge with blue and violet vertical lines (B). Next, draw a *horizon line* beneath the bridge with your blue pencil. The horizon line shows where land or water meets sky. Lightly draw some distant trees on your horizon line, and color them in with blue and green vertical lines (as illustrated in A). For water, draw long, broken, parallel blue lines (C). Finally, draw stones on the side of your bridge. Keep your stones in a straight line but give them different shapes. When finished, color them using at least three different colors for each. See how many different browns and bluish-grays you can make. You may want to try orange, violet and black; brown, violet and red; or green, orange and violet. Practice your colors in the stones on the bottom of the page and then write the colors used underneath each (D). You may want to check your color chart for interesting colors to use on your stones.

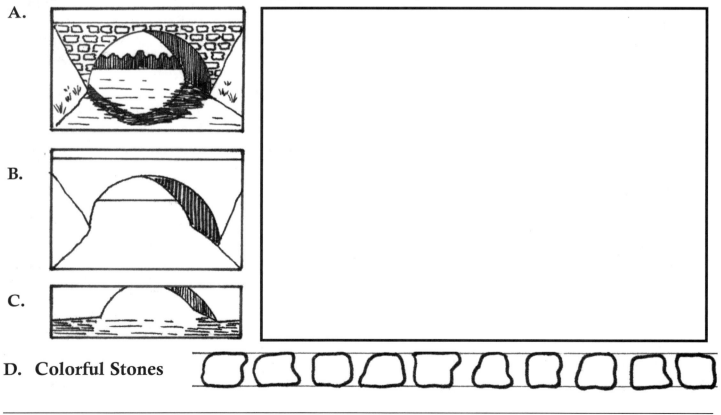

A.

B.

C.

D. Colorful Stones

> *"But when the Helper comes, whom I shall send to you from the Father, the Spirit of truth who proceeds from the Father, He will testify of Me."* — John 15:26

The Romans remained all-powerful for several centuries. However, during the life of Christ, the empire had spread itself too thin over its many territories and had trouble controlling the barbarian hoards who were invading its borders. This would eventually contribute to the collapse of the Roman Empire.

After the crucifixion of Christ, His disciples and the followers of the Christian faith were treated as enemies of the Roman Empire and persecuted. Some Roman Emperors, like Nero, had Christians thrown into large colosseums to be devoured by wild beasts for the entertainment of his subjects. Nevertheless, Christianity continued to grow in spite of the cruel persecution.

Barbarian tribes of Huns and Visagoths continued to attack Rome in the fifth and sixth centuries. For a brief period of time the devastation and destruction was so great that it is rumored that not a living soul remained in the once great city of Rome. It was during this time that people began to search for spiritual answers and hope. They realized that the Greek and Roman gods, goddesses, idols and ceremonies no longer held any meaning in their lives. People needed something to believe in. Thus, when they heard about the life and resurrection of Jesus Christ and the martyrdom of His followers, a new and pure faith began to spread throughout the civilized world.

Triumphal Arch of Tiberius (37 A.D.) Southern France
copied by Benjamin Iocco Age 12 Freeport, Michigan

173

After the crucifixion of Christ, Christians met in secret for fear of their lives. Many believe the first Christian worship services were actually held in *catacombs*, which were abandoned, underground quarries located throughout Rome. The stacked compartments in these cold, damp tunnels were also used as burial places for Christians and Jews who abhorred the Roman method of cremation for disposing of the dead.

Caleb Kennedy Age 8 Pittsburgh, Pa.

During the first and second centuries, the grip of the Roman Empire was beginning to weaken. The pagan emperors saw the Christian faith as a threat to their various gods and decreed that it was forbidden to practice Christianity. Even though many believe that Christians met secretly in catacombs to perform the outlawed mass and to preach the new gospel, most scholars disagree with this theory. There were so many decayed bodies in these underground tombs that the stench would have made it impossible to have worship services. It was also cold, damp and dark. Therefore, the catacombs were most likely a place where Christians met to bury those who had departed to be with God and to celebrate their arrival to heaven.

Whatever the reasons, it is known that early Christians celebrated the consecration of their faith by adorning the stuccoed walls of the catacomb with artwork. Since most early Christians were poor and could not afford to have artwork professionally done, they chose primitive carvings done in *low relief* (light carvings) and simple paintings. It is difficult to imagine why they did artwork in such underground chambers. Perhaps they decorated the walls to create a comforting environment for their departed friends.

The early Christian outlook on art was clearly different from that of the pagan world. The art of the catacombs was a simple language spoken by this new faith, created with a joyous style. There were no pictures of the crucifixion or depictions of the painful tribulations that Jesus and His followers went through. These decorations were of spiritual symbols, like the vine, which was often referred to in the New Testament. When Christian artists were called upon to paint biblical characters, they had no figures or forms of their own which could be recognized as symbols of their faith. So, in the beginning, they adopted the style of the Greek and Roman figures from mythological paintings.

"The Miracle of the Loaves & Fishes" (520 A.D.) copy by Ben Iocco Age 12 Freeport, Michigan

Adorning the Church was a slow and gradual process. As Christianity grew, worship services required more and more space. Art began to gain significance at these spiritual gatherings as the walls were decorated with paintings of stories from the Bible.

William Shelby Age 6
Shinnston, West Virginia

Kristen Miller Age 9
Minneapolis, Mn.

The image of Jesus would also change as the years passed. The earliest Christian art never portrayed Jesus, but illustrated simple, symbolic decorations. Christ was first depicted as the Good Shepherd, a beardless youth holding a lamb. This early image of Jesus looks similar to the Greek-Roman figure of Hermes, a youth with short, curly hair. It wasn't until the fifth century that the image of Jesus started to take on more unique qualities, like longer hair and a beard - the image that we are familiar with today.

Jewish tradition also influenced early Christian art, since their law forbade the creation of images in paintings or sculpture. However, the Jewish colonies which were relocated in cities near the Mediterranean, decorated some walls of their synagogues with stories of the Old Testament. Look at the copy of a wall painting in a Jewish synagogue in Dura-Europas, Syria (245-256 A.D.) on page 196 as an example of this type of Jewish artwork. Besides the Holy Temple, these were the first recorded examples of artwork in a building that was dedicated to God. Quite possibly, religious paintings found in early synagogues may have influenced the early Christian artists.

Most of the early Christian art may seem crude or unrealistic, but the artists were not concerned with expressing things in the idealistic Greek style. Instead their aim was for simplicity. The wall paintings were not intended to be a thing of beauty, but an illustration of the gospel and an encouragement to those in the faith. Anything that was not relevant to the gospel was deemed unnecessary and consequently left out.

Amber Theisen Age 11
Minneapolis, Minnesota

175

Christian Symbolism

The first illustrations that adorned the Roman catacombs were simple in design. Inscriptions were either scratched on the walls or painted in red. The symbols that were created included the *cross* (the anchor of hope), the Greek letters *IXOYE* (Jesus Christ, God's Son, Savior), the *dove* (peace), the *palm* (victory), the *ship* (the Church) and Jesus in the form of the Good Shepherd.

Even though most of these symbols were borrowed from pagan art, the artists incorporated them with new Christian meaning. For example, the four seasons, which were pagan in origin, were transformed into symbols for the cycle of life. Below are some of the symbols that early Christians used in their artwork.

....

Symbolism in Christian Art

The Lamb - Christ and His sacrifices
Amanda Bledsoe Age 12 Winter Park, Florida

The Snake or Serpent - Satan
Sarah Trevett Age 12
Livermore, California

The Cross - Emblem of Christ, Salvation
Erin Stahel Age 8 Plymouth, Minnesota

Sun - life giving force, symbolizes Jesus
Rainbow - symbol of union and God's forgiveness
John Yates Age 14 Melbourne, Florida

The Boat - symbolizes the Church
Angie Stoner San Diego, California

Symbolism in Christian Art

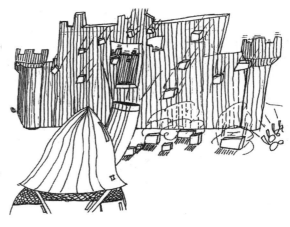

Rocks - the firmness and strength of God
Moon - passage of time and life
Flowers & Fruit - cycle of life, death and resurrection
Halo - the attribute of sanctity
Skull - reminder of death and that life is perishable
IXOYE - Greek word for fish,
    symbol for Christ in early Christian art,
    initials stand for *Jesus Christ, Son of God, Savior*
The Lily - purity of Christ
Dove - peace
Palm - the righteous man, victory

"The Walls of Jericho"
Student Drawing

....

Lesson #108: *Early Christian Art*

    Let's imagine that you are a Christian artist living in the first century after the crucifixion of Jesus. You meet with a group of Christians in a secret gathering place to worship God and you have decided to adorn a wall with artwork. Take some of the Christian symbols from the previous page and incorporate them into your picture. However, see if you can draw your own symbol for each, such as: the *boat* (the Church), the *cross* (universal emblem of Christ and salvation), the *lily* (purity of Jesus), the *sun* (life-giving force, symbolizes Jesus), the *moon* (passage of time and life), *rocks* (symbolizing the firmness and strength of Jesus). Draw your picture below with your colored pencils.

177

Lesson #109: *Symbolic Colors*

Christian art illustrated the Bible and used color to symbolize spiritual things. For example, purple represented royalty and was used mainly for kings and the robe of Jesus. However, it could also symbolize penitence or sorrow. Some of the colors used in Christian art and what they represented are listed below:

Blue - heaven

Red & Black - the devil

Yellow or Gold - God & divinity, truth

Purple - penitence or sorrow

White - purity

Let's once again pretend that you are living in the first century and that you must meet in secret to worship God. For this assignment, draw a story from the Bible in the large figure box below. Imagine that this is going to be painted on one of the walls where your Christian friends meet. Keep your Bible story simple and spiritual. Add some Christian symbols like the *sun* for Jesus, the *moon* for the passage of time and so on. Finally, use colors that have spiritual symbolism, such as blue for heaven, purple for penitence, or gold for God and divinity. Make your colors bright and rich by adding pressure to your pencils when applying color.

The Basilica - Roman Architecture & the Christian Church

The *basilica* (meaning royal room) derived both its name and design from the Greeks, but was popularized by the Romans. In early architecture, a basilica was simply a large roofed building. The Roman basilica served in many capacities such as a courthouse, a marketplace and a town meeting hall. The exterior of the structure was simple in design and rather plain in appearance. The first basilicas had no traditional design and were built in various sizes and shapes.

As time passed however, basilicas took on a standard pattern. They became rectangular and featured a long hallway that extended from one end of the building to the other (A) with aisles that did the same on either side (B). They also contained a raised platform near the front (C) where the leading authorities would be seated.

The early Christians were much like the ancient Jews who had been dispersed from the Holy Land. They too needed a place to worship, and the basilicas fulfilled this purpose nicely. Thus, the Roman basilica officially became the original *church* of the Christian faith.

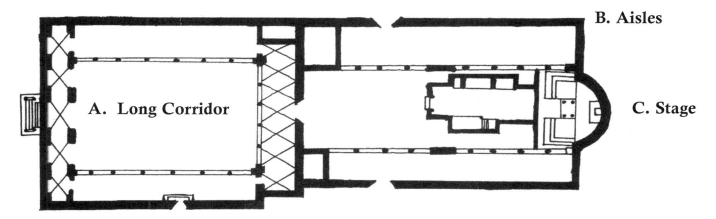

B. Aisles

A. Long Corridor

C. Stage

"Blueprint of a Basilica" Gregory Iocco Age 13 Freeport, Michigan

"Jesus Healing the Sick"
Dave Lee Age 12
Forest, Virginia

Student Art Gallery

Gemesen Carper Age 7 Litetz, Pennsylvania

Hannah Hancock Age 8 Monroe, N.C.

Carissa Hubert Age 11 Rock Island, Illinois

Jody Gramling Homeschool Mom Canton, Georgia

> *"It was the best of times, it was the worst of times; it was the age of wisdom, it was the age of foolishness; it was the epoch of belief, it was the epoch of incredulity; it was the season of Light, it was the season of Darkness."*
>
> Charles Dickens (A Tale of Two Cities)

The Middle Ages
The Dark Ages
Byzantine Art
Romanesque & Gothic Periods

"Bayeaux Tapestry" (1080 A.D.)
copied by Benjamin Iocco Age 12 Freeport, Michigan

"But the natural man does not receive the things of the Spirit of God, for they are foolishness to him; nor can he know them, because they are spiritually discerned."

I Corinthians 2:14

··

The Middle Ages

The *Middle Ages* is the period of European history from the fall of the Roman Empire until the beginning of the Renaissance (500 A.D. to 1500 A.D.). Many scholars believe that the Middle Ages was simply an insignificant bridge of time between the glorious ancient world and the late 15th century. However, the Middle Ages is a rather interesting period because of the other periods that also occupied this span of time. For example, do you know what the *Dark Ages* were? And what *Medieval* means? How about *Byzantine, Romanesque* and *Gothic?*

Briefly, here is a summary of what these periods mean. *Medieval* is a term that simply means having to do with the Middle Ages, and usually refers to the feudal life of kings, serfs and castles. This period of time lasted approximately from 500 A.D. until 1300 A.D. The *Dark Ages* was a period of 500 years within the Middle Ages (500 A.D. to 1000 A.D.) when barbarian hordes, like the Huns and Goths, roamed freely across Europe and destroyed everything in their path. *Byzantine, Romanesque* and *Gothic* refer to different periods of art which were popular in the Christian church during the Middle Ages.

The scholars who deemed this period as *insignificant* were mistaken. Actually, the Middle Ages could have been more appropriately titled The *Glorious Ages.* Even though it was a time of wars, pestilence and pagan gods, Christianity rose as a beacon of light and the greatest single purpose for art was to manifest the gospel of Christ. As the centuries passed and the faith grew, churches became magnificent museums of art, displaying the message of salvation to all who entered its doors. Instead of seeing this era as a time that yielded nothing of relevance, Christians can view the Middle Ages as a time when God was glorified.

Many Christian churches were constructed during the ninth and tenth centuries, which meant that artists, especially sculptors, were busy producing artwork for the interiors. Master artists, much like minstrels, would travel from village to village throughout Europe looking for work on the new churches being constructed. Also, *miracle plays* were enacted by travelling groups of performers. These plays proclaimed the word of God by bringing Bible stories to life. However, not all of the art that was created during the Middle Ages was for the Church. Many castles were being built, and the barons and feudal lords commissioned artwork to adorn the walls of their fortresses. Unfortunately, many of these great manors and castles were destroyed in battle along with their artwork.

Painting was not a major medium during the Middle Ages, as most of the artwork being created was by architects and sculptors. The only painting done during this time was by monks who drew and painted colorful pictures in religious texts and manuscripts. These artists have come to be known as *illuminators* because of the way they illumined written pages with bright illustrations.

Miniature paintings also adorned the calendars of this period. It was customary to illustrate calendars with the various seasons of the year by portraying activities like hunting, planting and harvesting. Since Christianity prevailed as the dominant faith throughout Europe, many of these calendars were attached to prayer books.

"Israelite Putting Blood on the Door before Passover"
Laura Bible Age 11 Statesville, N.C.

Lesson #110: *Being an Illuminator*

For this assignment, select from your *picture postcard gallery* the painting *St. Dominic*, by Gerard Horenbout and place it in front of you. This is a good example of an illuminated page in a manuscript. *St. Dominic* was completed in 1520 - long after the Middle Ages. However, thanks to the diligent work of monks, the style of the illuminators lasted for many centuries in various parts of Europe and *St. Dominic* is a delightful example of this style.

Observe the beautiful design of flowers going around the picture and the articulate penmanship. Also notice the illustration of *St. Dominic* studiously at work within the arched frame. What do you think he is reading? What is looming behind his chair? Is the work realistic? What do you think of the design and colors? What else do you see in the picture? Write your feelings about the artwork on the lines below.

_____

_____

_____

_____

A.

Next, copy the *picture postcard* of *Saint Dominic* in the figure box (A). Make sure to draw the flowers around the picture frame and neatly print the lettering. However, before you do the lettering, draw light guidelines with a ruler to keep your letters straight and the same height. Then draw each letter as precisely as you can with a pencil. When you are finished, go over your lettering with your black pen, except for the letters in red which you may want to do with your red colored pencil. To be an *illuminator*, simply press down more firmly on your colored pencils for deeper, richer colors. Do not forget to mix your colors.

Finally, draw and color some illustrations for a calendar, just as the illuminators did. You may want to select scenes from your neighborhood, or pictures of various seasons of the year from magazines. Draw and color four months of the year in the small figure boxes below (B).

B.
Calendar
Months

Tapestries were popularized during the Feudal times of kings and castles. Tapestry art was woven pieces of textile or fabric made to cover the interior stone walls of the castles. These tapestries were not only used for decoration and to keep the cold out, but also to tell a story. Different forms of narrative art has retold history through the ages. The ancient Egyptians told stories about the lives of the Pharaohs on the walls of their tombs; the ancient Greeks painted mythological stories or exploits of Greek battles on the sides of their vases; the ancient Romans painted and sculpted stories of their victories on buildings and monuments, and the early Christians used the narrative form of the gospel so the illiterate people could understand and believe. Likewise, Medieval artists interwove the stories of battle and great victories on large tapestries. One of the greatest surviving examples of this type of art is the *Bayeaux Tapestry*, which is more than 230 feet long.

The Bayeaux Tapestry tells the story of William of Normandy, or *William the Conqueror*, and Harold of England. Harold had been a leader in the fight to restore William to the throne. However, when William departed to fight wars in foreign lands, Harold claimed the throne for himself and refused to relinquish it. When William returned to England with his army, he killed Harold on the battlefield of Hastings in 1066. All this is illustrated on the large Bayeaux Tapestry. Like most narrative pictures, the artwork is simple, the figures are linear, and everything is outlined with bands of color. In summary, much of the artwork which came out of the Middle Ages, whether for the Church or for the lords and barons of castles, told a story.

Narrative Art

Ancient Egypt	- the walls of the tombs
Ancient Greece	- the sides of vases and jars
Ancient Rome	- paintings & relief sculpture of victories in battle
Early Christian	- telling the gospel
Medieval	- tapestries with stories of battle

"Bayeaux Tapestry" copied by Benjamin Iocco Age 12 Freeport, Michigan

184

Lesson #111: *Creating Narrative Art*

Throughout history, man has told stories in his artwork. For this assignment, draw a picture that tells a story from the Middle Ages. You may want to illustrate a story about the Crusades in the Holy Land, or life in a monastery, or the building of a church. Research the costumes that were worn during this time and the way the buildings were designed. Also, study the event that you are going to illustrate. Remember, great artists throughout time researched what they were going to draw, paint or sculpt before they began. The more you research, the better your artwork is going to be. An encyclopedia is a great place to find much of your information. Practice drawing some of your ideas in the figure boxes below (A).

Draw your final picture in the large figure box (B). Start by drawing lightly with your yellow colored pencil and then darken everything with your black pen. Color with colored pencils and print the event and the date it occurred above your artwork.

A.   **Thumbnail Sketches**

Event: _____ Date of Event: _____

B.

"Let your light so shine before men, that they may see your good works and glorify your Father in heaven."
Matthew 5:16

....

The Dark Ages

Nearly 1,000 years passed between the fall of the Roman Empire and the beginning of the Renaissance. The first half of that period is known as the *Dark Ages*, which lasted from about 475 A.D. (when Attila the Hun sacked Rome) to 1066 (when William the Conqueror invaded Britain). During this time, barbarians mercilessly pillaged and plundered Europe. It was a time of migration and bloodshed - only Christianity remained steadfast against this onslaught of ruthless heathenism.

There were two safe sanctuaries against these barbarian invasions. One was the seemingly impregnable Christian bastion of Constantinople, or Byzantium, located on the Bosporus Sea in what is now Istanbul, Turkey. Behind the walls of a strong fortress, this Christian nation warded off attacks by barbarians and Muslims alike, while highly trained artists kept art alive in the churches with beautiful mosaics, church decorations and metal works of remarkable quality.

Gregory Iocco Age 14 Freeport, Michigan

However, there was another little candle of faith burning in the monasteries of Ireland and France, far north of Constantinople. These monasteries were centers of architecture, sculpture and the *illumination* of sacred writings. Christian monks erected buildings with beautiful arcades and courts in which they developed stained glass. They also restructured the old, drafty Roman basilicas and converted them into Christian churches.

Cloistered in quiet, isolated areas, these monks were especially busy laboring over sheets of velum paper, articulately copying pages from the Bible. There were no copy machines, computers, or even printers during this time, and everything was articulately done by hand. Using the finest brushes, they painstakingly painted brilliant illustrations of biblical stories and decorated the margins of the pages with magnificent penmanship and colorful designs. Thus, while the emperors of Byzantium were exalting God through the adornment of their churches during the Dark Ages, the monks also gave glory to God through beautifully illuminated manuscripts.

"The Full Armor of God"
Sarah Barnett Age 12
Taylor Mill, Kentucky

186

"When His lamp shone upon my head, and when by His light I walked through darkness." Job 29:3

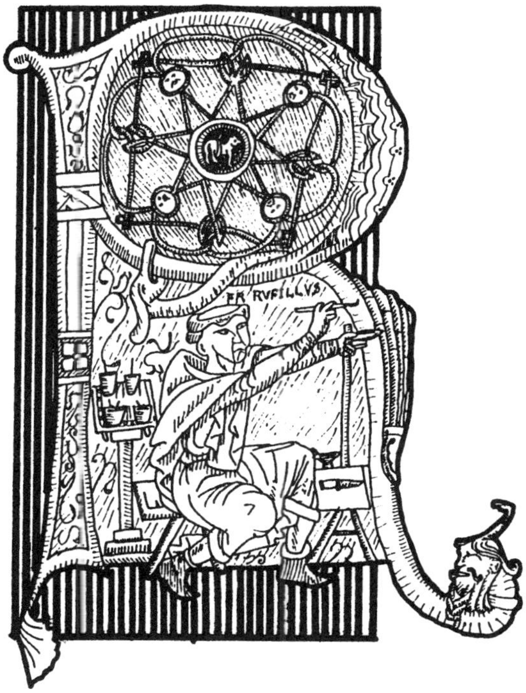

Lesson #112: *Designing Fanciful Letters*

Notice the beautiful design quality of the picture to the left, *Brother Rufillus Writing the Letter R.* Have you heard the saying that a picture is worth a thousand words? Well, this copy from a page in an illuminated manuscript from the Middle Ages certainly tells a story. One not only notices the wonderful design quality of the illustration, but also senses the discipline that went into the lettering. Penmanship, like drawing, takes practice, effort and control, and writing and lettering can be just as creative as drawing!

"Brother Rufillus Writing the Letter R"
13th Century (detail of illuminated manuscript)
copied by Greg Iocco Age 14 Freeport, Michigan

Now let's practice making fanciful letters in the figure boxes below. See what nice designs you can come up with for the letters *S, T, K, O, P* and *A*. Use controlled lines to draw your letters and place a floral design around each letter. You may want to look at pictures to find designs of flowers, vines and leaves. Finally, outline each letter and floral design with your black pen and color them in with colored pencils.

Lesson #113: *Making an Illumined Manuscript*

"*Saint Dominic*" Gregory Iocco Age 14 Freeport, Michigan

Let's now put your penmanship and creativity together just as the monks did centuries ago. Take another look at *Saint Dominic* in your *picture postcard gallery*. Create your own decorative design in the outer border of the copy of the picture to the left. Again, you may want to use leaves, flowers, animals, or anything else you find interesting and decorative. Then, in the rectangular figure box directly under the picture of the monk, letter part of Psalm 23. First, practice lettering your scripture on the lines below. Then place light guidelines in the figure box and letter part of the verse lightly to make sure of its placement. When you are finished, go over your lettering and designs with a black pen. Finally, add a bright array of colors with your colored pencils. Think about the colors you are going to use, mix your colors together, and color with lines. Practice mixing your colors in the circles below.

188

> *"Every man, however obscure, however far removed from the general recognition, is one of a group of men impressible for good, and impressible for evil, and it is the nature of things that he cannot really improve himself without in some degree improving other men."*
>
> Charles Dickens

....

Byzantine Art

As the Roman empire continued to weaken during the fourth century it began to lose much of its hold over the world. During this time there was a drastic move in the central location of both Christianity and the Roman dominion. Byzantium was a city located on the eastern end of the Mediterranean Sea, far removed from all the concerns and problems that confronted Rome. Eventually, a huge part of the Roman empire would shift to this far eastern outpost, changing the face of Europe forever.

Inadequate Roman leadership along with government infighting were quickly dividing the Empire. This caused Constantine, one of the three leaders of Rome during the time, to move his kingdom to the Sea of Bosporus and the city of Byzantium. Story has it that before a major battle against other Roman armies of the West, Emperor Constantine had a vivid spiritual dream. In his dream, an angel visited him who showed him the Cross of Calvary and said, *Under this sign you will be victorious.* The following day as his armies advanced, Constantine looked up in the clouds and saw a cross in the heavens with the inscription, *Holy, Holy, Holy.* Greatly inspired, the emperor of the Eastern Empire led his army to victory.

This victory sealed Constantine's dominion over the Roman Empire; however, he loved the city of Byzantium. With the western part of the empire (Rome) still in turmoil, Constantine realized his new location was too far away to rule both the eastern and western regions. After many years of war and inner conflicts, the Roman Empire split in two; one emperor ruled the eastern half, with its capital in Byzantium, and the other ruled over the western half, with its capital in Rome.

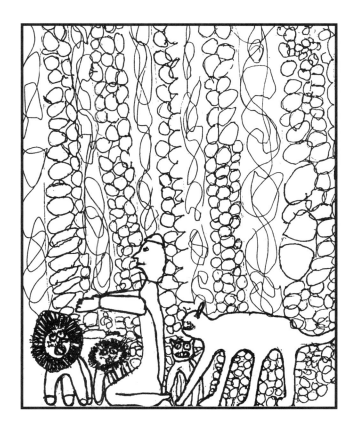

In 311 A.D., Emperor Constantine established Christianity as the official religion of the Eastern Roman Empire, renaming the city of Byzantium *Constantinople* (now known as Istanbul). Emperor Constantine gave the Church dominion over the land and his people. Thus began the *Byzantine Period*, and the Church began to fill its walls with radiant, colorful pictures of Christ and His disciples. This new Byzantine style of art was a unique blend of Roman and Oriental art which would last over a thousand years until this majestic city was finally destroyed by the Turks in 1453.

"Daniel in the Lions' Den"
Johnathan Blew Age 8 Ontario, Ca.

"Your carved images I will also cut off, and your sacred pillars from your midst; you shall no more worship the work of your hands."   Micah 5:13

There was really no dividing line between early Christian art and that of the Byzantine period because they had the same foundation. Both were initially influenced by Roman styles and ideas, and both served the purpose of evangelizing the message of the Gospel through simple, symbolic art. Furthermore, since Christianity during the Byzantine period was recognized as the established religion of the Eastern Roman Empire, the artwork focused even more on serving the Church. However, Byzantine art would be marked by brighter colors and more creative designs which would become its trademark.

During the Byzantine Period there was much trade with the Orient, and the christian artists in Constantinople became influenced by the styles of their oriental neighbors. Because of this, the court of Constantine was adorned with the rich decor of the Far East. This new style of Byzantine art would be a combination of the Oriental influence with all its curves and colors, and the old classical influence of Rome and Greece. The merging of these two influences would bring forth the unique art of *mosaics* - a kaleidoscope of colorful pieces of glass or stone put together like puzzle pieces to make a radiant picture.

"St. Basil" Early Christian/Byzantine Art
copy by Benjamin Iocco Age 12 Freeport, Michigan

Byzantine mosaics depicted characters from the Bible, however the figures were portrayed in a unique manner. The faces were elongated and wore trance-like expressions. The figures were no longer true to life as was characteristically Greek, but illustrated in proportion to their spiritual importance. Christ was always seen as larger than the figures around Him. Centuries before, the Egyptians had illustrated their figures in profile. Byzantine art would now illustrate the figure in the front view. The figures were flat and gave the illusion of weightlessness, not being able to imagine the true form of the body under the garments. They stood in rhythmic procession, giving no perception of depth.

Byzantine artists followed a strict set of rules in how they represented figures, much like the traditional ways handed down from one artist to another in ancient Egypt. Also, like the Egyptians, the Christian artist focused on portraying the afterlife. The human figure became rather abstract in form, striving more for a spiritual meaning. Finally, the nudity that was endorsed by the Greeks and Romans was now forbidden as the focus of art was on the Gospel of Christ and holiness.

"Shadrach, Mechach & Abednigo"
Tony Tarasoft Age 13 Virginia Beach, Va.

"I wisdom, dwell with prudence, and find out knowledge of witty inventions."

Proverbs 8:12

During the fourth century, magnificent churches were built to house the vast congregations of the faithful. Emperor Constantine wanted a spectacular, yet refined, style of art to adorn these churches. It was to be a style that was both simple and emphatic about Jesus Christ. Byzantine art was a statement that the spiritual realm was more important than the physical world, just as simplicity was more important than realism.

The Byzantine Period would contribute much to the art world and to the Church. The church buildings not only became galleries of inspired artwork, but also a place that revealed God's holiness. During this time many symbols of the Christian faith were established, such as the traditional representation of Jesus, the designs of the Crucifixion, the Holy Trinity, the Annunciation and the Resurrection. This would leave a rich inheritance for future Renaissance artists to use many years later.

The most outstanding quality of Byzantine art was its color, especially the vibrant colors made with *mosaics*. Mosaics were pictures consisting of small pieces of cut glass and marble called *tesserae*. These pieces of colored glass were usually about an inch thick and were glued onto the white walls of the church like puzzle pieces to form pictures with spectacular color. Byzantine artists were not concerned with making colors true to life, but rather with giving each color certain symbolic meaning. For example, blue, bright red and gold were colors generally given to Christ. Mary was often pictured with a blue robe.

Some of the greatest mosaic art was created during the fifth and sixth centuries. Just as the purpose of the earlier Christian artist was to spread the gospel of Christ, most of these mosaics were religious in nature. The backgrounds were a vibrant, flat color with no detail which made the figures and the message more significant. Jesus would usually be the focal point, ornamented with a vivid gold background of tesserae. If this Byzantine style appears childlike, it is because the artist's main desire was to keep the message simple and spiritual. Even though these religious figures seem stiff and unrealistic, one also senses something very spiritual. The Byzantine Period became a wonderful representation of the gospel and a permanent influence of the churches in the Eastern Roman Empire for many centuries.

Lesson #114: *Making a Mosaic*

A.

For this assignment, take your yellow pencil and draw a picture of Jesus in figure box (A). Divide your picture into many different sections as in (B). Then color it as if it were a mosaic, using very rich colors.

B. *"Habakkuk"* stained glass (1220 A.D.)

191

A.

Lesson #115:
Creating Your Own Mosaic

Now let's create a drawing for a mosaic picture. Can you draw Jesus and His disciples as shown (A)? Practice drawing the picture with your yellow pencil in the small figure box (D). Then, go over your drawing with your black pen using one continuous line. This is called a *contour drawing*, letting your pencil go in and out, over and under, not stopping from beginning to end (B). As you go over your drawing, allow your pencil to make little designs like puzzle pieces (C).

"Jesus & His Disciples" copied by Todd Leasure

B.

Many students are awkward with doing contour drawings; however, you can create some delightful artwork if you continue to practice. Do not forget to fragment your picture into a puzzle piece design using one continuous line. After you have practiced drawing like this in the small figure box (D), do your drawing again in the large figure box (E). Color all the mosaic sections with your colored pencils using a lot of bright colors.

C.

E. Draw Your Creative & Colorful Mosaic Below

D.

"Painting can do for the illiterate what writing can do for those who can read."

Pope Gregory the Great

....

Justantine ascended to the Byzantine throne in 527 A.D., becoming the first emperor of both the Eastern and Western Roman Empires. He lived in Ravenna, Italy, the capital of the Western Roman Empire. Even though the western part of the Empire still centered around Rome, it had become weakened by continuous barbarian invasions.

Like Constantine, Emperor Justantine was a Christian ruler. He built exquisite churches in Ravenna, much like the ones that were in Constantinople. They were also decorated with mosaic artwork which was more a mixture of the Roman style. When Constantinople finally fell to the Muslims in 1453, the beautiful art from the Byzantine period was destroyed. Fortunately, Ravenna remained safe and secure during the many invasions in Italy. Because of this much of the mosaic artwork in Ravenna has been preserved for us to enjoy today.

....

Pope Gregory the Great

Throughout the history of Christianity, the question has continually been raised: *What purpose should art have for the Church?* As the Church began to grow and establish itself as a powerful influence throughout Europe, the artwork in the Church had to be God-centered. Nearly all early Christians believed that there must be no idols in the house of God. This was a return to the Jewish belief, *"You shall not make for yourself any carved image, or any likeness of anything that is in heaven above, or that is in the earth beneath, or that is in the water under the earth"* (Exodus 20:4).

"Christ with Peter & Paul" marble relief/Rome
copied by Gregory Iocco Age 14 Freeport, Michigan

Probably no other Christian leader dealt with this issue more than Pope Gregory the Great, who was the head of the Church at the end of the sixth century. He was a man after God's own heart - having a compassion for his people and the things of God. Pope Gregory's main desire was to become a pope for the people. He frequently used Church revenues to feed, clothe and house the poor. He also desired to place art within the Church so that it could evangelize the gospel and edify the body of believers. The congregations at this time were largely illiterate, and Pope Gregory believed that the story of Christ and salvation had to be told as clearly and simply as possible. What better way than to have stories of the Bible painted on the walls of the churches? He once proclaimed, *"Images are the books of the laity."* The Pope believed that this form of artwork was by no means idolatry, but a type of storytelling.

Madalyn Siscu Age 8 Charleston, South Carolina

193

> *"...and I will uncover her foundations. All her carved images shall be beaten to pieces...all her images I will lay desolate."*   Micah 1:6,7

....

The *Iconoclasts*

Despite Pope Gregory's fervent efforts to bring art into the Church, there was another group known as the *iconoclasts,* or *image smashers,* who were equally adamant in their belief that there should be absolutely no art in the house of God. Icon means: *an object of devotion, a sacred image venerated in Christian churches depicting Christ, the Virgin Mary, or any of the saints.* In 2 Kings 18:4, the Bible reveals how Hezekiah destroyed everything that his people had set up to worship, which included the bronze serpent that Moses had made. Who could imagine that Hezekiah would destroy such a special symbol from the days of Moses? Nevertheless, the people came to worship that serpent and bowed down to it as if it had its own special powers. And that is what concerned the *iconoclasts* - that art, in any form, shape or style could become a source of idol worship.

The dispute over the use of religious images (icons) raged throughout the eighth and ninth centuries. Art representing Christ or the saints was constantly opposed by the iconoclasts. However, despite their efforts, the use of icons steadily grew in the Church, especially in the eastern Roman Empire.

In 726 A.D., the Byzantine Emperor Leo III took a public stand against icons, and in 730 A.D. they were officially barred from the Church. This decision remained law until it was repealed in 787 A.D., and the use of images was once again restored. A new group of Christian leadership was to follow Pope Gregory's beliefs about the importance of art within the Church, and promoted an even broader view of acceptance. To them, these images were not just useful, but holy. Art supporters believed that if God, in His mercy, could reveal Himself to mortal eyes in the human nature of Jesus, He could also reveal Himself through artwork and other physical images. Thus, artwork within the confines of the Church flourished anew.

When the iconoclasts were finally suppressed, the Church officially declared that the physical representation of Jesus Christ and the saints in art was important for the edification of the congregation. With this approval, art was embraced even more by the Church, achieving greater heights. Nevertheless, the argument about placing artwork within the church continues to this day.

Danielle Nobles Age 8 1/2
Charleston, South Carolina

194

The Romanesque Period

"St. Matthew" (800 A.D.)
Benjamin Iocco Age 12 Freeport, Michigan

On Christmas day in the year 800 A.D., the Christian Emperor, Charlemagne (shar-la-main), received the crown of the Roman Empire. After conquering many of the barbarian hordes and leading them to Christ, his desire was to once again restore the ancient walls of the Roman Empire. Charlemagne was a man of learning and great aspirations. He purposed to bring back the glory of the ancients both in the arts and the academics. He encouraged the monasteries to broaden their interest in classical learning, returning to the times of the classic Greek and Roman civilizations. This new era would come to be known as the *Romanesque Period*, and lasted for approximately two hundred years.

During this time, the people lived under the feudal system and were subjects of powerful lords who ruled over them and protected them from invaders. The Church continued to become more powerful in influencing the people. Hence, the Church became a center for the fine arts, spreading its ideas and influence across Europe and the Mediterranean.

Like Byzantine art, the Romanesque style followed rigid guidelines, but instead of using wall paintings and mosaics to tell the gospel, artists now used sculpture. Human figures were used to portray Christ and His followers. Like the Byzantine style, the hands were long and the faces were devoid of any emotion or expression. These stone figures were intended to show the sacredness of the spiritual kingdom instead of real life. While Byzantine art had prominent places upon the walls of the churches, the artwork during the Romanesque period filled in areas of blank spaces with heavy sculpted figures from the Bible. These somber stone figures lined the interiors of churches in rigid rows and were rather abstract in appearance.

Patrick Bennett Age 11 Troutville, Va.

Many symbols in Christian art were imported from other countries and religions. The eagle, which would become a Christian symbol, was actually duplicated from Syria, as was the image of Jesus with a beard. Roman patterns were used to create interesting designs and geometric shapes such as squares, triangles, and circles. Romanesque art would become, more or less, a hodge-podge of many different cultures from many different eras. Christian artists during the ninth and tenth centuries did not consider themselves artists in the same sense as artists do today. They perceived themselves as simply fulfilling their service to God to edify the body of Christ.

Wall painting/synagogue at Dura - Europa, Syria
copied by Gregory Iocco Age 14 Freeport, Michigan

The architectural design and structure of the Church took on new proportions during the Romanesque Period, created for the sole purpose of worship. The massive buildings were designed with thick, heavy stone walls making the interiors dark and dank. With only slithers of light entering through the small windows, worship became a rather somber experience.

"Jesus Turning the Water into Wine"
Bruno Sielaff Age 10 Dauphin, Pennsylvania

Charlemagne's vision of returning to the ways of the ancient classics was short-lived. Upon his death, many of his heirs fought for power, and the once-mighty Empire was divided. The one thing that did remain was his influence on art, and the Romanesque style prevailed until the 11th century. In the turmoil after his death, art managed to sink to an all-time low for a brief period, but was revitalized during the *Crusades*, or Holy Wars. These wars were fought against the Muslims in 3the Holy Land, or Palestine. During this time, there was great mobility as thousands of Christians went on pilgrimages to Jerusalem and other sacred locations. This widespread travel would lead to many changes.

"Truly the light is sweet, and it is pleasant for the eyes to behold the sun." Eccl. 11:7

The Gothic Period

During the 11th and 12th centuries, the artwork of northern Europe and the Byzantine style began to merge. As their styles influenced each other, a new approach and purpose for Christian art was created. With the Romanesque Period fading away, the large, stone Romanesque churches were replaced by another style of architecture. The new era came to be known as the *Gothic Period*. Whereas, Romanesque architecture resembled fortresses with their massive walls of stone, vaults and towers, this new Gothic-style of architecture seemed more sublime, light, and heavenly. In the face of this fresh, new approach, the old style seemed clumsy and obsolete.

To many of us, *Gothic* signifies the large cathedrals with towering spires, like the Cathedral of Notre Dame in Paris. This new style originated in France and quickly began to spread throughout Europe during the middle of the 12th century, lasting until the end of the 14th century. The Gothic Period brought about another intellectual awakening, similar in purpose to the ancient Greek and Romanesque philosophies. Once again there would be an emphasis on man's improvement through such pursuits as Latin, astronomy and mathematics.

"Gothic Cathedral"
drawing by Gregory Iocco Age 14
Freeport, Michigan

The Gothic Period was accented by the splendid churches which were being built with greater and greater proportions. The Church became a place where one could meet God; a place of reverence and holiness, much like the Holy Temple in Jerusalem. New churches rose in many towns and villages, proclaiming that the Dark Ages were officially over. Each church grew larger in size and splendor than the one before it, as the congregations stood in awe saying, *"Surely the Lord is in this place."*

European cathedrals became spacious houses of God with spirals that soared to the heavens! Along with these new, grandiose designs came the innovation of the *flying buttresses*. Flying buttresses were simply winged supports to hold the new, tall churches in place. The interiors had high ceilings with long, vertical walls that represented the omnipresence of God in Heaven. Where the old, stone churches of the Romanesque Period were dark and dank, large stained glass windows now radiated a wonderful, colorful light. The impression they gave was of a magnificent splendor which Ecclesiastes 11:7 exemplifies, *"Truly the light is sweet, and it is pleasant for the eyes to behold the sun."*

Much pride went into building these churches, some of which took centuries to complete. As a result, 13th century Europe became renown for its great cathedrals, spiritual revitalization, and a renewed appreciation for the arts. The Gothic Period would be a forerunner to the *Renaissance*, the great revival in the fine arts of the 14th and 15th centuries.

The Gothic Period witnessed a great rise in artistic appreciation as merchants began to prosper and support the arts. Yet, there was no formal education in the arts at this time. Instead, *guilds* were created for the artisans. These guilds were like unions - they promoted and protected the trade and services of the artists or craftsman in each specific guild.

Even sculpture went through a revival during the Gothic Period. As in the past, most of the sculpted figures were of biblical figures. Like Gothic architecture, Gothic sculpture seemed light and weightless when compared with the heaviness of the more solid and somber Romanesque figures. The carved stone figures of the Gothic Period seemed to have vitality and their own personalities. The bases of the large columns within the churches became ideal places to situate carved figures of Christ and His disciples as reminders of the truth of the gospel for all those who entered. Like Pope Gregory the Great in the sixth century, the Church believed that artistic renderings of biblical stories would encourage those in the congregation who could not read.

Lesson #116: *Drawing Drapery*

The Gothic Period brought forth a new desire to regain a classical approach to art. For example, sculptors wanted to understand the ancient formula for portraying draped bodies realistically. Among other things, artists were concerned with making drapery look as if it went around the body, showing the form underneath. For this assignment, find a doll or statue that shows folds in the clothing going around the body and draw it in figure box (B). When drawing clothing or drapery, it is good to draw the folds like curved rolls. Have a light source and show three different values: a light value, a medium value and a dark value (A). Start by drawing lightly with your yellow colored pencil and then darken with your black and brown pencils.

A.

B.

The Gothic Period was the last phase of art to come out of the Middle Ages. No longer was Christian art simply meant to be symbolic and spiritual. Artists were now more concerned with conveying the message of the gospel in a realistic manner. This new approach would influence the purpose and direction of art during the Renaissance.

Whereas, the Romanesque Period portrayed the saints as rigid and expressionless, the Gothic Period strived to show the human side of Jesus and His disciples. Jesus is portrayed with tenderness, and Mary is depicted as young, full of life and smiling with a spiritual glow. Likewise, the calm expressions of the disciples seems to convey their peace with the world.

Remember, the artists during the Gothic Period were mainly preoccupied with the building of churches and sculpting characters from the Bible. Though painting played a significant role with the ancient Greeks and Romans, the painters of this era were usually given the secondary task of illuminating manuscripts. Just as colorful mosaics became the dominant form of art during the Byzantine Period, sculpture and architecture dominated throughout the Romanesque and Gothic Periods. Painting would not come into its own until the 14th century during the Renaissance.

"Cathedral of Notre Dame" by Gregory Iocco

The 13th century, which was the height of the Gothic Period, has been claimed by many religious scholars to be the greatest of all centuries. It was a time when men were bound together by the same faith and philosophy. There was only one Church, one form of worship, one system of education, one approach to art and beauty, and one code for law and order. Most of the artists even had one job - creating inspiring cathedrals.

Ironically, the term *Gothic* was given to this period by the great Renaissance artist Raphael in the 1500s. He believed that the artwork, architecture and sculpture produced during the 12th and 13th centuries was strongly influenced by the barbarian tribe of Goths. In actuality, the Goths had rampaged Europe nearly 700 years before the Gothic Period and had very little influence on its style.

Raphael, like most Italians, believed that art had flourished during the times of ancient Greece and Rome; a time that man was truly enlightened both in the arts and academics and a classical approach to life. Raphael reasoned that much of the classical style of art and enlightened ideas had been destroyed during the Dark Ages. Hence, many Italians yearned to return to the ways of the ancient Greeks and Romans and revive the past.

In summary, the Middle Ages produced many different styles of art. It contained early Christian art, the Byzantine period, the Dark Ages, and the Romanesque and Gothic Periods. Despite the various styles of art, one thing remained steadfast - the focus was on the Christian faith and illustrating the Gospel. During these centuries, the Church raised the banner of Christ with Christian artists defining art as pure and simple, and striving to edify the body of believers.

"How lonely sits the city that was full of people! How like a widow is she, who was great among the nations! The princess among the provinces has become a slave! She weeps bitterly in the night, her tears are on her cheeks; among all her lovers she has none to comfort her. All her friends have dealt treacherously with her. They have become her enemies."

Lamentations 1:1-2

The Fall of Constantinople 1453

The city of Constantinople, nestled in the easternmost corner of Europe on the Bosporus Sea, was relatively cut off from the rest of the Christian world. It was also only a stone's throw away from Asia and the powerful Ottoman Empire. Constantinople served as a launching pad for many of the Crusades which had poured in from all over Europe. It had successfully defended itself and the Christian faith against barbarian and Muslim armies, and had become a symbol of hope for the rest of the Christian world. Constantinople's downfall would be a momentous and sad event in the history of Western civilization.

After ten centuries of prevailing against invading enemies, the once mighty Byzantine Empire was finally vanquished by Mohammed II and his Muslim army in 1453. When the walls of the city were breached, many of its citizens fled to the security of St. Sophia, a magnificent church filled with the artistic splendor of the Byzantine Period.

"Tree of Jesse" stained glass window
Chartres Cathedral (1270 A.D.)
copied by Benjamin Iocco Age 12
Freeport, Michigan

Earlier, a false teacher prophesied that the city would be entered by the Muslim nation, but that the citizens would be safe in the confines of this magnificent church. The prophet stated that God would send a warring angel to fend off the heathens, much like He had done to Sennacherib, King of Assyria when he approached the walls of Jerusalem. Unfortunately, this did not happen. The doors of the church were smashed in, its disillusioned inhabitants taken into slavery, and all the beautiful artwork was destroyed.

After conquering Constantinople, the Muslims converted all of the Christian churches into mosques and renamed the city, *Istanbul.* Though most of the city's glorious artwork was systematically eradicated, Byzantine art would continue to be a wonderful inspiration to the Christian faith, and its style is still flourishing in Greek and Russian orthodox churches.

> *"You also, as living stones, are being built up a spiritual house."* — 1 Peter 2:5

The Church - *A Spiritual Building*

Since the Church is such a major part of Christian art, let's review its growth and purposes. The Middle Ages would give birth to wonderful church architecture that would produce many various styles during the next thousand years. The Church would gradually evolve from the underground burial places in Rome to the magnificent stone cathedrals of the Gothic Period.

Yet, the Bible tells us that the *Church* is really a spiritual building made with a *spiritual head*. This universal Church includes the entire body of Christ, and its head is Jesus Christ. However, the physical church made with stone and mortar has two purposes: to *edify* the body of believers and to *evangelize* the gospel. In the early days, Christians did not have buildings in which to worship, but simply went from house to house and broke bread together. It would be several hundred years after the resurrection of Christ that the Church actually became a physical building and a focal point for worship. As this physical church continued to grow, it would become a museum of Christian art promoting the gospel through visual means.

Architecture - *The Birth of the Church*

Like painting and sculpting, architecture is a form of art, although it is not considered part of the fine arts nor affiliated with music, dance or literature. Yet, architecture is an enriching and essential part of the arts. The term *architecture* means *the art of designing buildings*. The purpose of architecture is to merge the *function* of a building with its *purpose*, meaning that a building should not only be beautiful but practical.

During the Middle Ages, the Church would be the main protector of the fine arts. Even as barbarians devastated European civilization, it remained steadfast in its protection and promotion of the arts. The Church's purpose was to glorify God by leading man to salvation through the design of its buildings and the artwork housed within them.

The Church was also devoted to faith and worship. It was built during a time when people considered beauty and art to be servants of truth. Nothing in the art of the church existed for its own sake, but only to transmit the saving knowledge of Christ, without whom all beauty is meaningless. The images that adorned the walls were to be a reminder of the timeless Christian message throughout the ages.

"Church Spire"
Benjamin Iocco Age 12
Freeport, Michigan

"So continuing daily with one accord in the temple, and breaking bread from house to house..."

Acts 2:46

Going from House to House - *The Breaking of Bread*

The church is a wonderful building for architectural study. The word *church* is derived from the Greek word *ekklesia* (meaning *a gathering of people*). The term was first given to the Jewish people of Old Testament times for their religious gatherings. These were held in places called *domus ecclesiae* which is also Greek for *meeting house.*

"The Infant Jesus" Annie Kate Sahlie
Age 8 Wilmington, N.C.

The Synagogue

Thus, the synagogue was actually the first *church*, or place of meeting. It had its beginning in Babylon with exiled Jews who needed a place to worship after being removed from the Holy Land. The term *synagogue* means to assemble, and also, the house of learning. With the gospel spreading, many Hellenist Jews converted to Christianity. They continued to congregate in their synagogues, but now came to worship Christ.

Although the Jewish faith did little to nurture the creative arts, the synagogues began to serve as galleries for early Christian art. With the synagogue becoming the church, or *meeting place*, for some of the early Christians, many would eventually become filled with paintings and altarpieces of Jesus Christ and the gospel.

The Basilica

The term *basilica* (meaning royal room) is of Greek origin both in name and design, but it was the Romans who really put this building to good use. In early architecture, a basilica was a large building used for a number of functions, like a courthouse, marketplace, or town meeting hall. The outside of the structure was simple in design and plain in appearance.

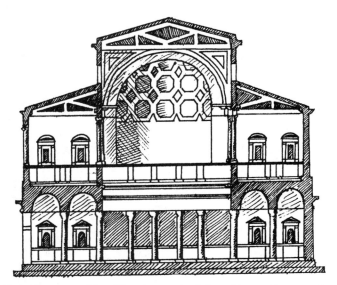

As time passed, the basilicas took on a more specific structure. They became rectangular in design and featured a long corridor, or hallway, that extended from one end to the other. They were also built with aisles on both sides and a raised platform, much like a stage, in the front and the rear of the building. Eventually the raised platform would become where the leading authority would be seated. It was during the first centuries after Christ that Christians began using these structures as their meeting places, and the new churches would follow this design.

"A Roman Basilica" copied by Greg Iocco Age 14 Freeport, Michigan

The Dome

Although the Greeks and Romans were aware of the dome as an artistic structure, it was the artists of the Byzantine Period who actually adopted the style. Since Constantinople was situated next to the Far East, the art and architecture of the Byzantine Period came under Oriental and Muslim influence, and served as models for the majority of the churches which Constantine built.

The *dome,* a larger hemispherical roof or ceiling, was given different names and purposes by various religions. It was called the *cosmic egg* and *heavenly bow,* but most often symbolized the dome of Heaven. The dome has also been identified with the Syrian tent, which was represented in many early ceiling paintings. As time passed, both tradition and symbolism from the East would establish the dome as an important feature of Church architecture during the Byzantine Period.

Sixteenth Century woodcut

The Christian Church in Constantinople became a spiritual building which strived to instill a sense of the sacred. Romans and other artisans were called on to fill the interior of these new churches with artwork that would exemplify the teachings of the gospel and stories from the Bible. Beautiful and colorful mosaics radiated from within the confines as the preacher would often point to these pictures to help him explain the *greatest story ever told*. Although all of the churches built by Constantine have been destroyed, other churches of this era marked with a similar style and design have survived the passage of time and give us an example of this type of architecture.

"St. Pierre Church"
Benjamin Iocco Age 12
Freeport, Michigan

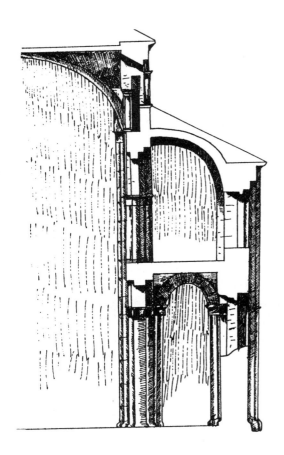

"...the place where you stand is holy ground."

Exodus 3:5

....

Although the Gothic style of architecture was used for town halls and municipal buildings in the southern countries near Holland and Germany, its main purpose was for the church. Each church had a *diocese,* or territorial jurisdiction, and the bishop had an official chair or throne called a *cathedra.* It was only logical, therefore, to call any important church a *cathedral,* or seat of a church authority.

In less than two hundred years (from the 11th to the 13th centuries), Europe had completely changed its approach to building churches. There were also many new Christian orders like the Franciscan monks who constructed churches on the outskirts of towns and villages. These new buildings became sites of creativity and inspiration, as artists would decorate the inside and design the outside of each new church or cathedral.

Nave and Aisle of Gothic Cathedral/St. Etienne, Caen
Gregory Iocco Age 14 Freeport, Michigan

....

The building of churches was a laborious process that took many years to complete. One reason is that they had to wait for good weather to do their work. Secondly, the heavy stones used in construction were brought from quarries by horse and mule - the only means of transportation.

The townspeople participated in the building of churches with all their hearts and souls. One abbot commented in 1115 A.D., *"Who has ever seen the like? Princes, powerful and wealthy, proud and beautiful women, bent their necks to the yoke of carts which carried the stones, wood, wine, oil and lime - everything necessary for the building and the men working at it. One saw as many as one thousand people, of both sexes, drawing wagons, pressing forward in the emotion which filled their hearts. Nothing could stop or delay them - and from dawn to dusk the sound of hymns arose."*

Gothic Cathedral Benjamin Iocco Age 12 Freeport, Michigan

What a beautiful time it must have been! There probably had never been a more glorious time in the history of Christianity except when Jesus walked the earth. Christianity spread like a sweet fragrance across all of Europe and the body of Christ seemed to dwell in perfect harmony. It must have been music to God's ear.

"The Lord was like an enemy, He has swallowed up Israel, He has swallowed up all her palaces; He has destroyed her strongholds, and has increased mourning and lamentation in the daughter of Judah."

Lamentations 2:5

Victor Hugo, the great French writer of the 18th century, would also commend the atmosphere that surrounded the body of Christ and the building of these marvelous stone churches during the Gothic Period, *"The spiritual history of the Middle Ages was written in the stones of the cathedrals -in the statues designed to clothe the idea of Christianity in forms which all could appreciate and to instruct the faithful in great truths. To enter the cathedral was to experience a great uplifting, like the partaking of a sacrament. The cathedral was a place of religious light colored by the stained windows; it was the symbol of faith and love, and within it the worshipers felt the mystical union with the body of Christ and the mingling of soul with soul."*

The End of a Glorious Era

Throughout the centuries, there had been many wars between the Muslim and Christian faiths. These Holy Wars would have a profound effect on Europe and much of the Middle East. Before the 11th century, Muslims had overrun the Holy Land and controlled most of the shrines in the Near East that were sacred to Christians. Then, in 1095 A.D., the French-born Pope Urban II delivered a monumental and emotional speech to the Christian Church. The crowd that came to hear him was so large that he had to address them in an open field. He urged both his countrymen and those of the Christian faith to take up arms against the infidels who were desecrating the holy places, and assured his listeners that this *holy war* would win those who participated a reward in Heaven and on earth. Thus began the first of a series of Crusades which continued for several centuries - one of the longest wars in the history of mankind. Vast armies of Christians sailed their ships to the Holy Land and fought against the Muslims in the name of God and for His glory. The First Crusade was led by Peter the Hermit, a simple man who rode bareheaded and barefoot on a small donkey at the head of a straggling mass of sinners, fighting to reclaim the Holy Land and to make restitution in God's eyes.

"Christ Calming the Storm" Brian Reddish Age 13 Awendaw, S.C.

205

Summary

In summary, as Christianity grew throughout the centuries of the Middle Ages, many of the new eras desired a return to the ways of the ancient Greeks and Romans. In the ninth century, Charlemagne called for a return to this classical approach which, in turn, inspired the Gothic artists, especially the sculptors, who began to sculpt the human form realistically in draped clothing. However, the era that would truly bring about a great *rebirth* in the arts and sciences (known as the Renaissance) was still to come.

The Middle Ages consisted of many various periods and styles of art. For example, the Byzantine Period lasted as long as the Middle Ages, but was a style and period confined to a certain location. Even though Byzantine art influenced churches as far away as Russia, its artists remained in and around the city of Constantinople. Other periods during this time were the Dark Ages, when illuminated manuscripts were created by monks in Ireland and France; the Romanesque Period, marked by the return to the classical approach in learning and the arts; and the Gothic Period with its grandiose cathedrals. Finally, there was Medieval art (with castles, kings and lords) which contributed with its colorful, narrative tapestries.

So the Middle Ages was more than a bridge that spanned the gap between the classical era of the Greeks and Romans and the new era of the Renaissance. It was a period, despite all its trials and tribulations, when Christ was glorified and everything focused around the Church and its faith in God. The Middle Ages was also a time when the Church became a gallery of simple and pure Christian artwork. If it is to be considered simply a bridge that connected more glorious times in the history of man, then it is certainly a splendid bridge indeed.

"Bayeaux Tapestry" copied by Todd Leasure

The Middle Ages

Early Christian	wall paintings
Byzantine	colorful mosaics
Romanesque	sculpted figures
Gothic	large churches
Dark Ages	manuscripts
Medieval Art	tapestries

206

Lesson #117: Examination #IV

I. Complete the sentence with the correct term: 3 pts. each.
   (Answers appear on last page of *God & the History of Art I.*)

1. The Middle Ages begin in the _____ century.
2. Colorful, cut pieces of glass used in mosaics were called _____.
3. The _____ Period was started by Charlemagne in the ninth century.
4. During the Gothic Period, a bishop's chair was called a _____.
5. A series of holy wars between the Christians and the Muslims was called the _____.
6. A type of woven art used to adorn castles is called _____.
7. _____ art is a form of storytelling.
8. The architecture of the _____ Period was light, sublime and heavenly.
9. The period when barbarians ravaged Europe was called the _____ _____.
10. The religious leader and patron of the arts in the sixth century was _____.
11. Jewish students who excelled in _____ became known as scribes.
12. Romans loved entertainment in open air arenas called _____.
13. _____ _____ were miniature paintings with bright colors.
14. _____ were image smashers.
15. The Roman _____ was the first building used by Christians as a church.

II. True or False. Place a "T" or "F" next to each statement: 2 points each.

_____ 1. Diaspora is a term for the Jews who remained in Palestine during Roman rule.
_____ 2. Rabbi means "teacher."
_____ 3. An aesthetic building is more practical than beautiful.
_____ 4. In Christian art, blue symbolized sorrow.
_____ 5. Early Christian art served to evangelize the message of the gospel through art.

III. Matching: Match the symbol with its meaning by placing the correct letter next to the term it represents: 3 points each.

1. Rainbow
2. Skull
3. The Boat
4. Flowers & Fruit
5. Sun
6. Moon
7. IXOYE
8. The Lily
9. Rock
10. Dove
11. Halo
12. Palm
13. Lamb
14. Serpent
15. the Cross

a. life giving force, symbolizes Jesus
b. symbol of union and God's forgiveness
c. symbolizes the Church
d. the firmness and strength of God
e. passage of time and life
f. cycle of life, death, and resurrection
g. the attribute of sanctity
h. reminder of death and that life is perishable
i. Greek word for fish; symbol for Christ in Christian art;
   initials stand for *Jesus Christ, Son of God, Savior*
j. purity of Christ
k. Christ and His sacrifices
l. peace
m. satan
n. the righteous man
o. emblem of Christ and salvation

Student Art Gallery

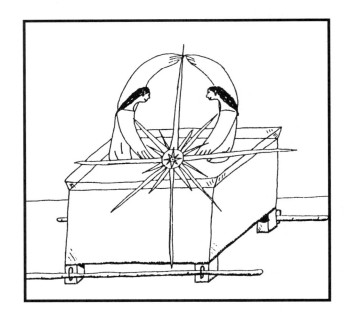

"Jesus & His Disciples"
by Hanah Kisner Age 7
Grafton, West Virginia

Ryan Thomspson Age 13
Stafford, Virginia

"Jesus Feeding the Thousands"
Sarah Marchmont Age 9
La Grange, Illinois

"Psalm 23"
Julie Dunham Age 15
Statham, Georgia

The Renaissance

"Madonna & Child" copy by Todd Leasure

··

The Early Renaissance

The Renaissance actually started with a small group of Christian men who wanted to bring glory to God. Such men were Dante, the classical writer; Cimabue, the great painter; and Giotto, the renowned sculptor and painter. Unfortunately, as time passed and philosophy changed, the Renaissance began to strive more for a perfection in art through a humanistic approach (glorifying man instead of glorifying God). In the beginning the changes were gradual. During the first half of the 14th century, the style of art was still simple as artists continued to strive for symbolism instead of realism. Like earlier Christian art, many of the human figures were still out of proportion, being rather long and thin, and most of the poses were stiff and statuesque. The first real change came early in the 1300s by the hand of the Italian painter Giotto (gee-ah-toe), who wanted to make his pictures more realistic. From then on, especially in the latter part of the 14th century, many artists would follow his example. Thus the art which began to fill the churches slowly started to change both in purpose and style.

The term *Renaissance* means rebirth, and refers to the period from 1400 to 1600 A.D. During this time, there was a great revival in the arts, mainly in Italy, as the spirit of adventure was taking hold of the art world. Once again the Italians believed that true art originated from ancient Greece and Rome and desired to imitate that style of artistic perfection. With this new attitude came the dismissal of old beliefs. Gone was their appreciation for the wonderful works of the Byzantine, Romanesque and Gothic Periods, which were now looked upon as primitive. Sadly, much of what had been accomplished in art throughout the past centuries was laid aside to make room for new ideas in architecture, painting and sculpture, along with the academics and sciences.

The Roman Catholic church was also changing. The seat of the papacy was now located in Rome, the heart of Italy. Many years before, in the sixth century, Pope Gregory had proclaimed that the purpose of art within the Church was to evangelize those in the congregation who were illiterate. During the Romanesque and Gothic Periods, Church art expanded its message to include frightful images of hell and damnation. This often resulted in the rejection of the gospel. However, as the Renaissance blossomed, the Church desired to show the gospel in a more spectacular way. Church buildings became magnificent and grandiose religious museums. Wall paintings were larger and sculpture bordered on the sensational. It was as if there were a contest to see who could build the most beautiful church and adorn it with the greatest artwork. The Church paid large sums to have these religious masterpieces created. It was a time of great production as *botteglias* were everywhere. These workshops of master artists were a place where young students, or *apprentices*, could learn the many secrets and techniques of the profession. Everyone seemed to have a guild from leatherworkers to goldsmiths, wood-carvers, barbers and metalworkers.

Through all the changes, the Roman Catholic church continued to be a dominant factor in everyday life as well as a major influence in the arts. Yet, as people prospered and became more independent, the Church's spiritual hold on the community began to weaken. Man began to break away from the authority of the Church and question not only his relationship with God, but also his quest for a better life. This was the reoccurring influence of humanism upon society. As the Italians dug up the artwork of the ancients, they also excavated the philosophy of the Greeks, which stated that man was the center of the universe. So as many artists of this era continued to create for the Church and the glory of God, others began to use ancient mythological figures as subject matter to fill their canvases.

A.

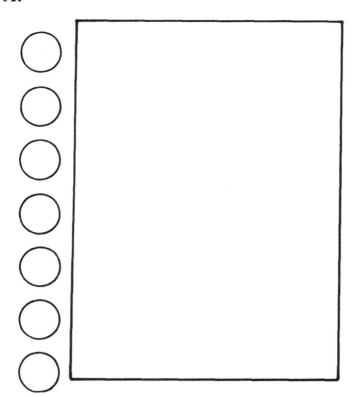

For this assignment, select *Saint Luke* (Constantinople, 1133) from your *picture postcard gallery* and place it in front of you. Notice how elongated the figure is and that the head seems rather small in proportion to the rest of the body. Notice also that the figure is rather *flat*, with little form or dimension, and the colors are basic and simple. Before the Renaissance, artists used a few select colors in their paintings that were intended to be symbolic, and chose not to express any *form* of the figure underneath the folds of the robe. Notice the face of Saint Luke lacks expression and seems to be meditating on spiritual matters as he ponders the Scriptures. Observe the swooping curves in the figure. Remember, Byzantine art was greatly influenced by the artwork of the Orient. Whereas the art of Western civilization was rigid, the artwork of the Orient was filled with curves.

Write your feelings about the picture of *St. Luke* below. Do you like it? Why? What about the colors? Does St. Luke look realistic? What do you think he is thinking about? When you are finished, draw the picture in the figure box (A) and color it with your colored pencils. Start by drawing lightly with either your yellow or orange colored pencil. Mix your colors in the circles on the side of the picture before using them. Can you mix a nice color for his flesh? What about mixing colors for the blue/green robe and gold background?

_____
_____
_____
_____
_____
_____
_____

During the Middle Ages, *serfs*, or peasants, maintained a certain loyalty toward their king and feudal lords. However, the feudal system was about to change drastically during the Renaissance. Villages, towns and cities began to prosper and business merchants became increasingly more influential than dukes and barons. Likewise, where the artist of the Middle Ages was basically a traveler going from job to job as cathedrals were being constructed, now artists were becoming more stable and centralized through *guilds* and commissions from the local community.

In order to be admitted to a guild, the artist had to show he was able to reach the standards needed to becomes a master of his craft. Guilds watched over the interests of their members, making sure they had work, and making it difficult for any foreign artists to gain employment or to settle among them. Only the most famous artists could break through this strong monopoly and travel freely from place to place to do artwork. As a result of this conglomeration of trades, even the roving minstrel of the arts during the Gothic Period vanished.

Florence - A New Athens

Italy, like Athens centuries before, was broken up into many individual, self-governing cities during the Renaissance. The most prominent of which were Pisa, Siena, Luca and Florence. With time, Florence would rise to be more majestic and powerful than all the others. In 1252, the Florentines began to mint their own coins, called *florins*, which became Europe's most dependable source of currency. By the end of the century, nearly 100,000 people lived in Florence, making it one of the largest cities in Europe.

For many years, powerful factions within Florence warred against each other. These factions were families that had grown to acquire much prosperity and power. To protect themselves the families built walled fortresses accompanied by towers much like those in castles. These would be used as a place of refuge and protection during times of trouble. Whenever one of these families was vanquished by another, the towers were demolished and others were built in their place.

"Florentine Tower"
by Gregory Iocco Age 14
Freeport, Michigan

"David & Goliath"
Ben Russell Age 9
Lenoir, North Carolina

212

Lesson #119:
Drawing Florentine Towers

A.

B.

For this lesson, draw the two towers (A & B) below (C & D). Start by drawing them lightly with one of your light colored drawing pencils. Keep your drawings small. Then, when everything is drawn in correctly, go over them with your black marker pen. Notice the shading in both. The shaded side of tower (A) is done with *cross-hatching* (criss-crossing lines that are placed closed together). The shaded side of the tower (B) is done with diagonal lines that give it a lighter value. Also, notice that some of the bricks are merely suggested - they are not drawn in completely. Finally, notice the dark value inside all the windows is done with cross-hatching.

"Florentine Towers"
copied by Gregory Iocco Age 14
Freeport, Michigan

C. Florentine Tower #1

D. Florentine Tower #2

213

Lesson #120: *Designing a Tower*

A.

B.

Renaissance artists were diverse, meaning they had the ability to excel in many different areas. For example, many painters were also architects and inventors. For this assignment, design and draw your own towers of fortification to the left and right (A & B). See if you can make them unique, yet sound enough to withstand an attack. Use a ruler to keep your lines straight and start your drawings lightly. Do you have a light source? Are you going to have a light and shaded side to your towers? Finally, color each tower with a bluish/gray or brownish/orange. Make these colors by mixing orange with brown and white, or mixing blue with black and white.

The Quattrocento

The Italians called this new era of the Renaissance the *Quattrocento* (meaning *1400 -* pertaining to the 15th century). And so, the Middle Ages was laid to rest and the pagan gods of the barbarians that had permeated Europe were seemingly buried. St. Francis had carried the gospel of Christ to the poor throughout towns and villages in Italy and people were once again free to live without the fear of invading armies. Commerce flourished, the Church and community prospered, and art was embraced with a deep reverence. Likewise, scholars were enthusiastically digging up the works of the ancient Greeks and Romans, and marveling over their creative skills and knowledge. With the *Quattrocento*, it was time to return to the ways of the ancients and hoist the flag of classicism once again. It was time for a real Renaissance to begin!

Although Renaissance artists desired to copy the style of the ancient Greeks, there was little artwork to study from as much of the artwork of antiquity had been lost or destroyed. Therefore, artists were forced to rely on replicas of Greek art done by the ancient Romans. No better praise could be placed upon an artist during the *Quattrocento* than that his work was *as good as the ancients.* It is not surprising that this fervent desire to reclaim the glory of the ancients would be a major goal of the Italian Renaissance since the Italians were very aware that, in the distant past, Rome had been the glory of the civilized world. In their minds, this revival would be a rebirth of the grandeur that defined Rome and Greece and part of their glorious inheritance.

Seth Hancock Age 9 Monroe, N.C

Lesson #121: *Creating a Triptych*

Around the year 900 A.D., an abbot of a newly founded monastery in Rabona, Italy carved an ivory relief from two panels. This two-sectioned panel was designed to tell a story from the Bible in two parts, called a *diptych*.

"Daniel in the Lion's Den"
Christy Ernesto Age 10 Wernersville, PA

"Shadrach, Meshach & Abednego"
Christine Zines Age 13 Chandler, AZ

Shortly after the innovation of the diptych, artists began to create narrative paintings in three sections, known as a *triptych*. Both techniques of showing a religious story in panels would become very popular during the Renaissance. In Lesson #36 you created a *diptych*. For this assignment, let's make a triptych. The borders, or frames, of your triptych are below (B). See if you can draw a narrative story from the Bible, showing part of the story in each section by illustrating three scenes from the life of Daniel. You may want to show Daniel praying before God; Shadrach, Meshach, and Abednego in the fire; Daniel in the lion's den, or any other scene you like. See how creative you can be. Sketch your ideas in the small frames first (A). Then, copy your best sketches in the opened areas of the large triptych (B) with a light pencil. Finally, go over your drawings with your black pen and color your pictures with colored pencils. Place nice designs like flowers or leaf patterns in your borders.

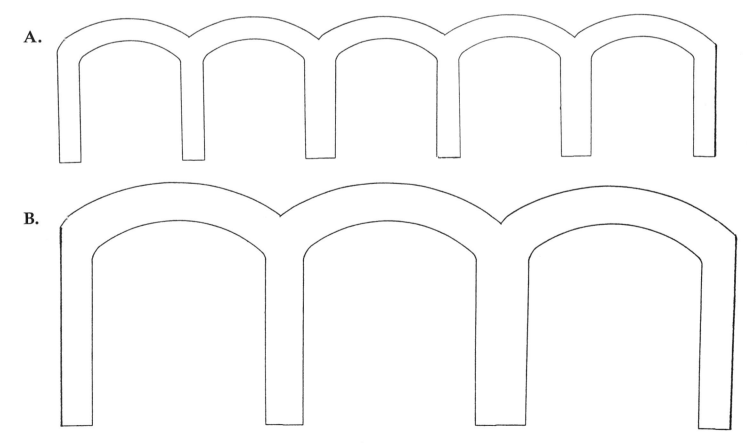

A.

B.

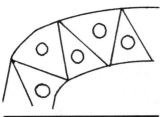

Lesson #122: *Painting a Diptych* B.

Place *Paint Card #VII* in front of you. For this assignment, we are going to draw and paint two scenes from the story of Ester in the panels to make a *diptych*. First, draw your two pictures lightly with your yellow colored pencil inside the curved frames on the bottom of the page .

Then, draw some creative designs or patterns in the picture frames as shown (A & B). Test the colors you mix with your colored pencils in the circles below before you put them in your diptych. When you are finished, draw and paint your pictures on the paint card.

As you learned earlier, it is always good to start with your larger brushes and to paint the background first, working your way forward. Most of the time, your background should be light with very little detail. With acrylic paints, you can paint over an area after it has dried. This is good if you want to paint over another color or if you make a mistake. Details in paintings are saved for last. After the paint has dried, you may want to redraw the details in using a fine brush or a fine black pen.

"Queen Esther" Esther Stoneypher
Age 6 Orlando, Florida

Before beginning, practice painting details on the faces above the two frames on your paint card. To make a flesh tone, mix yellow and red together to make orange. Then, add a speck of orange to white to make a very light skin color. Paint each face making sure sure you can still see the details underneath. You can do this by adding a drop of water to make a thinner layer of paint. Next, add a light violet to the shaded areas to create *form* for the facial features, like the nose. When your paint is dry, you may want to redraw the facial features with a pencil. Then, using your finest brush, put in the details. Try not to use black for details, but instead use colors that are softer and lighter, like brown or violet. Finally, paint your two scenes from the story of Esther in the diptych on the bottom of the paint card.

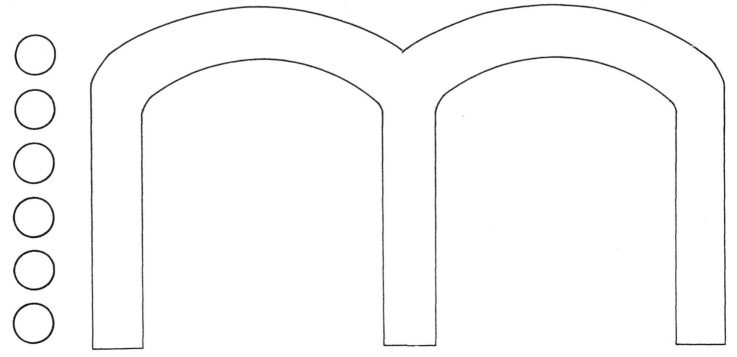

Lesson #123: *Touring the Picture Gallery*

For this assignment, place *The Farewell of Telemachus* by Jacques Louis David, along with *Saint Luke* in front of you. Even though Jacques Louis David was from France and born nearly 400 years after the beginning of the Renaissance, he gives you a good example of classical artwork that sought perfection. Much of the time, this classical style glorified mythology which also originated in ancient Greece. Mythological stories from centuries past would be excavated and become a major source of inspiration for many Italian artists, opening new avenues of creativity and passion.

The two *picture postcards* in front of you will give you an idea of the two main purposes for art during the Renaissance. The Church was still commissioning artists to glorify God. *Saint Luke* signifies the spiritual approach used to encourage members of the congregation with a simple, godly message. However, look at the contrast between this and the mythological painting, *The Farewell of Telemachus*. Granted, the latter painting is beautiful, perfect and very realistic. *The Farewell of Telemachus* seems to have an appeal that draws you in and is somewhat provocative, alluring and even romantic.

It's rather ironic that Jesus was a man of no reputation. His appearance had *"no form or comeliness; and when we see Him, there is no beauty that we should desire Him"* (Isaiah 53:2). Yet the world is quite the opposite with all its charm, attraction and allure. This contrast, between Christ and the world, is evident here with the simplicity of *Saint Luke* versus the beauty of *The Farewell of Telemachus*. Greek mythology comes in a subtle guise that can lead one away from the simplicity of a spiritual life. Study the two pictures and write what you think of each below. Is there anything else you notice about how the two contrast each other? Finally, write what you believe the purpose of art should be.

_____

_____

_____

_____

_____

_____

_____

Florence was the center of the Renaissance. Along with Athens, the jewel-city of the past, it became a nurturing place for aspiring artists and creative minds. The inhabitants of Florence were proud and prosperous. They were also capable of extreme good and evil, as most were absorbed in making money. Florence had powerful families that ruled and governed over the city. These families dominated with their great wealth. The *Medici* family was one of the most powerful and influential families in Florence, and would also rise to be great patrons of the arts.

"It is good for a man that he bear the yoke in his youth.   Lamentations: 3:27

....

During the 14th and 15th centuries, artists began to receive recognition for their profession. The names of the great Renaissance artists are known because of their reputation and through the signing of their works. As mentioned, before this time, artists were more or less like other workers - farmers, builders, bakers and so on. Art was simply a job, and they went about their work like everyone else. Artists were considered tradesmen and did not think highly of themselves. Ancient Rome had imported its artists, many from Greece, who were nothing more than slave laborers. The early Christian artists were doing what they were called to do out of a duty or responsibility. During the Middle Ages, monks were called upon to preserve manuscripts out of a sense of commitment, and artists of the Gothic Period traveled to and fro as churches were constructed. With the advent of the Renaissance, artists started to receive acclaim, and this recognition brought a return to signing their work as the ancient Greek artists had done centuries before.

One of the main goals of the Renaissance masters was to strive for recognition and acceptance. Their preoccupation with social acceptability may be difficult to understand, but it has been a deep concern for artists throughout history. Aristotle, the great Greek philosopher, classified art thousands of years ago in the category of *manual arts*, labeling it as menial because artists worked with their hands. It was the ambition of great artists from the Renaissance, like Leonardo da Vinci and Michelangelo, to show that art went far beyond menial work.

With the defeat of Constantinople by the Turks in 1453, the center for art gradually shifted to Florence. The Italian culture grew and prospered in the 14th and 15th centuries as it continued to embrace and encourage the fine arts. The young apprentices worked and boarded in their master's house for years. Their only pay was learning the secrets of their craft. As mentioned, this type of school was called a *botteglia*. Florence had no art schools during this time and talented boys *apprenticed* under a recognized master in order to be thoroughly trained in their profession. Both the apprenticeship of young art students and the creation of masterful paintings grew to become an organized business as monumental statues and architectural renderings for new buildings were being created everywhere.

In the beginning of apprenticeship, students were no better than janitors cleaning up around the shop. Eventually, the students learned carpentry, metalwork, masonry, the grinding of colors and other artistic skills. Each day he was disciplined in drawing and the study of the human figure. If the young man showed promise as an artist, he was then chosen, often in his teens, as the master's assistant and given a small salary. Finally, when he developed his talents and satisfied the requirements of the examiners, he was admitted to the *Guild of St. Luke*. (Luke, who had been a disciple of Christ, was the patron saint of artists.) It is said that Luke had not only been a doctor, but also an artist. The guild issued the license of a professional master to those who graduated. The graduate would then be introduced to trade secrets in the preparation of paintings, the use of color, nature studies, portraits and anatomy, statue making, metalwork and perspective.

Story has it, when Leonardo da Vinci was a young apprentice in a botteglia, the master assigned him to paint the face of one of the angels on a large painting. Leonardo painted such a sweet and beautiful face that, when the master walked into the studio, he paused and commented, *I never want to touch paint again.* Eventually the master quit painting and invested his labors in architecture. Years later, da Vinci would comment that he believed every student should eventually be able to surpass his teacher in excellence.

Lesson #124: *Perspective - Showing Depth in a Picture*

Throughout the 1400s, Florence remained a prosperous and progressive city that promoted the fine arts. One of the most important innovations of the Florentines was the use of *perspective*. Perspective is a mechanical technique using a *horizon line* and *vanishing points* to create *depth* in a picture. Since drawings and paintings are on a flat surface, like paper or canvas, they are basically *two-dimensional* - long and wide, but not deep. Perspective is a way of making artwork on a flat surface seem more *three-dimensional.*

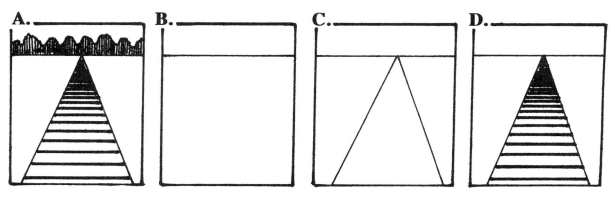

Let's start with some beginning exercises in drawing to create depth in your pictures, making them three-dimensional. The first exercise is to draw railroad tracks receding in the distance (A). The line where land meets sky is called the *horizon line* (B). Using your black colored pencil, draw a wide triangle with the peak going to the middle of the horizon line, however, do not draw a bottom line for your triangle (C). Next, draw the railroad tracks starting with the first one in the foreground, making your lines go straight across, or horizontally. As you draw the remainder of the railroad tracks going back in the distance, place them closer and closer together, creating the illusion of depth in your picture (D). A golden rule to remember is, as things recede in the distance, they become closer and closer together. Finally, draw distant trees on your horizon line by making different sized cloud shapes and coloring them with vertical green and blue lines, as shown in A. You can even add some violet and yellow if you like. Practice drawing the railroad tracks in B and C, and then draw your picture in the figure box below (F).

F. Railroad Tracks   G. Draw Wally the Worm

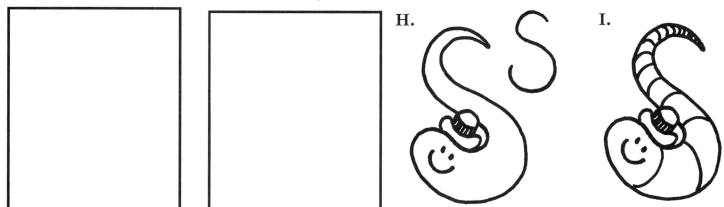

Now let's draw *Wally the Worm* in the figure box above (G), practicing *foreshortening.* Foreshortening means, *as things come forward, they become much larger; as they recede in the distance, they become smaller.* Take your red colored pencil and draw a large "S," making the bottom larger than the top. Then draw Wally's head and the front of his body fat, having it become thinner as it goes back into the distance, creating the illusion of depth (H). Finally, put stripes on his body, remembering two things: the stripes have to go *around* because his body is round, and secondly, as his body goes back in the distance the stripes must be closer together (I).

Lesson #125: *Foreground, Middleground, Background*

Another way to show depth in a two-dimensional picture is by drawing objects much smaller in the background and larger in the foreground. Objects in the background have very little color and no detail, whereas objects in the foreground have more detail and a lot of color. For this assignment, draw the picture below (A) in the figure box (B), and show depth by making the objects in the background smaller and objects in the foreground larger.

A.
Background

Middleground

Foreground

B.

Lesson #126: *One-Point Perspective*

You learned earlier that the *horizon line* (A) separates land or water from sky. However, the horizon line is also used in perspective to show where the *vanishing point* (B) is placed. The vanishing point is marked by an "X," and is where all the lines meet that go back into the distance.

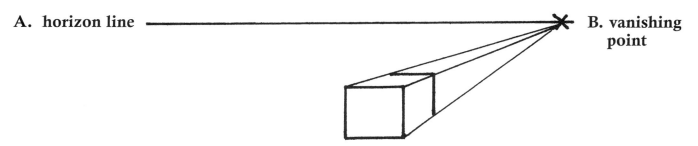

A. horizon line   B. vanishing point

To start, let's do a simple exercise with one-point perspective. In *one-point perspective*, all the lines recede to *one vanishing point* (B). Observe that three corners of the square have been connected to the vanishing point, or "X." Notice the horizon line below (C), and that the vanishing point is to the right of this line. To the left and beneath the horizon line is a square. Connect the three corners of the box to the vanishing point as illustrated above. It is always good to use a ruler to draw straight lines in perspective drawings. Whenever you use mechanical devices, such as a ruler, T-square or compass, it is called a *technical drawing*. Start your drawing using light guidelines until you have everything drawn in the way you like, and then darken your three-dimensional box with your black pencil.

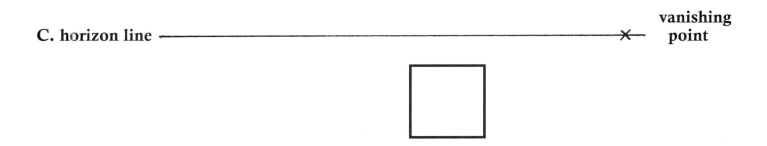

C. horizon line   vanishing point

Finally, on the bottom of this page (D), draw everything on your own as shown above (A). Start with a straight horizon line. Then, put your vanishing point to the right on this line, draw a square to the left and below your horizon line. Connect the corners and complete your three-dimensional box.

D. Draw Your Horizon Line Here

Lesson #127: *Vantage Point*

When using perspective, you can place objects anywhere on or below your horizon line. For example, you can draw a square to the left or to the right (A). This will give you a different *vantage point*, or position, from which you are viewing the objects. For the first part of this assignment, connect the two squares below to the vanishing point on the horizon line to make boxes with depth. (The line that is already drawn for you beneath the horizon line is for the back of the boxes.) After you connect the three corners of each square to the horizon line, draw the side of each box with a straight vertical line. Use your ruler and draw lightly, then darken your boxes with your black colored pencil.

A.

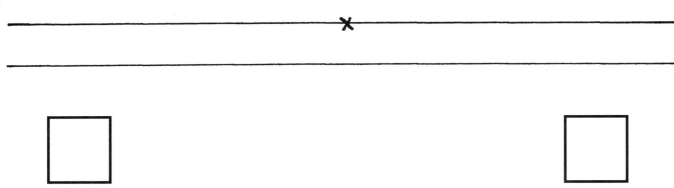

Where you are standing has a lot to do with your vantage point. For example, if you are standing to the left, you will see the left side of the object. If you are standing to the right, you will see the right side of the object. If you are standing directly in front, you will not see either side of the object (B).

B.

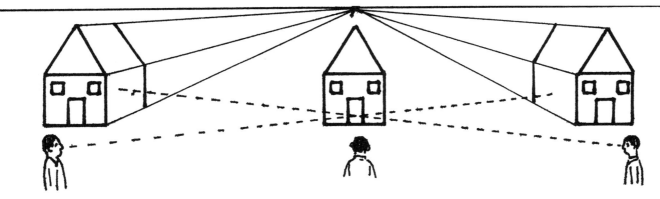

Draw a horizon line below (C), placing the vanishing point in the center. Then draw two squares beneath the horizon line, one to the far right and one to the far left as illustrated above (A). Connect the sides to the vanishing point and complete your drawings by making two three-dimensional boxes.

C. Draw Your Horizon Line Here

Lesson #128: *High or Low Vantage Point*

Another name for the horizon line is *eye-level*. Your eye-level is located at the same height as the horizon line. An easy way to remember where the eye-level would be is to draw a pair of eyes on the horizon line (A).

A. Horizon Line ——————— 👁 👁 ——————— **Eye Level**

If your eye-level is high, you will be looking down on the object (B). If your eye-level is low, you will be looking *up* at the object (E). For this assignment, complete the two boxes in the center below (C & D) by connecting the corners to the vanishing points: one looking down, and the other looking up.

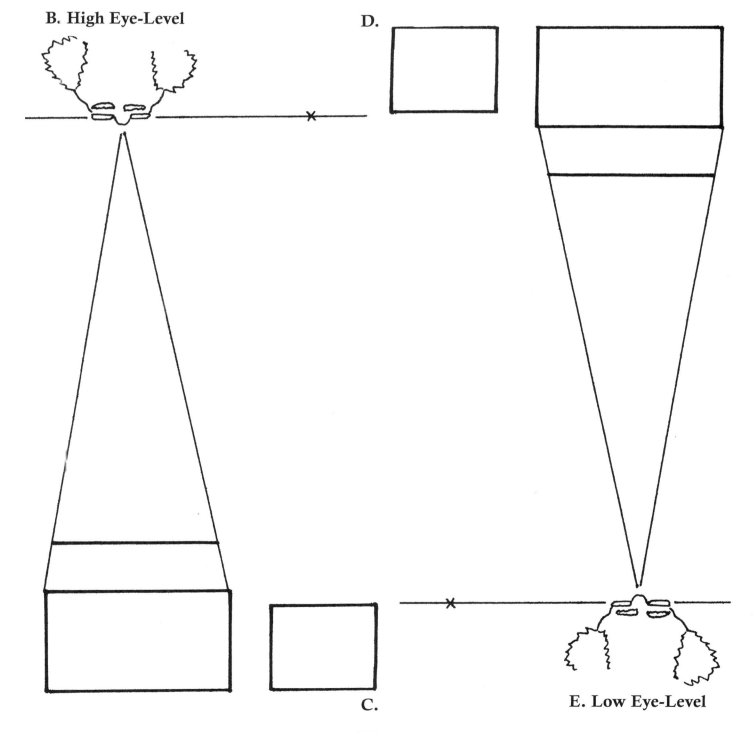

B. High Eye-Level

D.

C.

E. Low Eye-Level

Lesson #129: *People in Perspective*

There are many objects that can be drawn with perspective. For example, you can draw people, trees, telephone poles and railroad tracks. All you need to do is draw one person, tree or telephone pole in the *foreground* (closest to you), and then draw light guidelines from the top and bottom to the vanishing point (A). You can then draw two light horizontal lines going across your picture to show you the correct size of other people standing in the distance (B). For this assignment, draw the picture below in the figure box (C) adding people going back in the distance. Before beginning, draw some more people in the top picture by simply connecting the top and bottom of the person in the foreground with straight lines to the vanishing point and then adding more people inside those lines. Remember, *whenever things recede in the distance, they not only become smaller, but also closer together.*

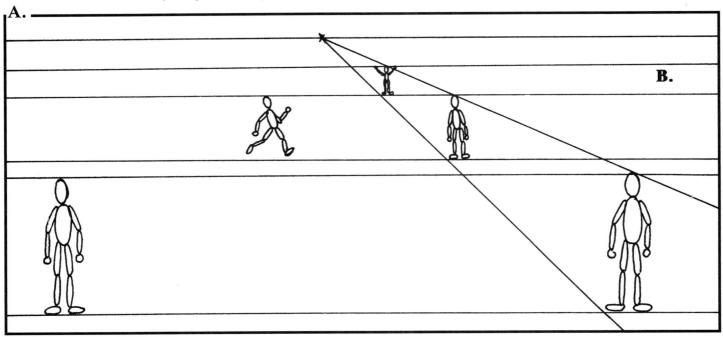

224

Lesson #130: *Drawing a House with Perspective*

Let's now draw a house using one-point perspective. First, draw a square to the far right of the horizon line below (A). Then, draw a triangle on top of the square for the roof of your house. Using a ruler and a light colored pencil, connect the top of the triangle and two corners of the square to the vanishing point. For the back part of your roof, simply draw a line at the same angle as the front line, keeping them *parallel*. Then, draw the back side of the building, keeping the line vertical like the front. Draw your house below and to the far right of the vanishing point (B).

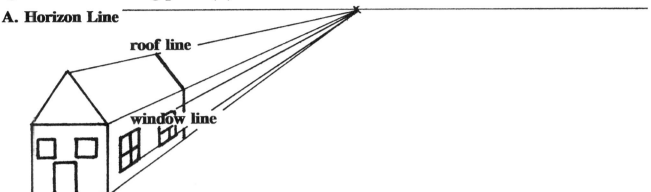

A. Horizon Line

roof line

window line

B. Draw Your House Here

Next, add some details to the house. First, put a window on the side of the house by drawing a short vertical line that shows how long you want it to be. Then, connect the top and bottom of this window line to the vanishing point. Finally, draw a vertical line for the back part. You have just put a window on the side of your house using one-point perspective! See if you can place another window on the side of your house.

With one-point perspective only one side goes back in the distance. This being the case, the front of your house doesn't go anywhere. All the lines on the front of your house are straight up and down (*vertical*) or straight across (*horizontal*). Thus, when you draw the door, windows, and siding on the front, all the lines will either be vertical or horizontal. Draw a door and two windows on the front of your house using vertical and horizontal lines.

When you are finished, see if you can draw another house below, but this time to the left of your vanishing point (C). Add windows and other details. Complete your picture by adding trees, animals, flowers and a fence. Last of all, place small marks 1/8" on the corner of your house. Then, using your vanishing point and a ruler, draw wood siding on your house as shown below.

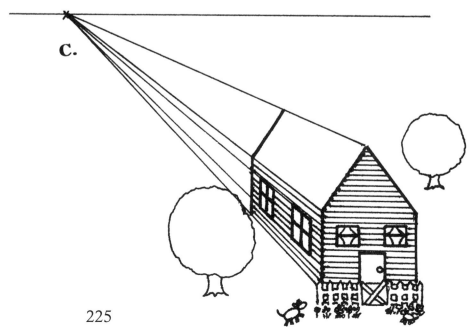

C.

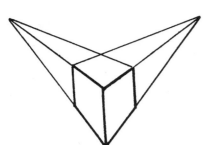

A.

Lesson #131: *Two-Point Perspective*

Two-point perspective is when the lines go back to two vanishing points (A). Have you ever stood at the corner of a building and observed how both sides go back in the distance? Well, that is two-point perspective. For the first part of this exercise, use your yellow colored pencil and draw a box below (C) by connecting the top and bottom of the vertical line below to both vanishing points as shown (B). Then draw the sides to your box by drawing a vertical line for each side.

Finally, connect the top right corner of your box to the left vanishing point and the top left corner to the right vanishing point. Since your horizon line, or eye-level, is high you will be looking down at the box. When you are finished, darken your box with your black pen and your light guidelines will disappear.

B. Two-Point Perspective

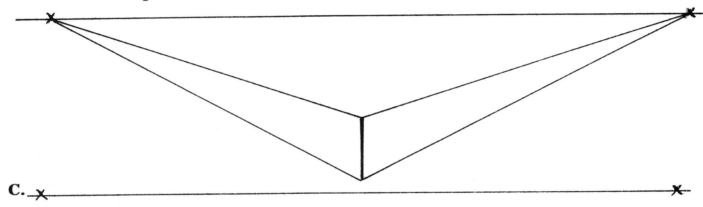

C.

Likewise, your box can be above the horizon line, depending on your vantage point. See if you can connect the vertical line below (E) to the vanishing points, and then complete the box as shown (D). This time you will be looking up at the box and see its bottom. Complete your box in the bottom right.

D.

E. Draw Your Box Here

Lesson #132: *Boxes & Paper Bags*

Do you know how to draw a box without using a vanishing point? Let's start by drawing a very simple, basic box. First, draw a rectangle (A). Then draw a short, diagonal line that extends from each of the three corners. Make sure these lines are at the same angle, or slant (B). Connect the top two lines with a horizontal line and the two lines on the side with a vertical line. You have just made a nice box (C). This is good for cereal boxes, a block of wood or even paper bags. To make a bag out of this shape, simply give your box a few wrinkles, a zig-zagged top, and shade the inside (D).

For this assignment, draw two boxes on the bottom of the page (E & F) as illustrated. Make one a cereal box and the other a paper bag. Start your drawings lightly with your yellow colored pencil and then go over them with your brown colored pencil. You may even want to draw a label on your box.

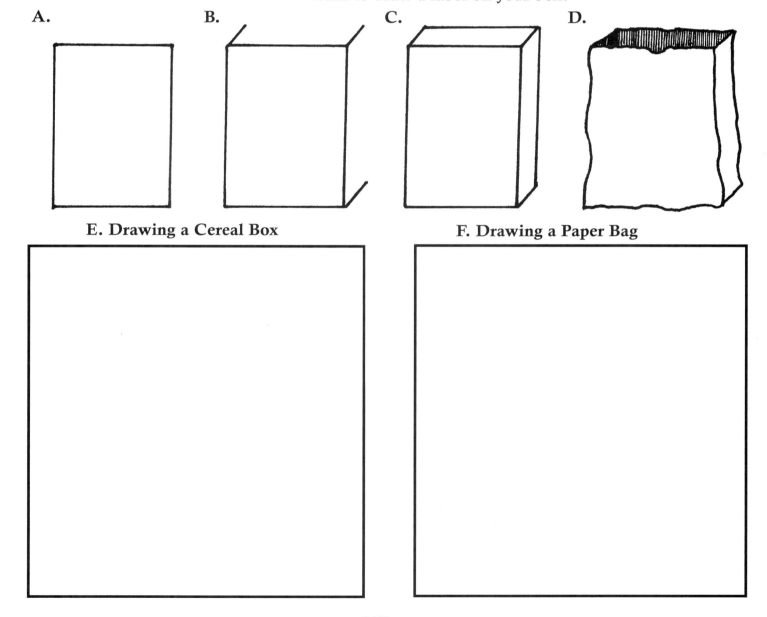

A.

B.

C.

D.

E. Drawing a Cereal Box

F. Drawing a Paper Bag

Lesson #133: *Books & Bibles*

Technically speaking, whenever lines go back in the distance (as they do on the sides of boxes and books), they will have to connect somewhere in the distance (A). Therefore, all the lines that go back in the distance will be on a slight angle, leaning in and eventually connecting at some invisible vanishing point. If your lines do not slant in, your drawing will be incorrect (B). For this assignment, let's draw some books and boxes, keeping this basic principle in mind as illustrated below (C). First, draw the basic shapes of four thin boxes on the bottom of the page (E), remembering that the lines going back in the distance will slant in. Then change each shape into a book by rounding the two front corners (D). Finally, add the finishing touches to your books or Bibles by making the cover a little larger and adding pages with long, straight lines. Start your drawings with your yellow pencil and complete each book with either your black pencil or black pen.

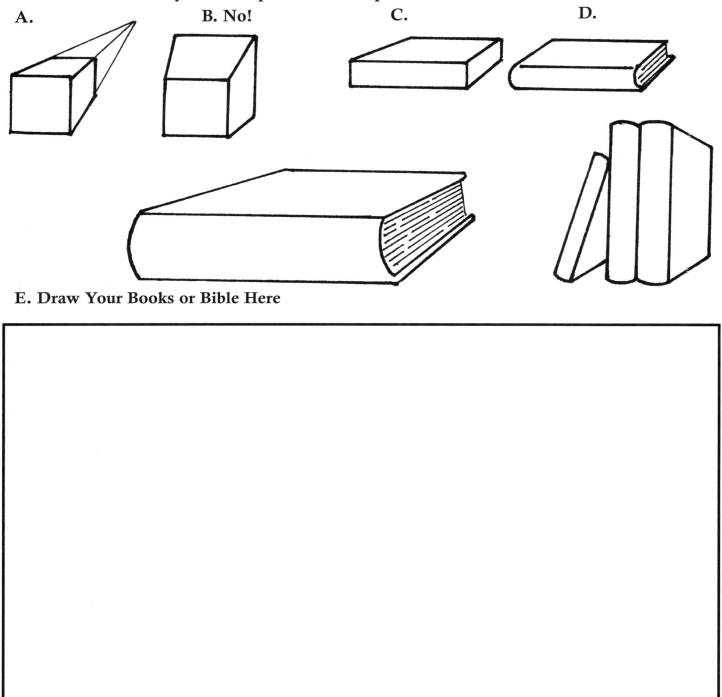

A. B. No! C. D.

E. Draw Your Books or Bible Here

Lesson #134: *Drawing Cubes*

Now let's practice drawing cubes. First, connect the four corners of the two squares below (A) with straight diagonal lines to make a cube as illustrated (B). Next, let's see if you can draw a square in the space provided (C). Then *overlap* another square by placing it slightly behind the first square as illustrated (A). Pretend that these squares are transparent, or see-through, as if they are made of glass, one going through the other. Finally, connect the four corners with straight, diagonal lines as shown (B). Next, let's draw an *opaque* box. Opaque means it is not transparent, or see-through, like a cardboard box. First, lightly draw another cube with your yellow pencil. Also, see if you can draw a lid for your box (D). Then take your black pen and outline just the front, side, top and lid. Shade inside the box with vertical lines (E); however, only bring the shading to the corner, so one side of the inside will be in shade and the other in light. When you are finished, see if you can draw other cubes, or boxes, in the same manner, changing some into opaque boxes by shading inside the boxes with vertical lines.

A.   B.   **C. Draw Your Square Here** D.

E.

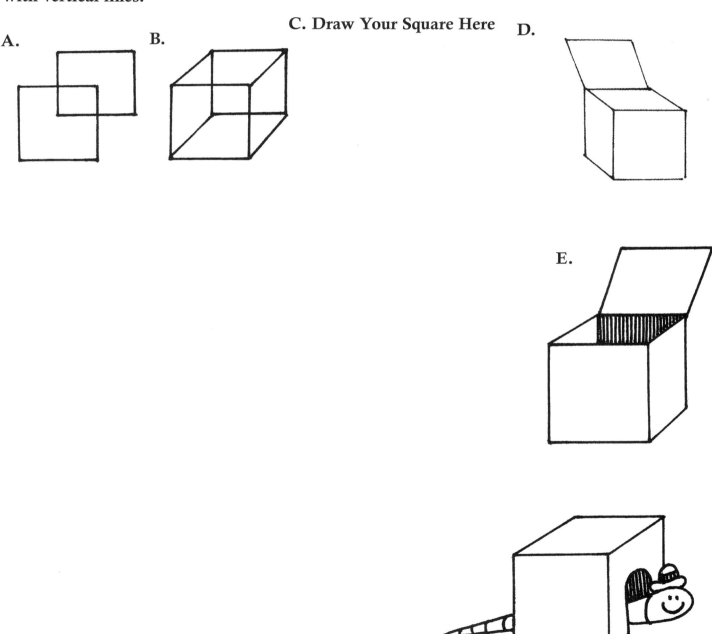

A.

"The Crucifix" Cimabue

Cimabue (1240-1301 A.D.)

One of the great painters of the Early Renaissance was Cenni di Peppi, better known as Cimabue (chim-a-boo-ee). During the latter part of the 13th century, he was the most revered painter in Italy. He was also one of the first to depart from the Byzantine style and paint in a more creative and realistic manner.

During the Renaissance, an artist's profession was still looked down on by the upper classes. It seemed to attract boys from lower-income families, as the more well-to-do families tried to persuade their sons from pursuing this profession. The success of Cimabue would have a profound influence on raising the status of artists in the eyes of society.

B.

Gregory Iocco Age 14 Freeport, Michigan

Lesson #135: *The Crucifixion*

The *Crucifixion* as an icon dates back to the fourth century. Jesus on the cross has been created for centuries in a variety of mediums, including mosaics, fresco paintings and sculpture. Many were placed in the sanctuary for an altarpiece as a reminder to believers of the crucified Christ.

Great masters like Cimabue created beautiful altarpieces for churches, such as the elaborate cross above called, *The Crucifix* (A). This cross can still be seen in the church of San Domenico located in Arezzo, Italy. In crucifix designs like this, the disciples and Mary were often portrayed in the smaller figure boxes to the sides and top of the cross. For this assignment, complete *The Crucifixion* by drawing Jesus on the cross (B). Then draw two people who were close to Jesus in the small figure boxes to the left and right of the cross. Start your drawing lightly and then complete your picture with bright colors. You may want to use a rich black behind Jesus by blending a dark blue, some red and a little black. In the larger area near the bottom of the cross, you may want to use a *reddish/orange*. Finally, make a light flesh tone for the body of Jesus.

230

Giotto di Bondone (1266-1337)

Giotto (gee-ot-toe) is known as *the father of modern painting.* He was born in a small, mountainous village not far from the city of Florence. Little is known of Giotto's childhood except for this story. One day, while looking after a flock of sheep, Giotto began to sketch the head of a goat on a rock as the great master Cimabue was passing by. Cimabue was so impressed by the boy's talent, that he invited him to apprentice under him in his workshop in Florence.

"Portrait of Giotto"
copy by Benjamin Iocco Age 12

At the age of 15, with the urging of his father, Giotto went to Florence to learn the wool trade. However, the aspiring artist spent so much time in the workshop of Cimabue, that his father finally relented and allowed him to pursue a career as an artist. While a young apprentice under the great Cimabue, Giotto's duties were those of the average houseboy. Gradually, the young student was given more responsibility in preparing materials for the master. In time, he assisted in creating Cimabue's paintings.

"He is Risen" Rachel Holland 13 Athens, Georgia

Giotto's most famous works are wall paintings, or *frescoes*, named for the way they were painted on a wall while the plaster was still wet. His paintings were the first since Roman times that rendered human forms so realistically, suggesting both weight and roundness. However, Giotto's style was still influenced by the Byzantine masters and the great sculptors of the Gothic Period. These new realistic figures had a great impact on Italian society because they had life, expression and form. During Medieval times, religious stories were told in the form of miracle plays. Giotto incorporated this dramatic approach to his artwork by presenting Bible stories as if they were on stage. When requested to draw a saint, he made him appear more human and less rigid. This marked the beginning of a new era where man, once again, sought a more artistically accurate interpretation of the world around him.

It is said that Giotto was the author of the first great paintings in the history of art. He was very skillful in the way he composed the subject matter of his paintings to create the maximum impact. Giotto was also an excellent draftsman. After nearly seven centuries, he is still considered one of the world's great masters.

Giotto was the first Italian painter to study from nature. This was revolutionary, though today nature study is considered a basic requirement in art. He also observed the habits and postures of men and women as they went about their daily business, gleaning from their every emotion.

"The Walls of Jericho"
Joshua Morrison Age 15
Phoenix, AZ

Lesson #136: *Lamentation*

Look at the painting on the back cover. The title of this is *The Lamentation*, by Giotto. Lament means, *to cry out loud in grief.* Compare this painting with your *picture postcard* of *Saint Luke*. Notice the emotions in Giotto's faces compared with that of *Saint Luke*. Also observe how creative Giotto's composition is in comparison to the background of *Saint Luke*. Do you see more form in Giotto's figures? Likewise, observe the colors in the two paintings. Write a summary comparing the two styles on the lines below. When you are finished, draw a scene from the Crucifixion that displays the grief on the faces of Jesus' disciples. To make a sad expression, you can draw a curved line on the sides of the eyes and also *furrow* the brow by placing several wavy lines on the forehead (A). Practice drawing expressions of sorrow in the small figure boxes (B) before doing your complete drawing in the large figure box (C). You may want to copy a sad expressions in the mirror, find sad faces in books, or simply copy those by Giotto on the back cover. Start your picture by drawing lightly with a yellow pencil, and then use the rest of your colored pencils to complete your picture.

A. Sad Expression

B.

C.

Giotto's fame as an artist quickly spread throughout Italy and he was hailed as a creative genius. Artists who emulated him proudly signed their paintings, *Disciple of Giotto, the good master.* Giotto's portrayal of realism would be one of the biggest turning points in Western art. However, there is never any one artist who is responsible for great change. Art has always been a gradual transition from one subtle change to the next.

Unfortunately, big changes in art bring about losses as well as gains. What Western art gained through Giotto's realism and dramatic compositions resulted in a loss of the innocence, beauty and simplicity that were prevalent during the Byzantine and Gothic periods.

··

St. Francis of Assisi

The church of St. Francis of Assisi was built to honor the great saint who had died in 1226. St. Francis abandoned wealth and high society to live among the poor and to care for the oppressed, both physically and spiritually. When Giotto was 30 years old, he was commissioned to paint a multi-paneled tribute to St. Francis' life on the walls of the Upper Church of St. Francis located in the town where the saint was born and died.

God has used many men and artists in various ways throughout the ages to glorify Him. Most Christians do not believe in sainthood, trusting that we join in the fellowship of the saints through Christ Jesus. Christians had questioned this doctrinal belief of the Catholic church even before the Protestant Reformation. However, faith in saints was, and still is, a common practice. Paul told believers in the New Testament to test the spirits, saying, *"Beloved, do not believe every spirit, but test the spirits, whether they are of God."* Even with divisions and various doctrines, believers who love Jesus and serve Him with all their heart and soul have been found in every denomination. St. Francis was such a one, loving God fervently. What God desires most from His people is a pure, servant's heart.

"The Death of St. Francis" Giotto Bardi Chapel, St. Croce, Florence
Drawing by Gregory Iocco Age 14 Freeport, Michigan

233

"O Divine Master; grant that I may not so much seek to be consoled as to console; to be understood as to understand; to be loved as to love; for it is in giving that we receive, it is in pardoning that we are pardoned, and it is in dying that we are born to eternal life."

St. Francis of Assisi

St. Francis was not a Florentine, but spent much of his time in and around Florence. He enjoyed life and delighted not only in his fellow man but in animals and nature. He was a modest man, and his humility and simplicity touched the hearts of many Florentines. His sacrifices and Christ-like compassion for his fellow man are a model for all of us to follow.

St. Francis started the Order of Friars with only eleven members in 1209. The order grew after his death, and its existence was encouraged by the Roman Catholic Church because it helped keep many dissatisfied groups from breaking away.

"Two Monastics Monk" by Gregory Iocco
Age 14 Freeport, Michigan

As the Franciscan Order continued to fill the churches and monasteries that were being constructed, the life of St. Francis became a major source of inspiration for artists during the 14th century.

Lesson #137: *Telling the Story of St. Francis of Assisi*

Draw St. Francis wearing a frock, as shown above, in the figure box below. Draw him in a kindly manner, showing him with the love of Christ in his relations with mankind or animals. Decorate your picture frame with birds, flowers, and other objects from nature. Draw lightly, and then color with colored pencils.

A.

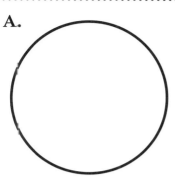

Lesson #138: *Drawing Circles*   B.

Giotto was very disciplined in the art of drawing - a skill in which he excelled. Visari, the great historian of the Renaissance, commented that, as a young student Giotto could draw a perfect circle without the use of any mechanical devices. As a matter of fact, *"as round as Giotto's circle,"* became a popular saying of the time.

For the first part of this assignment, see if you can draw a perfect circle (A) in the figure box (B). In Lesson #7 you learned how to draw a circle by lightly going around four or five times. However, this time see if you can draw a circle by using just one solid line from beginning to end. It is not easy to do, and should make you appreciate Giotto's talent. But even Giotto would tell you, the more you practice, the better you will become.

Now, let's practice drawing circles again by lightly going around and around in a circular motion (C). Draw four circles in figure box (D) using a different colored pencil for each.

C. Circle

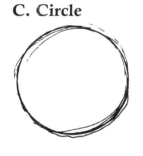

D. Draw 3 Circles Below

E.

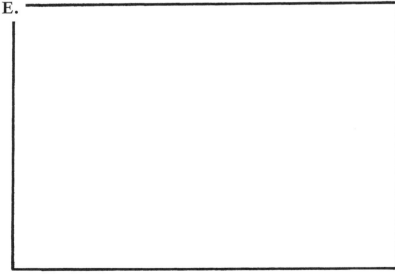

Next, fill the figure box to the left (E) with circles by overlapping them. Overlapping means placing one slightly in front of another. When you overlap circles they will look like rings. Draw them different sizes as shown below (F). Start with a light colored pencil and go around in a circle four or five times to make them round. Using two different colors, color each with vertical lines (G), placing some circles in front of others to create depth.

G.

F.

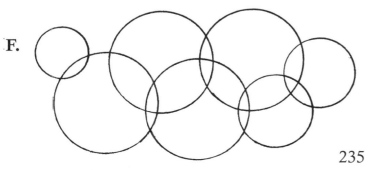

Lesson #139: *Into the Picture Gallery*

As you read earlier, before the 14th century artists were mainly concerned with showing the story of the Gospel in a simple and spiritual way. The backgrounds of paintings were left plain and flat, often gold in color. Giotto would be the first painter of the Early Renaissance to show an interest in *landscape* painting. Landscape means drawing and painting scenes of natural formations of land; like hills, valleys, mountains, trees, lakes and rivers. Other artists soon followed his example and filled backgrounds with realistic landscapes that placed the subject matter in a more down-to-earth setting.

For this assignment, select *Saint Luke* and *Flight into Egypt* by Jacopo da Ponte from your *picture postcard gallery*. These are good examples of the two different styles. On the lines below, express which style you like best and why. When you are finished, create a picture using each method in the figure boxes below (A & B). You may want to color a golden background around a simple drawing of Jesus. (Can you make gold with your colored pencils?) In the other figure box (B), draw Joseph and Mary leaving Egypt and place a landscape behind them. Notice that the distant mountains in *Flight into Egypt* are very light and almost blend into the sky. Remember, things in the distance have very little color and detail. As objects come forward, they have more color and detail to create depth in your picture. Practice your drawings on a sheet of paper before doing your final pictures below.

A.

B.

The dress of the figures in paintings also began to change during the Early Renaissance as Giotto began to adorn figures in everyday Italian attire. This was a major departure from the Roman togas of earlier art. His new approach appealed to the hearts of the people, allowing them to identify with the figures and their lifestyles more easily.

A.

B.

Lesson #140: *Drawing the Human Form*

One of the major accomplishments of the Renaissance was its adoption of the Greek rendition of the human form, a style which showed every muscle, twist and curve of the figure. For this assignment, let's practice drawing more *hot dog* figures in various positions below. Start by lightly drawing a stick figure with your orange colored pencil. Then draw a large, hot dog shape for the *torso* (upper body); two thin, hot dog shapes for each leg, and two thinner, hot dog shapes for each arm. Finally, draw an oval shape for the head, a small circle for each hand, and a small, fat, hot dog shape for each foot (A).

Copy each of the stick figures below. Then, lightly go over each with hot dog shapes to put meat on their bones. Finally, draw robes on your figures, showing the folds on the bottom by shading one side of each fold to show form. Place a rope around the waist, tying the robe loosely to the figure. You may even want to put sandals on their feet (B). When you are finished, go over only the areas which will be seen with darker colored pencils.

"And he received the gold from their hand, and he fashioned it with an engraving tool, and made a molded calf. Then they said, 'This is your god, O Israel, that brought you out of the land of Egypt.'"

Exodus 32:4

"The Crucifixion"
Drawing by Todd Leasure

The Renaissance-*The Cinquecento*

The term *Cinquecento* means 1500, especially with respect to the Italian art and literature of the 16th century. Although Florence had been the center of the Renaissance in the 1400s, it gave way to Rome in the 1500s as the cultural center of the fine arts. The reason for this move from Florence to Rome is attributed to its growing prosperity and the many art commissions that could be found through the churches in Rome. Italy truly entered its *awakening* during the *Cinquecento*, seeking new knowledge just as, in ancient Athens, the artists had sought many centuries before them. The artwork of ancient Greece was being excavated with a new fervor, along with its style of perfection and humanism. This influence would be like the golden calf of the Old Testament, with art of the Renaissance becoming an idol.

The classical poets of ancient Greece were known and studied during the Middle Ages, but it was only during the Renaissance that Greek prose and mythology really became popular. The Italians were so convinced of the superior wisdom of the ancient Greeks that they believed classical legends, like those of Homer, contained profound and mysterious truths. This would be another subtle turning away from the truths of God.

The Church would remain the paramount authority throughout the land, as well as the major patron of the arts. However, the *humanistic* philosophy which began to come forth, encouraging people to honor the accomplishments of man over the supremacy of God, had a great influence on society, philosophy and religion. Aided by new technical knowledge and a deep drive to learn more, artists achieved great heights in portraiture, landscape, mythological and religious paintings, as well as mastering the drawing and painting of the human form. These accomplishments in art created a stir throughout Europe. Painters and patrons alike became fascinated with art that not only illustrated the sacred stories from the Bible, but also showed man in a glorious state.

Neither religion nor God would be rejected outright during the Renaissance, though many believed that life had been too religious in the past and that man should have a freer choice in his existence. This would be a gradual departure from the philosophy of the Middle Ages where, for nearly 1000 years, life revolved around the Church and the Christian faith. Jesus stated that, *"No man can serve two masters."* (Matthew 6:24). Man cannot serve God and the world at the same time. Even though God was still glorified in the artwork that adorned the churches during the 14th and 15th centuries, humanism and the ancient Greek way of life had been resurrected. Italy, along with other European countries, was beginning its subtle decline away from Christ.

Painting

Throughout the centuries, painting had always taken a back seat to architecture and sculpture. Grandiose buildings and sculpted images had been prominent in the ancient Egyptian, Greek and Roman societies. During the Middle Ages, painters struggled for recognition, being used only sparingly for religious manuscripts and calendars. Even throughout the Romanesque and Gothic Periods, architecture and sculpture reigned. However, with the advent of the Renaissance, painting would rise to become the most popular form of art as many artists eagerly strived to master this medium. Fresco painting had been popular within the Church, but now great paintings were also being done with a new medium - the innovation of oil paint on canvas.

In the 15th century, painters did not have ready-made colors in tubes. They had to prepare their own *pigments*, mostly from minerals and colored plants. These were ground to powder between two stones, usually by an apprentice, then liquid was added to make a paste. The main ingredient of the liquid used for this purpose was egg white. That is why it was called *egg tempera*. However, egg tempera wasn't an ideal mixture for many artists because it dried quickly.

Oil painting originated in northern Europe out of the necessity for paint to dry more slowly, allowing the artist to work longer on a painting while it was still wet. Oil painting was first mastered by the Flemish artist, *Jan van Eyck* (1390-1441) of the Netherlands. Van Eyck realized that this innovation would allow him to make transparent layers of color called *glazes*. Applications of one thin layer of color over another made it possible to paint the most exact details with the point of a small brush, something that was much more difficult with fresco painting.

Throughout Europe, art guilds had been established as workshops for masters of many trades, including painting. These guilds had trade secrets for techniques of painting which they closely guarded. As an apprentice, or student, grew in maturity and ability, he would learn these guarded methods. The techniques were handed down from one trustworthy master to another. Thus, each guild became quite unique with its own techniques and personality. During this time, an Italian apprentice working in a Flemish workshop in northern Europe, learned of this new medium of oil painting and quietly returned to Italy to reveal the wonderful technique to his countrymen.

Nevertheless, the *fresco* style of painting on walls and ceilings remained popular. This technique had originated in ancient Greece but was revitalized during the 1400s. Fresco paintings hold up best in warm climates, like that of the Mediterranean, making oil painting more popular in northern Europe. Fresco painting was not practical in northern Europe because the wet plaster often froze before the painter had an opportunity to complete his work.

"Le premier copie la nature, le second copie le premier." ("One landscape artist copies nature, the second copies the first.") Daumier/French 1865

Lesson #141: *Into the Picture Gallery - Understanding Color*

Color also began to change during the Renaissance, moving from the symbolic colors of gold, blue and red to a broader palette of more realistic colors found in nature. For this assignment, take out the picture postcard, *St Luke*; Raphael's, *Sistine Madonna*, and Leonardo da Vinci's, *Mona Lisa*. Notice the difference in the use of color from the earlier period and that of the Renaissance (Raphael and da Vinci). The painting of *St. Luke* is done with symbolic, spiritual colors, while the artists of the Renaissance favored more realistic colors. What do you think of the two styles of painting? How do you feel about their use of color? Is their anything you miss about the earlier methods of painting in Christian art? Write your thoughts on the lines below.

_____

_____

_____

_____

_____

_____

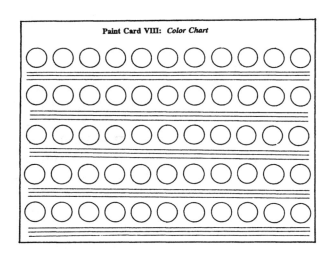

Paint Card VIII: *Color Chart*

Lesson #142: *Color Chart*

Learning to mix colors is one of the most important disciplines for an art student to learn. As you peruse your collection of works by the great masters in your *picture postcard gallery*, you will notice that each painter had a great understanding of color. Learning to mix colors does not take any talent. It is very scientific, like mixing two chemicals together. You have practiced mixing colors in every painting assignment, starting with *Paint Card #I*. Now let's become scientific, just as the artists of the Renaissance were, seeing how many colors you can make by simply using various combinations of the primary colors and white.

The number of colors you can create are limitless! You can make colors lighter by adding white or yellow, or darken a color by adding black. (To make a black, try mixing some red to blue and add a touch of yellow.) Underneath each color you have made note the colors you used, beginning with the color you used most and ending with the color you used least. For example, let's suppose you made a pink by adding a little red to white. You would print W + R, because you used more white and less red. A *color chart* is to assist you in making a certain color again.

Place *Paint Card #VIII* in front of you and see how many nice colors you can create. Make as many as you like, and then, as time passes and you learn new colors, add them to your color chart. Finally, look through some of your finished painting assignments to see if there are any nice colors that you mixed and try to make them again, noting them on your color chart. Your color chart should be something you are proud of, displaying the scientific research you have done in order to understand color theory better. Do not forget to use these beautiful colors in your next painting!

Lesson #143: *Painting with Tones*

Place *Paint Card IX* in front of you. Whereas in the previous assignment you practiced mixing colors, today we are going to practice making *tones*. Tones are different gradations of color from light to dark. For example, a light blue is a tone of blue. Tones are very important in learning more about painting because they can help you show the *form* of an object. For example, if you were going to paint an apple that sits in the light, you would have a light tone, a middle tone and a dark tone.

Tones also teach students how to break a color into many variations. You would be amazed at how many light blues you can make with various amounts of blue and white. Finally, tones are important for learning to mix colors. Many students like to return to their old habits of dipping their brush in red and painting an apple, or dipping their brush in blue and painting a river. There is no limit to the amount of colors you can create when you learn to mix your colors.

First, let's see if you can make different tones from light to dark for each of the colors listed on the paint card. Remember, mixing colors is scientific and takes no talent. The important thing to remember is: add only a very little of the darker color to the lighter color. Thus, when we say a *speck* of paint, we literally mean a speck. You will continually be reminded of this because many students are heavy-handed and make their colors too dark.

To make a color dark you can add black. Another good way to make a color darker, or duller, is by adding a speck of its complement. Do you remember your complementary colors (Lesson #20)? Complementary colors are colors which are opposite each other on the color wheel. For example, blue is the complement of orange.

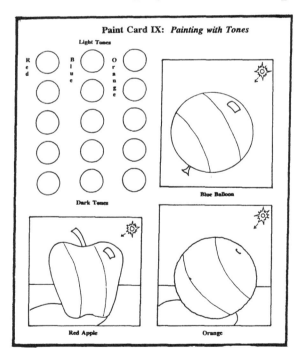

Part of a student's education in painting is learning how to make colors lighter. To do this, simply add white. However, you can make other light variations of some colors by adding yellow. Yet, you cannot add yellow to blue to make it lighter because it will make green. Red is also a little different. You may want to add some white and yellow to make red lighter. Remember, all you need is a speck of the darker color and white to make a light color. To make a color darker, just keep adding a little more of the darker color. Before beginning, see how many tones of red, blue and orange you can make in the circles below with your colored pencils. Then paint the circles on the top of your paint card with a variety of tones from light to dark. Finally, paint the three objects with a light tone, medium tone and dark tone of each color. Notice where the light is coming from in each picture to tell where your light and shaded sides will be.

Light Red ◯ ◯ ◯ ◯ ◯ ◯ ◯ **Dark Red**

Light Blue ◯ ◯ ◯ ◯ ◯ ◯ ◯ **Dark Blue**

Light Orange ◯ ◯ ◯ ◯ ◯ ◯ ◯ **Dark Orange**

Answers to Examinations

Examination #I (page 34)

I. Matching

1. q	11. e
2. k	12. l
3. g	13. c
4. f	14. o
5. s	15. t
6. p	16. m
7. i	17. j
8. d	18. h
9. a	19. r
10.b	20. n

II. Fill in the Blanks

1. yellow
2. y/o
3. orange
4. o/r
5. red
6. r/v
7. violet
8. v/b
9. blue
10. b/g
11. green
12. y/g

III. True or False

1. T
2. F
3. T
4. T
5. F
6. T
7. F
8. T

Examination #II (page 122)

I. Matching

1. e
2. l
3. f
4. j
5. b
6. m
7. i
8. o
9. k
10. c
11. h
12. g
13. d
14. n
15. a

II. Fill in the Blanks

1. graphic
2. Reformation
3. Martin Luther
4. three
5. Millet

III. True or False

1. T	9. T
2. T	10. F
3. F	11. T
4. T	12. F
5. T	13. F
6. F	14. F
7. F	15. T
8. F	

Examination #III (page 163)

I. Matching

1. g
2. k
3. q
4. h
5. b
6. m
7. f
8. i
9. n
10. a
11. e
12. p
13. j
14. l
15. d
16. o
17. c

II. Fill in the Blanks

1. city
2. shame
3. atheist
4. capital
5. Greece
6. teracotta
7. proportion

III. True or False

1. T
2. F
3. F
4. T
5. F
6. T
7. T
8. T
9. T

Examination #IV (page 207)

I. Fill in the Blanks

1. thirteenth
2. tesserae
3. Romanesque
4. cathedra
5. Crusades
6. tapestry
7. narrative
8. Gothic
9. Dark Ages
10. Pope Gregory
11. writing
12. amphitheaters
13. illuminated manuscripts
14. iconoclasts
15. basilica

II. True or False

1. F
2. T
3. F
4. F
5. T

III. Matching

1. b	9. d
2. h	10. l
3. c	11. g
4. f	12. n
5. a	13. k
6. e	14. m
7. i	15. o
8. j	